'This book is most welcome for many reasons. It comprehensively examines a rarely analysed region, covering the policy background to African aviation, explores the airlines and their networks, and assesses the infrastructure, labour market and efficiency problems they face.'

—*Peter Forsyth*, Monash University and Southern Cross University

The Economics and Political Economy of African Air Transport

Africa is the smallest of the 'regional' aviation markets but one that Boeing and others expect to expand over the medium term. Developments on the continent that require the creation of robust and efficient air transport include growth in tourism, the export of 'exotics', and the emergence of modern manufacturing and high-tech industries. Africa's regional aviation markets generally lack good airports and air traffic control, viable airlines, and adequately skilled labour. Airline safety is also a major concern.

Written by a 'Who's Who' of aviation specialists and policy makers, *The Economics and Political Economy of African Air Transport* fills an emerging void in the literature regarding Africa's aviation markets. Its original papers focus explicitly on the economic and political dimensions of the subject, although with relevance to the strategic planning and management of airlines and their associated infrastructure. Topics discussed include external and internal market efficiencies, air service liberalization, the emergence of new carriers, safety and security, low-cost airline and other business models, and airport economics.

Focusing on the broader issues surrounding the subject, this book will be of interest to both the aviation community and those with an interest in economic and social development.

Kenneth Button is a University Professor of Public Policy at the George Mason School of Policy, Government, and International Affairs, USA, and a world-renowned expert on transportation policy. He has published, or has in press, some 80 books and over 400 academic papers in the field of transport economics, transport planning, environmental analysis and industrial organization.

Gianmaria Martini is Professor of Economics at the University of Bergamo, Italy, and Head of the Department of Economics and Technology Management. His recent research focuses on methods to estimate technical and economic efficiency in the air transportation and healthcare sectors, published in international journals and presented at many international conferences.

Davide Scotti is a Research Fellow at the University of Bergamo, Italy, with a focus on technical efficiency and productivity studies regarding airport activities.

The Economics and Political Economy of African Air Transport

Edited by
Kenneth Button, Gianmaria Martini, and Davide Scotti

LONDON AND NEW YORK

First published 2018
by Routledge

2 Park Square, Milton Park, Abingdon, Oxfordshire OX14 4RN
52 Vanderbilt AVenue, New York, NY 10017

Routledge is an imprint of the Taylor & Francis Group, an informa business

First issued in paperback 2019

Copyright © 2018 selection and editorial matter, Kenneth Button, Gianmaria Martini, and Davide Scotti; individual chapters, the contributors

The right of Kenneth Button, Gianmaria Martini, and Davide Scotti to be identified as the authors of the editorial material, and of the authors for their individual chapters, has been asserted in accordance with sections 77 and 78 of the Copyright, Designs and Patents Act 1988.

All rights reserved. No part of this book may be reprinted or reproduced or utilised in any form or by any electronic, mechanical, or other means, now known or hereafter invented, including photocopying and recording, or in any information storage or retrieval system, without permission in writing from the publishers.

Notice:
Product or corporate names may be trademarks or registered trademarks, and are used only for identification and explanation without intent to infringe.

British Library Cataloguing-in-Publication Data
A catalogue record for this book is available from the British Library

Library of Congress Cataloging-in-Publication Data
Names: Button, Kenneth, 1948– editor, author. | Martini, Gianmaria, 1960– editor, author. | Scotti, Davide, editor, author.
Title: The economics and political economy of African air transport / Kenneth Button, Gianmaria Martini and Davide Scotti.
Description: New York: Routledge, 2017. | Includes bibliographical references and index.
Identifiers: LCCN 2017018362 | ISBN 9781138203600 (hardback) | ISBN 9781315471297 (ebook)
Subjects: LCSH: Aeronautics, Commercial—Economic aspects—Africa. | Aeronautics, Commercial—Political aspects—Africa. | Airports—Economic aspects—Africa. | Infrastructure (Economics)—Africa.
Classification: LCC HE9882.A35 E26 2017 | DDC 387.7096—dc23
LC record available at https://lccn.loc.gov/2017018362

ISBN: 978-1-138-20360-0 (hbk)
ISBN: 978-0-367-88413-0 (pbk)

Typeset in Bembo
by codeMantra

Contents

List of figures and tables

Figures

Tables

List of contributors

Joseph Amankwah-Amoah is Reader in International Business at Kent Business School, University of Kent. He received his PhD in Business Studies (IB and Strategy) from the University of Wales, Swansea.

Kenneth Button is a University Professor in the Schar School of Policy and Government at George Mason University, Virginia. He has a PhD in Economics from Loughborough University.

Stephan Heinz is a Senior Consultant at the Seabury Group. He has an MBA from INSEAD.

Stefano Leidi is the Project Manager and Head of Customer Care at Mida Informatica and collaborates with University of Bergamo on aviation research. He holds a MSC in Management Engineering from University of Bergamo.

Berendien Lubbe is a Professor and Head of the Tourism Management Division at the University of Pretoria. She has a DCom (Communication Management) from the University of Pretoria.

Gianmaria Martini is Professor of Economics in the Department of Management, Information and Production Engineering at the University of Bergamo. He has a PhD in Economics from the University of York.

Rui Neiva is a Policy Analyst at the Eno Center for Transportation and holds a PhD in Public Policy from George Mason University, Virginia.

John F. O'Connell is a Senior Lecturer in the Centre for Air Transport Management at Cranfield University. He has a PhD in Airline Strategy from Cranfield University.

Gordon Pirie was Professor in the African Centre for Cities at the University of Cape Town until retiring in 2016. He has a PhD in Geography from the University of the Witwatersrand, Johannesburg.

Charles Schlumberger is the Lead Air Transport Specialist of the World Bank. Previously he was Vice-President of the Union Bank in Switzerland. He holds a PhD in Civil Law from McGill University.

Davide Scotti is a Research Fellow in the Department of Management, Information and Production Engineering at the University of Bergamo. He holds a PhD. in Economics and Management of Technology from the University of Bergamo.

Svetlana Shornikova is a Senior Project Development Associate: Air Transport, Hospitality and Tourism at AHT Research and Consulting. She has a DCom in Tourism Management from the University of Pretoria.

Eric Tchouamou Njoya is a Senior Lecturer in the Department of Logistics, Operations, Hospitality and Marketing at Huddersfield University. He has a PhD in Applied Economics from the Karlsruhe Institute of Technology.

David Warnock-Smith is Director of the Department of Aviation Tourism and Events at Buckinghamshire New University and holds a PhD in Air Transport from Cranfield University.

Preface

The motivation for collecting these original papers was an appreciation of just how under researched some air transportation markets are. The aviation sector, and especially since the global spread of economic deregulation began nearly 40 years ago in the United States, has attracted immense academic interest as a sort of test-bed experiment for the way market forces can cause industry to evolve and stimulated new managerial practices. At a very rough guess, however, we would say that about 95 percent of this work was been focused on North America and Europe, with a gathering body of analysis looking at the Asian situation. Africa, and to a lesser extent South America, have attracted less interest.

This is understandable because data on Africa is sparse and the amount of both passenger and freight traffic is, by global comparisons, small. But on the other hand, Africa represents a large part of the global landmass and has a growing population that is also enjoying a degree of economic development. It is a place where air transportation would seem to have a role to play even now, let alone in the future.

With this in mind, we asked a set of experts in the aviation field, who also have some considerable knowledge of Africa, to write papers that address some of the main issues regarding the interacting economic and political economy features of the African aviation situation. The papers are all non-technical in the sense that they are designed more to explain what is going on, and likely to go on, in the African aviation scene, than to develop and estimate complex technical models. They are aimed at the proverbial broadly educated person rather than the narrow expert, although we do hope the latter may find interest in them in that much of the material is designed to set specific trends and issues in a broader context.

Assembling a set of papers of this sort inevitably means a certain amount of nagging and prodding of contributors, and we hope we have not been excessive in doing this. Indeed, the various writers have been generous with their time in preparing their material and, when requested, modifying and editing to produce a relatively even level of presentation and analysis for readers.

We hope that readers will find the finished result both interesting and useful.

KJB, GM, DS.

1 Introduction

Kenneth Button, Gianmaria Martini, and Davide Scotti

It is rather ironic that while modern economists generally trace the origins of the current core of their subject to Adam Smith's *Wealth of Nations*, they are not very good at explaining why some nations are wealthier than others, or why some are growing faster. Abstract models abound that point, in various degrees, to the roles of natural resources, stable political regimes, access to markets, cultural traits, and so on, but experience suggests that none is better at forecasting the next big economic superpower, or the timing of a major recession than simply tossing a die.

But going back to Adam Smith, his main explanation revolves around the economic progress that accompanies the division of labour and the economies that accrue from specialization. He uses his famed labour specialization in pin production as empirical evidence of this. But with this comes the need for trade, the people who spend their time sharpening the pins need to be able to trade with those who card them or add the cap. Trade is, in this sense, at the core of wealth creation; without it there can be no specialization or division of labour. And here we are not talking about international trade, which in the day of short-hand journalism is often seen as the only form of trade, but the more generic, everyday trade that takes place between individuals, firms, and government, and every combination thereof, at the micro level.

Most trade in physical goods involves some form of transportation, and this includes, in the modern world, electronic transportation of money and information. What emerges from this, when approached from this generalized framework is that, in general, the parts of the world with the greatest wealth are also those with the most efficient transportation systems. Of course, one can debate issues of causality – does transportation lead to wealth creation, or does the acquisition of wealth facilitate investment in transportation? But at the mega, geographical level there is clearly correlation, and at the very least, appropriate transportation does seem to act as a facilitator, if not always the driver, of economic growth and wealth creation.

Remaining at the mega level, the part of the world that has the least wealth per capita is Africa; e.g. while according to the United Nations, in 2000 (the last year data is available) North America held 27.1 percent of the world's net wealth in purchasing parity terms but only had 5.7 percent of the population, and Europe 26.4 percent of the wealth with 9.6 percent of the population, Africa share of the wealth was only 1.52 percent with 10.7 percent of the global population. If one looks at the dynamic situation, rather than Smith's focus on stocks of wealth, then there is little evidence of convergence. The wealthier parts of the world have the largest increases in absolute money GDP, although for periods, in percentage terms, their increases may be slower.

Of course, there may be many reasons for this distribution, but, by looking at the very basic statistics, the pattern corresponds with the quality of transportation in the various continents. Africa has, for example, by all the measures used by the World Bank, the worse road, railroad, and airport infrastructure, both in terms of quantity and quality of any Continent (Gwilliam, 2011). It also has the least number of cars, trucks, and commercial aircraft.

While there are important differences in the roles of the various forms of transportation in facilitating the trade that fosters the growth of wealth, the focus here is on the aviation sector. Of course, given the network nature of transportation, together with the multimodal nature of most trips or goods movements – you cannot ship flowers by air without adequate surface transportation to and from the airports involved – this does involve drawing a rater artificial boundary, but it is a practical one and institutionally aviation does tend to be treated separately, even if this is often inappropriate from an economic perspective.

The papers in this volume, all of which are original contributions, and that are outlined at the end of the Introduction, cover some of the main themes that have become important in ongoing debates about the African air transportation market, and the political economy of its development. Before moving on to explain the justification for the structure of the book, in the following pages the papers are essentially set within the larger context of African aviation. To this end we begin with a look at the larger picture of African air transportation in the early part of the 21st century, and to highlight some of the ongoing trends that would seem of an enduring nature.

African aviation

Over the past 15 years or so, Africa in general, and especially sub-Saharan Africa, has, albeit unevenly, been enjoying something of an economic boom. The demand for its raw materials has been one factor in this, as has the relative political stability of many of its constituent countries. Outside aid and investment strategies may also have removed some of the burden of limited local resources. This economic situation both provides resources for upgrading the continent's infrastructure while at the same time placing increasing demands on it. In this context, there has been considerable interest by non-African countries, in addition to former colonial powers, both for political-military and commercial reasons, in investing in African infrastructure and production. For example, China has shown considerable interest, as have other non-ex-colonial countries, such as Iran and North Korea, but actual financing has been rather limited, and often difficult to disentangle from investment in non-aviation activities (Infrastructure Consortium for Africa, 2014).

Despite its landmass of 11,730,000 square-miles, a population of 1.02 billion and population density of 87 persons per square-mile, Africa makes the lowest use of air transportation of any of the major continents. African air transportation represents somewhat less than two percent of world passengers, and less than 1.5 percent of the cargo market by tonnage. Put another way, Africans only fly 0.3 trips a year, compared to 1.7 in the "developed world" and over five times that in the US. These data should, however, be put in the context of recent growth trends in air traffic that have, in the case of sub-Saharan Africa (depicted in Figure 1.1), been faster than most other mega-regions. The political difficulties in Northern Africa, basically the Maghreb countries, have more recently been disrupted by political factors that have seen breakdowns in many of their internal and external markets, and other institutions.

Averaging across this, overall the forecasts for aviation activities are somewhat optimistic. Boeing Commercial Aeroplane (2015), for example, predicts that intra-Africa revenue passenger miles flown will grow an average of 6.7 percent a year between 2015 and 2034, and those between Africa and the Middle East and Asia by 7.3 and 7.1 percent, respectively. Physically, air cargo is projected to grow by 6.6 percent a year compared to global growth rate of 5 percent. The UN's International Civil Aviation Organization

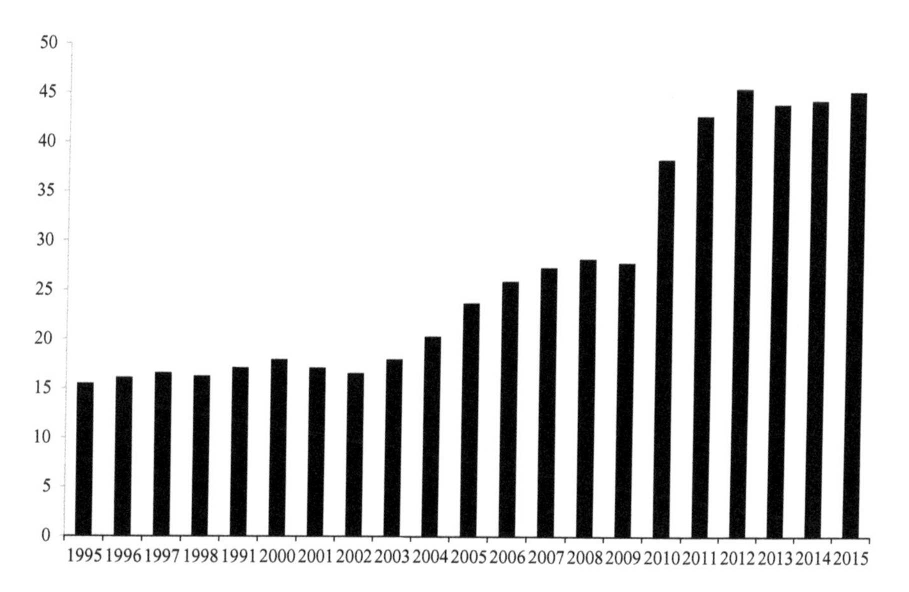

Figure 1.1 Sub-Saharan Africa air traffic (million passengers); 1995–2015.
Source: International Civil Aviation Organization.

indicates steady growth with passenger traffic to, from, and within Africa increasing at an annual average rate of 5.3 percent until 2030, while cargo traffic is projected to grow at 5.6 percent. Africa-Middle East traffic is forecast to expand at 9.9 per cent, the most rapid in the world. The forecasts produced by Airbus offer a similar picture. Where the forecasts differ is more at the micro level than in terms of the overall pictures being painted.

This economic dynamism in many of the continent's markets, and the expectation of the continuation of stable political conditions, largely explains the longer terms scenarios of Boeing, Airbus, and others regarding the future. They, when combined with the need to replace the region's aging fleet, are predicting a demand for between 1, 117 (Airbus) and 1, 150 (Boeing) new airplanes, with majority of them being single-aisle over the next 20 years. This in turn raises questions of how these purchases are to be financed.

The historically low level of economic development and income across most of the African Continent obviously provides a major explanation for the relatively small size of its commercial aviation sector, but geography and political history are also important (Pirie, 2014). Many of the African countries are artificial creations stemming from colonial days with limited internal political or economic cohesion. Large areas of virtually uninhabited, and probably uninhabitable, land could with natural barriers have made surface transportation difficult and costly, and especially so in the case of the land-locked nations (Limdo and Venables, 1999).

A major change in Africa's lot is that incomes on average have been rising, albeit with local geographical variations. Added to this, recent adjustments to National Income Accounts indicate that the base levels are higher than thought only a year or so ago. Nevertheless, whatever methodology is used, most of the populations of African countries come within the lower spectrum of material welfare.[1]

Furthermore, the gains have yet to produce a large middle, professional class in most of Africa, and it is this group that elsewhere tend to fly the most. Taking other things as being equal, there is a high positive correlation between countries' per capita income and their use of air transportation although this relationship is not linear. In general, it follows a sigmoid path over time. Incomes outpace air travel initially, there is then a more rapid growth in air travel, which, as in the case of North America and Europe, tends to fatten out at higher levels of income. At lower levels of income, those relevant for most African states, growth is relatively slow for a variety of reasons, such as a lack of adequate infrastructure and, not uncommonly, misguided aviation policies. But even allowing for this, the distributions of income are important; at lower levels these tend to be bimodal involving a relatively small middle class, ultimately the main users of air transportation.

In virtually all countries in Africa the main users are from higher income groups and this, because of their relatively low demand elasticities, incentivizes airlines to charge high fares and not to operate at maximum efficiency, a fact compounded by the lack of effective completion in many local markets (Button *et al.,* 2017). Airline costs in Africa are also generally above the global average, partly caused by fuel taxes that can be 50 percent or even 100 percent higher than the global average, but also due to the higher levels of state involvement in supplying infrastructure and restrictive regulatory environments.

In terms of its "network geography", African has little of the advantages of either the US/Canada market or that of Europe, or indeed that of China. Africa is an awkward "shape" for airline networks. The US is ideal for hub-and-spoke systems with its 48 contiguous states forming a virtual square embracing large populations at each corner. These entry points can be considered gateways for international traffic as well as large markets for domestic traffic, and major cities in the centre to act as hubs. Equally, Europe is almost ideal for discrete, short-haul, non-connecting services emanating from bases, Ryanair's model, with the bulk of its population and economic activity in a dense corridor stretching from North West England across London to the Benelux states and along the German Rhineland, Southern Germany, and Switzerland to Northern Italy; the "Blue Banana". China, with its concentration of economic activity in the south and west, is, in many ways, like the internal European market. The linear networks found in places such as Norway that facilitate "bus-stop routes", with planes maintaining their load factors by picking up and dropping passengers as they move along routes, are also not viable in sub-Saharan Africa, although possibly technically so in parts of the Maghreb. Notwithstanding the current political situation, the Maghreb is more akin to Europe and in terms of its air networks, although much less dense, and with a lower income.

Added to this, there are not the levels of economic ties between the African states that are a feature of the countries of the Europe Union or the states in the United States. Historically there has been more trade between the Maghreb countries than between those within sub-Saharan Africa, and especially the land-locked countries, but it is still limited (Button *et al.*, 2016). Complementarity between markets is a key component for fostering trade and, *ipso facto,* aviation, and this is limited within the Continent. Indeed, much of Africa's trade is with countries external to the continent.

The history of Africa, and especially that of 19-th and 20-th century colonialism, has done little to foster wider economic integration in sub-Saharan Africa. In consequence, the degree of integration of airline markets and their infrastructure leaves much to be desired (Button *et al.*, 2015b). This seems so regarding external commercial aviation markets. Overall, while African registered airlines now provide about 92 percent of the intra-sub-Saharan African annual seats on offer, only about 35 percent of the 11 million African/European seats are provided by African airlines, and 37 percent of the six million African/Middle East seats.

But within these aggregates are a series of sub-markets. For example, much of the external capacity serving Africa has traditionally been provided by the flag airlines of the former colonial powers associated with individual states, making any widening of external markets difficult, especially when overall aviation is growing slowly. Equally, the high proportion of intra-continental capacity offered by African airlines disguises very significant levels of spatial market segmentation.

Institutional problems caused by a lack of market liberalization are widely understood by governments across Africa, as well as international agencies like the International Civil Aviation Organization. Until the 1990s, intra-African air transport services were regulated by highly restrictive, bilateral agreements, with nearly all carriers state-owned and lacking the commercial focus for profitability. The African airlines were characterized by mismanagement of national carriers, political interference, high operating costs, and outdated equipment. The focus of carriers has also remained on international traffic, with the intra-African network taking a secondary role.

In 1999, as a follow-up to the 1988 Yamoussoukro Declaration, 44 countries adopted the Yamoussoukro Decision seeking to address this, although national ratification has been slow. The Decision was a commitment to deregulate air services and to open regional air markets to transnational competition. Using simulations, InterVISTAS (2014) suggests that if the Decision were fully implemented, increased air services between 12 sample markets across the continent could provide an additional five million passengers per annum, $1.3 billion in annual GDP, and 155,000 jobs.

The expected gains have, however, yet to materialize (Schlumberger, 2010). In practice while there has been a degree of operational integration that, for example, contributed to the 69 percent increase in traffic between South Africa and Kenya in the early 2000s and to the 38 percent reduction in fares between South Africa and Kenya, public policies have not been integrated to the extent envisaged. Overall, however, comparing those regions where Yamoussoukro has been implemented, frequencies have grown faster; new, privately funded airlines have emerged; and services improved more than where that was not the case (Njoya, 2016).

Infrastructure

Africa's transportation infrastructure, and particularly that of the sub-Saharan region, is poor, and this certainly extends to aviation (World Bank, 2009). In 2013, the Secretary General of the African Airlines Association summed it up thus, "deficient, dilapidated and not coping with the growing airline industry". The pressure for improving the quality and quantity of air transportation infrastructure is not just being driven by macroeconomic growth in Africa – seven of the world's ten fastest-growing economies in percentage terms are African and in sub-Saharan Africa – but also by the emergence of "airport megacities" such as Accra, Lagos, Luanda, Addis Ababa, Nairobi, and Johannesburg, with demands over 10,000 daily long-haul passenger trips. Jomo Kenyatta International Airport in Nairobi, for example, opened in 1958 with capacity of 1.5 million passengers a year. But the annual passenger flow has reached 6.5 million and it is forecast to reach 25 million by 2025.

When discussing commercial aviation infrastructure, it is normal to divide it into airports, and air navigation and control systems – often referred to as air traffic control (ATC), although this is only part of their function. Infrastructure, as in all sectors, is relative to those interested, and in this case all three elements are included; aircraft are uses as far as airports are concerned but infrastructure in the view of airlines. Because airports and ATC clearly fall under most definitions of infrastructure we look at these initially, and treat airlines more as mobile capital and as the hardware of the industry (aeroplanes are often referred to as 'metal'). This also largely conforms to the institutional structure in situ.

As with all matters regarding civil aviation, under the 1944 Chicago Convention each country controls its own air space and because of this is responsible for its air navigation system. Most such systems are state owned, although some are institutionally separate from government; e.g. South Africa's Air Traffic and Navigation Services Ltd is a not-for-profit joint-stock corporation, although a ministerial committee regulates its rates. Countries do co-ordinate their ATC systems with the Agency for Aerial Navigation Safety in Africa and Madagascar (ASECNA), founded in 1959, having 19 members. It manages 620 thousand square miles of airspace (1.5 times the size of Europe) covering six Flight Information Regions-Antananarivo, Brazzaville, Dakar Oceanic and Terrestrial, Niamey and N'Djamena – with ASECNA control centres located at the main international airports in each region.

The quality of the ATC systems deployed and their operations vary widely between countries and within them. In general, in North Africa, Morocco and Egypt have reasonable infrastructure, in west sub-Saharan Africa, Senegal, Guinea, Ivory Coast, and Ghana are adequately served, as are Kenya, Rwanda, and Tanzania on the east coast, and South Africa in the south. Indeed, South Africa's ATC is ranked 15th in the world by the World Economic Forum in terms of its air transport infrastructure, while Tunisia, Mauritius, Ethiopia, Morocco, Seychelles, and Namibia are all in the top 60. The African interior, on the other hand, and especially the vast expanses of the Central African Republic and the Republic of the Congo, is largely devoid of radar and good radio communications. Inter-aircraft communication in this case is the main way of maintaining separation (Esler, 2015).

Most of the evidence on performance, however, is largely anecdotal, and very little systematic analysis has been conducted into the efficiencies of Africa's ATC systems. Systems, like that of South Africa and, at the more micro level in locations around more economic developed parts of the continent, are often on a par with Europe and North America. For example, a comparative study of 11 ATC systems from higher income countries around the world, recorded no significant difference between that of South Africa and rest of the sample (Button and McDougall, 2006). Elsewhere, serious deficiencies seem likely.

One of the major problems in operating all infrastructures in most of Africa, including ATC, is that of labour supply. The implications of a shortage of suitable equipment in many parts of Africa are worsened by a shortage of skilled labour, and this is a problem that extends to other elements of the aviation supply chain (African Union, 2011). There have been efforts to upgrade the African aviation labour force, and especially traffic controllers. These have not always proved successful. For example, a 2012/2013, $7 million US programme involving Federal Aviation Administration officials being used to retrain the Djiboutian air traffic controllers, that as part of their responsibility serve the US base at Camp Lemonnier, collapsed after the Djiboutians stopped going to classes and locked the trainers out of the flight tower.

Although there are vast differences between countries, many of Africa's major airports are geriatric, and particularly so in sub-Saharan Africa. Furthermore, even among the older airports there is considerable variation in their efficiencies (Barros, 2011). In many cases, they are also poorly used, and in some, there is demonstrable underutilization (Stephens and Ukpere, 2011). The problem came to the attention of international agencies such as the World Bank, that had previously played an active role in upgrading airports in the immediate decolonization period, and the African Development Bank about 15 years ago, and more recently has engaged the interests of the China-Africa Development Fund. Aid has subsequently increased.

Added to this, there has been an increasing engagement of non-African countries and international agencies in providing aid, technical inputs, and soft loans, and this also extends beyond the ex-colonial nations. There has been a recent push by China to become more engaged in African aviation, that began as a complement to wider trade and geopolitical interests 50 years or more ago. Now at least 17 sub-Saharan African countries have or will have Chinese-built airports partly because China Airports Construction Group Corporation has considerable domestic experience in building and expanding the types and scales of airports suited to the various African subclimates and terrains. China's main involvement has largely been in East and West Africa, and in countries replete in the natural resources required for its economic growth. In the past six decades, but mainly since 2000, China has been involved in airport projects in Ethiopia, the Comoros, Angola, Tanzania, Kenya, Mali, Mauritius, Mozambique, Nigeria, the Republic of Congo, and Togo.

For example, the $550 million expansion of Addis Ababa Bole International Airport is being undertaken by China Communications Construction Company with funding provided by Export-Import Bank of China, and a new international terminal at Nnamdi Azikiwe International Airport Abuja, the main airport serving Nigeria's capital, is being partly financed with a soft loan provided by China. The Export-Import Bank of China provided a concessional loan and preferential buyer's credit to help with the $150 millions of investment in new facilities at Lomé-Tokoin, Togo.

Overall, the Centre for Aviation finds that $33.8 billion is being invested, or earmarked to be invested, in construction and associated projects at existing airports in 77 projects in Africa with an average price tag almost $440 million. Examples include Angola (30 projects costing $2.16 billion); Nigeria ($870 million on multiple passenger and cargo terminal projects); Senegal (a new airport at Dakar costing $700 million); Rwanda (a new airport at Kigali, $650 million); and Kenya (new terminals and a second runway at Nairobi, $1 billion).

Airlines

The carriers themselves, in part because of political interference, state ownership (about half of Africa's airlines are at least 51 percent state owned), and subsidies that have tended to allow less efficient airlines to remain in the market and prevented natural hub-and-spoke system from evolving, have often found market forces hostile. African domicile carriers often find it difficult to compete with non-African airlines. Indeed, if we combine both intra-Africa and inter-continental traffic involving Africa, then 80 per cent of traffic goes by non-African airlines (Heinz and O'Connell, 2013).

The result is that many African airlines are poorly managed and financially insolvent (Figure 1.2). Between 2001 and 2004, for example, saw the collapse of some of the legacy carriers and consolidation of the strongest ones like Ethiopian and Kenyan. The route network has grown significantly since then

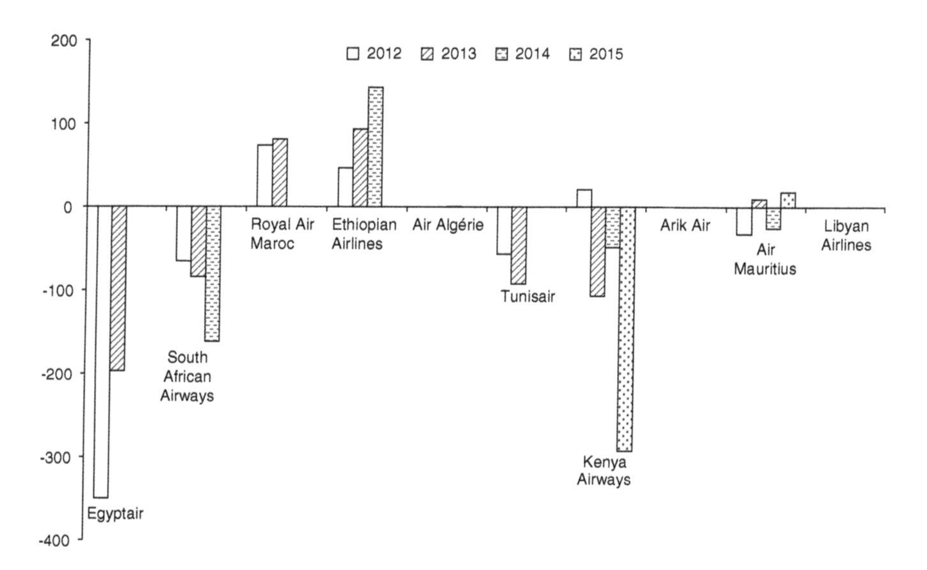

Figure 1.2 Net profits, from left to right of the ten largest airlines by passengers carried ($ million).

Note: Non-records indicate lack of data.

Sources: Company reports.

as many of countries have seen strong demands, at least to the late 2000s, for their primary products and airline-based industries like tourism and the export of exotics (flowers and fruit) has expanded (Dobruszkes and Mondou, 2013). There are short-term fluctuations, for example, Africa's economic activity slowed from 3.4 percent in 2014 to 3.0 in 2015, but macroeconomic growth, as pointed out earlier, is still anticipated.

In a bid to develop economies of scope and density that would help with financial viability, there have been several efforts to create multi-national African airlines (in addition to there being more conventional mergers between airlines from the same country). Few, though, have succeeded. West African and East African Airways, both pan-African entities comprising former British colonies, were dismantled when the various participating countries became independent. The first post-colonial pan-African airline was Air Afrique that was owned by a fluctuating number of West African countries and was intended as official transnational carrier for francophone West and Central Africa. It was formed because individually the countries did not have the capability to maintain a national airline. A major problem was that each investing country wanted its own offices and ground handling using its own staff, and several wanted a large share of services. The airline closed in 2002 (Amankwah-Amoah and Debrah, 2014).

More recently, at a conference of the Economic Community of West African States and the West African Economic and Monetary Union in Niger in 2004, it was decided to create a private, commercially oriented pan-African airline. Set up in 2005, it began operations in 2010 as ASKY Airlines and is based in Lomé, Togo, with 80 percent of its shares held by private investors, and 20 percent by public financial institutions. Ethiopian Airlines has a 40 percent stake in the company as a technical and strategic partner under a management contract for the first five years of operation. In 2015 it was operating services to 18 destinations in West and Central Africa.

Currently, the main airports serve to link Africa's major cities but, in a global context, only Cairo and Johannesburg rank in the world's top 150 airports in terms of the traffic handled. The important major hubs in the sub-Sahara are Johannesburg, Nairobi, Lagos, and Addis Ababa with large secondary airports such as Cape Town and Durbin offering feed. The increase in mainline services should be taken in the context of a consolidation of number of airlines and by 2012, EgyptAir, Royal Air Maroc, South African Airways, Ethiopian Airlines and Kenya Airways accounting for around 80 percent of scheduled capacity within Africa. The trend has been for increasing connectivity between African cities and with large urban area more generally (Otiso *et al.*, 2011). These networks also correlate with the trade patterns between the major urban areas in the mega-region (Button *et al.*, 2015a). The major hubs in the Maghreb are Cairo, Casablanca, and Algiers, with these often serving as feeder airports for services into Europe.

In terms of inter-continental traffic, while the former colonial powers tend to still provide the largest share of capacity, their relative position is changing. In particular, the Gulf carriers and Turkish Airlines have very rapidly developed a network of services based on their hubs that link Asia, and to a lesser extent Europe, to major African markets. Dubai-based airline, Emirates, is barely one-third the age of most of the world's legacy airlines but is now bigger than Air France, KLM, and Lufthansa combined. Similarly, Qatar Airways and Etihad Airways have leveraged territorial wealth and geography to grow based on large fleets of new and fuel-efficient aircraft. The Gulf carriers also fly from airports that have been expanded and updated. In 2014 Dubai International Airport became the world's busiest international airport in terms passenger numbers and, in 2015, 13 African airlines flew to it from 29 origins in 20 countries.

African air traffic is increasingly global traffic passing east-west through the Gulf, with relatively little capacity offered in a north-south direction. For example, in 2005, only about 11 percent of traffic transiting through Dubai on Emirates was connecting onwards to Africa (O'Connell, 2006). Africa accounted for 5.5 percent of available seat kilometres outbound weekly from Abu Dhabi, Doha, and Dubai together, but by 2009 this had increased to 8.1 percent.

The Gulf carriers and Turkish Airlines are being supplemented by Chinese and Asian airlines. Hainan Airlines, for example, has in the past served Luanda with more limited services to Cairo and Khartoum, and in 2013 it announced it would begin a Beijing to Dar es Salaam flight while China Southern Airlines announced a Guangzhou to Entebbe service, but neither materialized. The latter did inaugurate services to Nairobi in 2015, having abandoned its four-year Beijing-Dubai-Lagos route in 2010. In 2015, Air China started non-stop flights from Beijing into Addis Ababa and Johannesburg. It began Beijing to Johannesburg code sharing with South African, and to Addis Ababa services in 2015. The Johannesburg flight is costly with weak premium yields and poor connections from Johannesburg. The Addis Ababa service (because flights are shorter, allowing smaller aircraft, and the Ethiopian Airlines network offers a wide range of attractive connections) is more commercially viable.

Foreign investment in African airlines from outside of Europe has been limited, with alliances and agreements generally being preferred to financial entanglement. One exception is Air Seychelles that is 40 percent owned by Etihad Airways under a strategic equity partnership. China's interest in linking with African airlines really began in 2012 with Hainan Airlines' parent group and China Africa Development Fund forming a joint venture to purchase a controlling stake in Ghana's Africa World Airlines that had been incorporated in 2010, and started operations in 2012.

The airline situation is not helped by the inherent nature of African's industry. There is a shortage of skilled labour in Africa, corruption, overstaffing, a strong travel agency network that takes 7 percent commission, thin routes, low Internet penetration, and poor and lack of investment opportunities for fleet modernization. One result of this is low average utilization of aircraft-some 6.9 hours a day compared to 9.9 for European carriers-and low load factors-71.3 percent in 2015 compared with a global average of 78.8 percent. This has led to considerable market instability with 37 new airlines being launched in the decade from 2000, and 37 failing. The continent also has a poor safety record with 23 percent of the world's jet hull losses occurring there in 2010, or put another way, in 2012 African airlines had one accident for every 270,000 flights whereas the industry average was one accident per five million flights.

The book

This book of original papers fills an emerging void in the literature regarding aviation markets. Africa contains most of the least developed of these markets but it is a mega region that is of increasing importance to the aviation community and to those, such as the World Bank, that have an interest in economic and social development. We have seen that it is the smallest of the "mega-region" aviation markets but the one that Boeing and others that produce aviation traffic forecasts, expect to expand, at least in percentage terms, quite rapidly over the medium-term. The growth in tourism and demands for "exotics" are major drivers of development and require air transport. Modern manufacturing and high-tech industries also rely on air transport more than the more traditional, low value added extractive sectors.

The topics covered in the book are designed to provide a good, although not an impossibly comprehensive, set of examinations of ongoing issues. They are explicitly focused on the economic and political dimensions of the subject, although with relevance in many cases to the strategic concerns of airline management and infrastructure providers and operators. The authors are largely academics who have been active in thinking about and researching the African aviation sector. The papers are largely drafted in a way that are relatively easily accessible to allow for their assessment and discussion. Basically, as the great English economist Alfred Marshal put it, and we paraphrase, write a paper in mathematics, if the outcome cannot be translated into good, straightforward English, burn it and start again.

The substantive content of the book begins by providing an overview of the longer term and more recent trends in African aviation. Berendien Lubbe and Svetlana Shornikova take a broad perspective and look at the ways in which aviation, with its various sub elements of airlines, airports, and air traffic control, has developed in sub-Sahara Africa beginning in the immediate post-World War I period. This involves the movement away from the colonial period when, albeit very limited, air services were largely designed to meet the needs of their respective colonial powers and takes us up to the present day. This period of almost a century saw major changes in the sector, not only in terms of the technology deployed, but also in the objectives of the political authorities with oversight of their national air transportation systems and the regulatory tools that have been applied, with divergent degrees of success, in seeking to achieve these objectives.

Key elements of this larger perspective are then examined in more detail in a series of contributions. Chapter 3, by Davide Scotti, Gianmaria Martini, Stefano Leidi, and Kenneth Button complements Chapter 2 by looking specifically at the emergent airline network configurations within Africa and discussing the ways in which they have evolved. It pays attention to the more recent period over which many of the countries in sub-Saharan Africa have enjoyed relatively rapid growth and when more liberal economic regulatory regimes have come to the fore. Following this, David Warnock-Smith and Eric Tchouamou Njoya turn to more institutional matters and outline and discuss the ways that air service agreements have evolved in the Continent. They also, and this is very much linked to the more physical network material outline in Chapter 3, consider how these agreements have impacted on the various African aviation markets. The conclusion is that "regulations matters".

The next two chapters by Gordon Pirie, and Rui Nieva and Charles Schlumberger, respectively, consider two important developments in the African market. Pirie focuses on the very rapid and considerable growth in the long-haul Gulf Carriers, and the extent to which they have penetrated the African market at a very rapid rate. The conclusion here is not one of optimism for the majority African airlines, although there are some encouraging signs for Ethiopian Airlines. Nieva and Schlumberger look at a different issue, the emergence of low-cost carriers in short-haul markets as the regulatory regimes in Africa are being liberalized. The issues here, although institutional obstacles remain, often lie in the inadequate aviation infrastructure that is a feature of much of the continent, and in the generally higher prices of fuel that are found there compared to many other economically emergent parts of the globe.

Finally, the last two papers move to even more micro-issues, namely the ways in which individual airlines operate in the African context. Stephan Heinz and John F. O'Connell look at the market features that pose challenges to those operating airlines in Africa and seven types of business models that are being developed to handle these making use of airline data. The African market has proved extremely inhospitable to many airlines and large numbers have been forced from the market. Joseph Amankwah-Amoah examines the case of Air Afrique, an undertaking of several former French colonies to meet the challenges of thin markets and limited resources to cooperate in creating an airline. The airline failed, and the contribution provides an account of what happened.

Note

1 https://she.mumc.maastrichtuniversity.nl/sites/intranet.mumc.maastrichtuniversity.nl/files/she_mumc_maastrichtuniversity_nl/2014_wesp_country_classification.pdf.

References

African Union (2011) *Capacity Building. Impact of Brain Drain on African Aviation*, African Union, Luanda.

Amankwah-Amoah, J. and Debrah, Y.A. (2014) Air Afrique: The demise of a continental icon. *Business History*, 56, 517–46.

Barros, C.P. (2011) Cost efficiency of African airports using a finite mixture model. *Transport Policy*, 18, 807–13.

Boeing Commercial Aeroplane (2015) *Current Market Outlook*, 2015–2034, www.boeing.com/resources/boeingdotcom/commercial/about-our-market/assets/downloads/Boeing_Current_Market_Outlook_2015.pdf.

Button, K.J., Brugnoli, A., Martini, G. and Scotti, D. (2015a) Connecting African urban areas: airline networks and intra-sub-Saharan trade. *Journal of Transport Geography*, 42, 84–9.

Button, K.J. Martini, G. and Scotti, D. (2015b) African decolonization and air transportation. *Journal of Transport Economics and Policy*, 49, 626–39.

Button, K.J. Martini, G. and Scotti, D. (2016) Impacts of the Arab Spring on trade in airline services. *Applied Economics Letters*, 23, 532–5.

Button, K.J. Martini, G., Scotti, D. and Volta, N. (2017) Fare elasticities of demand for direct and indirect fights in sub-Saharan Africa. *Applied Economic Letters*, 24, 523–6.

Button, K. and McDougall, G. (2006) Institutional and structural changes in air navigation service-providing organizations. *Journal of Air Transport Management*, 12, 236–52.

Dobruszkes, F. and Mondou, V. (2013) Aviation liberalization as a means to promote international tourism: the EU-Morocco case. *Journal of Air Transport Management*, 29, 23–34.

Esler, D. (2015) Assessing Africa's aviation infrastructure. *Aviation Week*, October 26.

Gwilliam, K.M. (2011) *Africa's Transport Infrastructure. Mainstreaming Maintenance and Management*. World Bank, Washington, DC.

Heinz, S. and O'Connell, J.F. (2013) Air transportation in Africa: toward sustainable business models for African airlines. *Journal of Transportation Geography*, 31, 72–83.

Infrastructure Consortium for Africa (2014) *Infrastructure Financing Trends in Africa-2014*. ICI, London.

InterVISTAS (2014) *Transforming Intra-African Air Connectivity: The Economic Benefits of Implementing the Yamoussoukro Decision*, InterVISTAS, Bath.

Njoya, E.T. (2016) Africa's single aviation market: The progress so far. *Journal of Transport Geography*, 50, 4–11.

Limdo, N. and Venables, A.J. (1999) *Infrastructure, Geographical Disadvantage, and Transport Costs*, World Bank, Policy Research Working Paper, 2257, Washington, DC.

O'Connell, J.F. (2006) The changing dynamics of the Arab Gulf based airlines and an investigation into the strategies that are making Emirates into a global challenger. *World Review of Intermodal Transportation Research*, 1, 94–114.

Otiso, K.M., Derudder, B., Bassens, D., Devriendt, L. and Witlox, F. (2011) Airline connectivity as a measure of the globalization of African cities. *Applied Geography*, 31, 609–20.

Pirie, G. (2014) Geographies of air transport in Africa: aviation's 'Last Frontier', in A.R. Goetz and L. Bud (eds) *The Geographies of Air Transport*. Ashgate, Farnham.

Schlumberger, C.E. (2010) *Open Skies for Africa-Implementing the Yamoussoukro Decision*. World Bank, Washington, DC.
Stephens, M.S. and Ukpere, W.L. (2011), Airport capacity utilization in Nigeria: a performance and efficiency analysis. *African Journal of Business Management* 5, 11104–15.
World Bank (2009) Africa Infrastructure Country Diagnostic: Air Transportation Challenges to Growth, Report 49194, World Bank Washington, DC.

2 The development of African air transport

Berendien Lubbe and Svetlana Shornikova

Introduction

This chapter covers five main periods in the development of aviation in Africa, the political history of which determined much of the direction in which aviation developed on this vast continent, both from an international and regional perspective.

It begins with the colonial period that, amidst the empire-building ambitions of the colonial powers, served to provide Africa with the fundamental tools of an aviation system. The second period, commencing after World War II, marked a turning point in civil aviation in Africa because of both technological advances and the beginnings of the process of decolonisation. Several regional airlines were developed under the wing of the national carriers of the colonial powers and, albeit not always realised, profitable operation became possible.

The third period saw the attainment of independence where African states established their own national carriers and divested themselves from their colonial masters. The fourth period ushered in the beginnings of the deregulation and liberalisation efforts to lift the restrictive air service agreements under which the airlines were operating and to provide an environment of cooperation within Africa, but which has achieved less than satisfactory success. Finally, the current aviation landscape in Africa is beset with numerous challenges that impede further development in African aviation.

The colonial period: 1919–1939

Civil air transport evolved in the 1920s as a by-product of military aviation with the military aircraft of the First World War being adapted for civilian use. The main area of development during this first decade of air transport was in Europe, more specifically Britain, France, and Germany, each having purchased several small airlines which progressively amalgamated with other small airlines to form national flag carriers such as Imperial Airways in 1924, Lufthansa in 1926 and Air France in 1933. By the end of the decade the European continent had a comprehensive network of government-subsidised air services (Brooks, 1967). These developments provided the means for the major colonial powers such as Great Britain, France, Belgium, and Portugal to extend their international interests beyond the European continent with colonial Africa, particularly south of the Sahara[1]. The period between the two great wars was dominated by imperial ambitions in Africa, occupying a significant place in the overseas ambitions and itineraries of European airlines in the 1930s (Budd, 2014).

> People and nature may or may not have to be subdued, but remoteness positively must be subdued. Links are required to create and maintain an empire – to breach the horizon, spread into new land, occupy and unify distant territory, and then to manage, defend and exploit it. Transport is a key tool of empire.
>
> (Headrick in Pirie, 2011: 1)

The first decade of flying saw many constraints in the equipment used. Before the First World War flying machines were for recreational purposes (Pirie, 2011).

By 1924 most aeroplanes were converted or modified war machines from the huge inventories left over from the war. It was not until 1925 that the industry truly began to design aircraft to meet the requirements and the special needs of colonial aviation (McCormack, 1989), spurring British industry and the British Government on to harness the new technological possibilities. Pirie (2011) describes the beginnings of civil aviation as 'flights of discovery' into the Empire in 1919–1920, followed by mail-only military services, then air services for military personnel, and onto 'headline-grabbing' flights by senior public officials and private citizens. Commercial passenger Empire flying started in the early 1930s but were not without problems such as configuring aircraft appropriately for passengers and airfreight over long-distances, and acquiring permission to fly over non-imperial territory. This was a major obstacle to be overcome by protracted and delicate negotiations (Pirie, 2011).

Commercially most travel by air was work-related and where leisure tourism was the purpose it was mainly restricted to the very wealthy (Pirie, 2009). Freight made up a very small proportion of the payload. In the 1920s, profitable operation was quite impossible (Brooks, 1967) and while the metal monoplanes of the 1930s put airlines within reach of profitability, only the most efficient carriers could recover approximately 80 percent of their costs. In colonial Africa, the long distances, low density of traffic, and less favoured economic areas made profitability even less likely. Great Britain also did not favour government support with Winston Churchill famously declaring that "civil aviation must fly by itself" (McCormack, 1989: 377).

McCormack (1976) talks about the development of air transport in Africa during this first decade as another "dimension to the traditional processes of empire-building and colonial rule". This is best illustrated by Imperial Airways which was the 'chosen instrument' of Empire Civil Aviation in 1924

(Pirie, 2011), charged with carrying "*aloft the banners of imperial prestige and power, particularly through Africa where competition for air routes, services, and traffic was not "unlike" the 'scramble' for territory in the late nineteenth century*" (McCormack, 1989: 374–375).

In the years between the First and Second World War, activity in air transport development in Africa increased and by 1939 the major colonial powers could boast several successes across Africa, despite more than a decade of disappointment and frustration due to technological, economic and political difficulties. Belgium established the first internal air-service of any European colony in Belgian Congo in 1920 (Brooks, 1967). By 1925 France had extended its Toulouse-Casablanca air mail service to Dakar and in 1929 was able to run an experimental mail service through to Madagascar. In 1925, the German Junkers firm was negotiating with Egypt for air rights in Egypt and bidding on a tender to provide air mail services in South Africa. Germany scored what McCormack (1976) refers to as a *coup* when Junkers obtained a controlling interest in Union Airways, a privately owned airline formed in South Africa in 1929. Germany successfully tendered for an air mail contract in South-West Africa, putting Great Britain under pressure to support its claims to central and South African traffic (McCormack, 1976). The late 1920s saw Britain's Imperial Airlines extending its international air links with long haul services across Africa between Egypt and South Africa and commencing a weekly service connecting London and Central Africa in 1931 (Pirie, 2009), with this route being opened fully to the Cape in 1932. Air transportation in Nigeria commercial aviation started in 1930 with Imperial Airways inaugurating the first international air service to Nigeria under colonial rule, linking six towns, namely Maiduguri, Kano, Kaduna, Minna, Oshogbo, and Lagos (Akpoghomeh, 1999) using the DH.86 aeroplane. A full French Belgian trans-Saharan air service was in operation linking Europe with West Africa, the Congo and Madagascar by 1934. By 1939 Air France was serving 20 destinations in West and Central Africa and flying through Dakar to South America (Cumming, 1962). During this period, German civil aviation was aiming for commercial air paramountcy in Europe, Asia, South America, and Africa. After 1935, Italy entered the air transport arena competing with Great Britain in Egypt and the Sudan. Egypt was seen as the greatest prize of all due to its location across potential routes linking Europe with Africa, India, and the Far East, inviting almost every powers' attention (McCormack, 1976). In 1936 Imperial Airways had brought British West Africa into the fold by providing a service from Khartoum to Lagos and Accra using a DG.86 biplane which took two and a half days to do the trip carrying 14 passengers. Imperial Airways and Deutsche Lufthansa were also using flying boats to connect the continent with Imperial Airways flying boat[2] to Durban and Lufthansa using Bathurst, Natal, on its South American flying boat service (Cumming, 1962). By 1939 both the French and Belgian lines were linked with British airlines at Broken Hill in Northern Rhodesia (now Zambia).

Cumming (1962) stated that apart from the carriage of passengers and mail across Africa, it was the ability to carry freight that had a special interest in the geographical and geophysical circumstances of Africa, although the goods consigned to and from Africa was still limited during these early years the rate of increase was highest on the internal and regional services.

Despite the progress, frustration was deeply felt in some African countries. Kenya, which is described by McCormack (1989: 374) as the most 'air-minded' of the British colonies, and South Africa, which was the most ambitious and a 'challenging rival to British air interests throughout the colonial period', were at the forefront in their pursuit of establishing local air interests in Africa. Several attempts were made by the white Kenyan community and its governors who were 'air enthusiasts' to focus on local interests and in 1929 Wilson Airways, a private locally-owned airline, was established amidst deep hostility from Imperial Airways. Wilson Airways became Kenya's own instrument and 'flag carrier' for route development at a local and regional level successfully operating, without subsidy, throughout Kenya and Tanganyika and also linking Zanzibar to the mainland. With the outbreak of the War, Wilson Airways was liquidated. Further south commercial aviation first started in Nyasaland (present day Zimbabwe, Zambia, and Malawi) in 1930 with the formation of Christowitz Air Services Nyasaland Limited, which was used solely for charters for government officials, distinguished visitors, and private firms to carry passengers and freight (Florence, 1958). The year 1933 saw the formation of the Rhodesian Airways and in February 1934 this company amalgamated with Christowitz to form RANA and connect Nyasaland, Southern Rhodesia, and Northern Rhodesia and by expanding the carriage of mail by air opened a number of new routes in central Africa (Florence, 1958). In South Africa, by the 1930s, Oswald Pirow, South Africa's Minister of Defence, had made air policy the imperial policy of the Union of South Africa, with claims to predominance in all of Africa south of Nairobi. In 1934 the South African government took over the assets and liabilities of Union Airways, the privately owned airline formed in South Africa in 1929, and renamed the airline South African Airways, at the same time introducing the first multi-engine aircraft for use on domestic routes (www.flysaa.com/us/en/footerlinks/aboutUs/briefHistory.html).

By the late 1930s, South African Airways had built up a fleet of modern twin and tri-engined Junkers aircraft that were superior in speed and capacity to any available British landplanes (McCormack, 1989). South Africa also made claim to full partnership in the running of mainline African air services which, according to McCormack (1989: 382), "British authorities felt difficult to deny politically and even more difficult to challenge operationally". South Africa, under Oswald Pirow, aimed at dominating commercial flying in British Africa, at least as far north as Kenya, pushing Imperial Airways into retreat.

By early 1941, South Africa and Southern Rhodesia were running scheduled services to Kenya, "crowding the skies already busy with BOAC, SABENA,

RAF, and allied military aircraft". Furthermore, the already existing small local carriers such as Wilson Airways and Rhodesian and Nyasaland Airways (RANA) were vulnerable to South Africa's aggressive onslaught to expand into Africa. The type of aircraft operating during the period between the two great wars comprised mainly single-engined de Havillands and Dragonflies and aeroplanes such as the three-engined Westland Wessex. Aeroplanes such as the Dakota DC3, while flying in Africa during the War as military aircraft, were not employed for passenger transport (Cumming, 1962).

As air interests in the colonies increasingly came into conflict with Britain and Imperial Airways a growing sense of community evolved between Kenya, South Africa, and the Rhodesia's for air transport cooperation. By the outbreak of the Second World War a joint Kenyan/Rhodesian air transport organisation was being explored and in 1941 Kenya welcomed a proposal by South Africa to run a circular air service out of Johannesburg through Entebbe and Nairobi (McCormack, 1989). As far as domestic aviation was concerned within states, small aircraft would often flourish as a way to overcome distance, geographically challenging terrain, and lack of other developed transportation systems, but there was no concerted effort to develop domestic aviation (Rhoades, 2004).

While the air transport thrust into Africa was driven largely by colonial interests, according to McCormack (1989), the aim of imperial air policy and the attitudes of Imperial Airways implied a certain willingness to leave the colonies to their own devices while Belgium, France, Portugal, and Spain served their respective colonies through their national carriers. Button, Martini, and Scotti (2015) assert that the differing attitudes of the colonial powers towards their domains influenced the ways transportation was viewed which subsequently impacted the ability of African states to develop their own transportation policy in the post-colonial period.

In summary, it cannot be argued that the colonial period provided Africa with the fundamental tools of an aviation system – routes and terminals, wireless and meteorological organisation, experienced personnel – upon which independent Africa was to build (McCormack, 1976).

The commercialisation period 1945s–1960s

The war marked a turning point in civil aviation in Africa and Cumming (1962) ascribes this to both technological advances in the equipment used and the period of decolonisation. Brooks (1967: 171) says that the 1950s was also a period when profitable operation became possible.

Technological advances saw the coming of long-range aircraft with new large four-engine monoplanes coming into service most notably, according to Brooks (1967), the American Douglas DC-4 and Lockheed Constellation. Brooks (1967) says that the most important feature of the new aircraft was their much greater range with a worthwhile payload (40–60 passengers compared to the 20–30 passengers of the DC-3).

> In the face of this relentless technological advance, flying, from the passenger's point of view, has lost much of its earlier romance, if it has gained immeasurably in convenience. Flying over the long African routes is no longer an adventure in which the weather, the idiosyncrasies of the machine, the maps, the visible fauna below and the captain, on what was almost the quarterdeck, were the passengers' preoccupations. Now the question is whether the filet mignon has been cooked to a turn or whether the aircraft is half an hour late on a journey which has demolished thousands of miles in under half a day.
>
> (Cumming, 1962: 34)

The fierce competition for air supremacy amongst European and African rivals in the colonisation period was displaced by co-operation, at least until the emergence of the independent states after 1957. The Second World War saw changes in air policy with the British now arguing for assistance in Africa, which was contrary to the pre-war orthodoxy of colonial self-sufficiency, this to assure a continued British air presence and control of air transport development in the African colonies (McCormack, 1989). McCormack (1989) suggests that this change could be ascribed in part to British fears for the future of British aviation in Africa after the war as competition had heightened with the entry of the Americans into Africa,[3] the aggressive South Africans, the French, and the Belgians, all of whom were developing or maintaining air services in Africa during the war and preparing for post-war expansion. According to Cumming (1962) African airlines carried a proportionately smaller amount of local traffic compared with the traffic on the long international routes, but the internal airlines were steadily developing their local and regional services all over the continent, with the network of the former French territories of West Africa being particularly comprehensive.

A local African feeder service, West African Airways Corporation (WAAC) was established in 1948 to serve Nigeria, the Gold Coast, Sierra Leone, and Gambia. To encourage regional growth, the Kenyan settlers and their British patrons, with support from BOAC,[4] established a regional airline, East African Airways Corporation (more commonly known as East African Airways) as a replacement to Wilson Airways in 1946 (Irandu and Rhoades, 2006) to be operated by three East African countries namely Kenya, Uganda and Tanzania. East Africa Airways carried 9,500 passengers in 1946 compared with 150,000 in 1960. Central African Airways was established in 1946 to cater for the local air transport needs of three territories of the Central African Federation (Southern and Northern Rhodesia and Nyasaland) which saw as much as a 7,200 percent increase in passenger traffic from 1948 to 1957 (Florence, 1958). Both EAC and CAF managed to operate profitably (Cumming, 1962). In North Africa Air Algérie was founded in 1946 merging with the Compagnie Air Transport, a subsidiary of Air France, to form the Compagnie Générale de Transports Aériens (CGTA) six years later.

South Africa saw Britain's overseas airline (BOAC) reviving the London-Johannesburg service in 1945 with other west European airlines quickly re-establishing themselves in this new passenger market. The incorporation of SAA into the world airlines map of the late 1950s occurred without political restriction despite there being a minority government espousing harsh and blatant racism in South Africa since 1948 (Pirie, 1990: 232). Airline operations in South Africa were only affected some 14 years later at the onset of decolonisation and the independence of black Africa and South Africa's withdrawal from the Commonwealth to become a Republic in 1961.

The system of bilaterally negotiated traffic rights between nations, which had applied generally before the war, was reaffirmed in 1944 by the Chicago Convention (which also set up the International Civil Aviation Organization, ICAO, as the United Nations organisation controlling air transport). The International Air Transport Association (IATA) was subsequently established in 1945 to set the economic rules of engagement for international air transport. Airlines sought profitability with the long-haul European airlines entering partnerships, or 'pool' agreements with African airlines. Brooks (1967) asserts that the fare-fixing environment of IATA, which worked subject to the approval of governments, who themselves negotiate bilaterally all traffic rights between them, had the effect of holding most airlines to just below the level of profitably and dependent on direct and indirect government subsidies

For passengers, the 'pool' agreements and partnerships between airlines provided high-frequency and convenient timetables and for the partners economies accrued and the services could be sold by all the partners as one. Traffic in this period increased substantially, for example, traffic on the route between Britain and the Cape increased from 10 percent in 1955 to 24 percent in 1960. Although Cumming (1962) suggests that the results of the partnerships were of considerable importance to the African airlines, Bickley (in Sochor, 1988) questions whether the newly-emerging nations would have had a real opportunity to participate in international air transport since these nations were not represented in the Chicago negotiations. Their absence had the effect of making them the overall losers in negotiations in this heavily regulated economic environment. According to Sochor (1988: 1307) participants at the Chicago Convention could not agree on the economic rules for international air transport and it was left to the newly created IATA, where "most of the constructive work of IATA was done by about a 'dozen larger carriers' whose opinions and examples carry very much weight'" (Sochor, 1988). As a result, when recommending tariffs a 'determined carrier' could use its vote under the unanimity rule to exact a more favourable compromise. Kenya was particularly critical of the unanimity rule claiming that despite the ostensible encouragement of intense bargaining it inevitably results in the major players having their way.

Given the need to compete globally with larger, better carriers, and the limited funding for aviation developments, African nations attempted to join together (Rhoades, 2004). In 1961 ten African nations signed the Treaty on

Air Transport in Africa, popularly known as the Yaoundé Treaty, which has its roots in Articles 77 and 79 of the Chicago Convention (providing for joint or international operating organisations). These ten nations established Air Afrique[5] to operate international services between contracting states and other nations and to provide domestic and regional services in the former French colonies in West and Central Africa.

In summary, this period saw aviation in Africa developing within an environment of increasing assistance and cooperation from colonial powers. East, West, and Central Africa experienced several amalgamations of smaller airlines into single airlines to better serve regional interests, some of which operated profitably. Flag carriers of the colonial powers provided financial, technical, and management support to the emerging airlines in Africa and negotiated partnerships with African airlines, but these partnerships were confined by a rigid economic system of Bilateral Air Service Agreements, which appeared to favour the more powerful airlines in the partnership.

Independence and the national pride 1960s–1980s

The decolonisation of Africa must be seen as less a historical period than it is a process which began at the close of World War II. Pressure for independence grew rapidly after World War II with the Belgian Congo gaining independence in 1960, and by the end of 1968, all the British and French colonies were independent with Portugal withdrawing from Angola and Mozambique by 1975 (Button, Martini and Scotti, 2015). Decolonisation and its effect on African aviation must be seen against the background of the international conventions on aviation. Under these conventions states exercise sovereignty over their air space but in the African colonies this sovereignty was exercised by the European colonial powers, which claimed the traffic between their colonies and the home country. However, as soon as a colonial territory becomes independent, it is entitled to accede to the Chicago Convention and to exercise sovereignty over its own airspace. According to Cumming (1962) this required considerable re-adjustment for the airlines of the former colonial powers because "one of the first things a newly independent state wants to do is demonstrate its independence by having its own airline and to show its national colours on other independent countries' aerodromes".

A common way of re-adjustment was for the former colonial power to come to agreement with the newly created African states for providing their national airlines with capital and technical assistance. For example, in Nigeria West African Airways Corporation was divided into two main units in 1958, Ghana Airways and Nigeria Airways, both of which had initial capital investment from BOAC (Cumming, 1962). In 1963 Nigeria Airways became a fully-fledged government-owned company when the government bought out the other shareholders (BOAC and Elder Dempster Lines) to provide domestic air services in the country and, along with other international airlines, services along the West African coast, Europe, and America (Akpoghomeh, 1999).

In 1961 the Ghanaian government bought out BOACs share in the airline. In the former French territories airlines such as Air Mali, Air Ivoire, and Air Cameroun were established with Air France going into partnership with Air Afrique (Cumming, 1962). With the attainment of independence, Kenya renegotiated all the Bilateral Air Service Agreements previously entered into on her behalf by the then colonial government of the United Kingdom, which involved the review of traffic rights for all scheduled foreign airlines operating into and out of Kenya. Kenya Airways was subsequently established in 1977 to provide both international and domestic services[6] (Irandu and Rhoades, 2006). In the wake of the decolonization of Africa and the African independence movements, the Federation of Rhodesia and Nyasaland was dissolved on 31 December 1963. In 1964, the independent states of Zambia and Malawi were proclaimed in Northern Rhodesia and Nyasaland. Zambia Airways and Air Malawi were founded as wholly owned subsidiaries of Central African Airways, taking over the route network in the respective countries. In 1965, Air Rhodesia was founded as a third CAA subsidiary. In the early sixties scheduled air services within the Continent were carried out by about 43 airlines supplemented by numerous charter companies. A survey conducted in 1959 showed that 35 airlines of all kinds were registered and based in Africa with 393 out of 1,800 aircraft operating scheduled passenger services (Cumming, 1962).

However, there was little or no coordination between airlines operating parallel routes in Africa. Robert Gardiner, Executive Secretary of the Economic Commission for Africa, in his address to the African Air Transport Conference in Addis Ababa in 1964, stated that this resulted in "poor load factors, unbalanced services to the public, and inefficient utilisation of the fleet" (Weeks, 1965). He further argued for continued support and interest from the experienced airlines.

South African Airways was rather a special case, wholly owned by the South African Government since the 1930s, it had built a strong international route network, been a founding partner of IATA, and emerged as Africa's strongest airline. However, because of Apartheid, the early 1960s saw the beginning of various attempts to isolate South Africa and induce political change, through curtailing the travel of mostly white business travellers, tourists, sportsmen, and state officials by, as Pirie (1990) states 'the strangulation of air traffic'. Pirie (1990) describes the envisaged blockade of the Republic as entailing the severance of air links between South Africa and hostile nations, disruption of international services, and threats to curtail the rights of other airlines flying between South Africa and states uncommitted to sanctions. Black African states also blocked SAA overflying their airspace forcing SAA 'around the bulge' of Africa en route to European and American destinations. A complete ban on air traffic to and from South Africa was not possible due to its geographical position on the world map and the profitability of the route for foreign airlines, although America and Australia withdrew their landing rights from South Africa in the 1980s.[7]

African nations mainly followed the European approach of government ownership, subsidies, and protection from competition only to find themselves competing against larger, better funded airlines of the old colonial powers. Most African national air carriers pursued a business model that consisted of using profitable international routes to and from the territories of their former colonial masters to cross-subsidise their costly, yet extensive, domestic route networks (Guttery, 1998). Many of these airlines failed.[8] However, national airlines were recognised as one of the essential trappings of independence, whatever the economic consequences (Brooks, 1967). This is aptly illustrated in the words of Kwame Nkrumah (the then prime Minister of Ghana) in 1964:

> In connection with the founding of Ghana Airways, it was maintained that there were enough international airlines to serve our needs, and that the formation of a new one was unnecessary multiplication which would only serve to satisfy our national pride. Even if this were true, which it is not, it was an argument that did not appeal to us. Naturally it increases our self-confidence to observe our own people helping to control the intricate mechanisms involved in the functioning of our airways services, and we certainly experience a glow of pride in seeing our flag flying on planes and ships travelling to other countries.
>
> (Weeks, 1965: 28)

In summary, prior to gaining independence, most African countries had air services that were primarily based on the European relationships and agreements. Only in the 1960s, when many colonies became independent countries, did African states start negotiating and concluding their own air services agreements. Following the international example at that time, intra-African air transport services became regulated by the traditional framework of bilateral air services agreements (BASAs).

Deregulation and liberalisation 1980s–2016s

The typical BASAs of 1960s were based on the traditional predetermination model, by which market access and capacity were predetermined. This model controlled the market through effectively restricting competition (Doganis, 2001: 16). Whereas liberalisation had been actively pursued in the United States since the late 1970s and in Europe since the late 1980s, African air services remained generally restrictive, costly, and inefficient (Schlumberger, 2010: 2).[9]

In November 1984, the Economic Commission for Africa of the United Nations Economic and Social Council (ECA) organised a conference in Mbabane, Swaziland, to discuss the reasons why African carriers faced difficulties in obtaining traffic rights in other African states. The conference ended with the Declaration of Mbabane, which called for the creation of a technical committee that would develop "a common African approach for the exchange of third and fourth freedom rights" and "encourage the exchange of fifth freedom rights". It further proposed an additional set of measures that focused primarily on closer cooperation between African carriers. These measures later became the core of the Yamoussoukro Declaration (United Nations Economic Commission for Africa, 1988) which included comprehensive proposals for a general framework of air transport reform in Africa, the unification of the fragmented air transport market, and commitment from the governments represented to make all necessary efforts to integrate their airlines within eight years (United Nations Economic Commission for Africa, 1988, 2001).

During the 1980s and early 1990s air traffic in Africa grew much slower than in the industrialised world. Between 1985 and 1995 the number of revenue earning passenger-kilometres from Africa grew from 43,037 in 1985 to 57,178 in 1995, less than 3 percent per annum. As a result, it dropped from 4.2 percent to 3.4 percent of the world total. Since the mid-1990s African traffic increased more rapidly largely due to traffic growth to and from South Africa as the embargo on South Africa was lifted and many of the smaller international airports in sub-Saharan Africa have stagnated. In addition, many African airlines failed partly because the intra-African traffic dropped from 21 percent of the African traffic in 1985 to only 15 percent in 1996. Out of 18 African airlines only 9 operated in 1997 with a load factor above 60 percent, with others performing around 40 percent (Goldstein, 1999). Liberalisation and privatisation of the African airlines during the 1990s have reduced both the international and especially the domestic route networks. For example, in Nigeria the number of domestic air routes dropped from 63 in 1985 to 15 in the mid-1990s with a slight reduction in passenger movements (Akpoghomeh, 1999). After the deadline of the Declaration in 1996 no significant progress was accomplished and the air transport policy in Africa was inadequate. The market was heterogeneous, fragmented, and still governed by a highly regulatory environment.

A further important step towards intra-African air transport liberalisation was taken in 2000 with the Yamoussoukro Decision (YD), which became fully binding in 2002 and was ratified by 44 African countries to overcome the restrictive and protectionist intra-African regulatory regime based primarily on BASAs, which hampered the expansion and improvement of air transport on the Continent (Meshela, 2006).

The main aim of the Decision was to provide a continent-wide aviation agreement to liberalise the African air transport market and eventually create an "open skies" environment in Africa. The YD is a multilateral agreement amongst most of the 54 African states and allows the multilateral exchange of up to the fifth freedom air traffic rights between any African YD-party state using a simple notification procedure (Schlumberger, 2010).

YD is not mandatory to all members and ten[10] of the 54 African states remain non-signatories. Two of the non-signatories, namely South Africa and Equatorial Guinea (Schlumberger, 2010), have implemented the YD by means of their Regional Economic Communities (RECs). The YD has its legal basis in the Abuja Treaty of 1994, which established the African Economic Community. The Treaty was the culmination of more than 30 years of initiatives all aimed at achieving greater economic, social, and cultural integration among African countries.

While the implementation of the YD has made little progress over the past 15 years on a continent-wide basis, varying levels of progress has been achieved on a regional basis. In general, African states have acknowledged the importance of the YD for the Continent and recognised its precedence over BASAs and national policies and have individually or collectively taken steps to internalise the principles of the YD (United Nations Economic Commission for Africa, 2005). Many countries, including South Africa, Kenya, and Ethiopia, have recently revised existing BASAs with their African counterparts to align the provisions of the YD. For example, by the end of 2010, South Africa had entered into 45 BASAs with African states of which 17 were in line with the key YD principles (Surovitskikh and Lubbe, 2015).

Implementation of the Decision has encountered two opposing realities. Execution in terms of carrying out public policy has seen little progress at the intra-African level; at the same time, in terms of operational implementation, many examples can be seen of countries (Uganda, Ethiopia, Kenya, South Africa) opening up by applying the YD at the bilateral level (Schlumberger, 2010). Despite heterogeneous and slow progress of liberalisation, several positive examples have taken place in the domestic, intra-African and African-international air transport markets (Myburgh *et al.*, 2006; Schlumberger, 2010; Inter*VISTAS*, 2014).

The liberalisation of the domestic South African market in 1991 increased passenger volumes by 80 percent.

The agreement of a more liberal air market between South Africa and Kenya in the early 2000s led to a 69 percent rise in passenger traffic.

Operation of the low-cost carrier service between South Africa and Zambia resulted in a 38 percent reduction in fares and 38 percent increase in passenger traffic.

Ethiopia's pursuit of more liberal bilaterals has contributed to a fare reduction between 10 percent and 21 percent and a 35 percent to 38 percent frequency increase compared to restricted intra-African routes.

The 2006 Morocco-EU open skies agreement led to a 160 percent rise in traffic and the number of routes between the EU and Morocco increased from 83 in 2005 to 309 in 2013.

The 2001–2004 period was characterised by the collapse of some major legacy carriers, significant drops in seat capacity, and the supply of air services. The impact of the YD only became sizable post 2004, with the relative strengthening of stronger African carriers,[11] marginalisation and disappearance of weak carriers, consolidation of networks, development of fifth freedom traffic, especially in regions that lacked strong local carriers, and significant development of sixth freedom traffic driven by the liberalisation of third and fourth freedom capacities within Africa and in some cases with intercontinental counterparts (Schlumberger, 2010).

Additional efforts over the years by a number of RECs, sub-regional bodies, AFCAC, and the AU have resulted in the adoption and implementation of several key cooperation initiatives and milestones to further African air transport integration with the main outcome of the continent-wide YD implementation towards the establishment of a Single African Air Transport Market (SAATM) by 2017 as seen in Table 2.1. To date, 20 member states have signed a Solemn Commitment for the actualisation of the SAATM, namely Benin, Cape Verde, Republic of Congo, Cote D'Ivoire, Egypt, Ethiopia, Kenya, Nigeria, Rwanda, South Africa, and Zimbabwe as champion states in 2015.Later, these countries were joined by Ghana, Sierra Leone, Gabon, Botswana, Mali, Swaziland, Togo, Mozambique, and Republic of Guinea.

Although intra-African air transport liberalisation has been partial and slow, its impact has generally been seen as a positive stimulus to the overall growth of African economies. The main benefits of the implementation of the YD that have been cited and empirically assessed[12] are increased air service levels and lower fares, which in turn stimulate additional traffic volumes, facilitate tourism, trade, investment and other sectors of the economy, and bring about enhanced productivity, economic growth, and employment.

Africa's aviation landscape

Africa's air transport industry has always been a relatively small player compared to the global one. Africa represents less than 2 percent of the world passenger aviation market and less than 1.5 percent of global air freight shipments. It is projected to account for 294 million passengers or 4 percent of global air passengers by 2034. This growth is dismal, especially when compared with traffic for Asia Pacific with an overall market size of 2.9 billion or 40 percent. Air freight is forecast to grow at 4.5 percent per annum for the next 20 years from a base of 781 thousand tons (Boeing, 2015).

Air passenger traffic carried by African airlines increased by 100.3 percent from 38.3 million passengers in 2000 (year the YD came into force) to 76.7 million in 2014. Freight shipment increased by 53.1 percent from 510 thousand tons in 2000 to 781,000 tons in 2014. In 2014, the intra-African market share was 32.4 percent of the number of passengers carried by African carriers, an increase from 21.3 percent in 2000 and the combined fleet size of African airlines was only 690 aircraft, half the size of American Airlines, with 1,494 aircraft (Chingosho, 2015). In 2014, 61.4 percent of aircraft in operation in Africa was made up of single-aisle type, while wide body (large, medium, and small) constituted 21.4 percent and regional jets constituted 17.2

Table 2.1 Key cooperation initiatives and milestones implemented to further African air transport integration: post-YD to present

Year	*Initiative*	*Outcome*
2005	First African Union Conference of Ministers responsible for Air Transport held in Sun City, South Africa	Resolution aimed at accelerating the implementation of the YD was adopted
2006	Second African Union Conference of Ministers responsible for Air Transportheld in Libreville, Gabon	Adoption of the Libreville Plan of Action, which set targets for accident rates, considered an African external policy for negotiation with third parties and set up an action plan with regards to YD implementation
2007	Third African Union Conference of Ministers responsible for Air Transport held in Addis Ababa, Ethiopia	Adoption of a Resolution entrusting the functions of the Executing Agency of the YD to the AFCAC; Declaration on civil aviation security in Africa, which reviewed and updated the action plan adopted in Libreville
2011	Second Session of the African UnionConference of Ministers responsible for Transport held in Luanda, Angola	Adoption of the African Civil Aviation Policy
2012	Ministerial Conference on Safety held in Abuja, Nigeria	Abuja Declaration on Aviation Safety in Africa, which included a Plan of Action and High Level Safety Targets for African Union states
2014	Fourth Meeting of the Bureau of the Conference of African Ministers of Transport held in Malabo, Republic of Equatorial Guinea	Endorsement of the report of the Third Session of the Conference of African Ministers of Transport (CAMT): "Regulation on Dispute Settlement Mechanisms relating to the implementation of the Yamoussoukro Decision"; "Regulation on the powers, functions, and operations of the Executing Agency of the Yamoussoukro Decision"
2014	Route Network Coordination Project	Launched by the AFRAA, incorporating 19 participating airlines with the aim of increasing intra-African flight frequencies and offering flexibility to travellers while increasing airlines revenue at minimum cost
2015	African Union Executive Council, Addis Ababa, Ethiopia	Adoption of the Regulatory and Institutional Yamoussoukro Decision documents
		Competition Relations; Dispute Settlement Mechanism; Consumer Protection Regulations; Regulatory and Enforcement Powers of the Executing Agency

(*Continued*)

Year	*Initiative*	*Outcome*
2015	Assembly of the African Union, Twenty-Fourth Ordinary Session, held inAddis Ababa, Ethiopia	Solemn Commitment by African Union Member States to the Implementation of the Yamoussoukro Decision towards the Establishment of a Single African Air Transport Market by 2017 involving Benin, Cape Verde, Congo Republic, Cote d'Ivoire, Egypt, Ethiopia, Kenya, Nigeria, Rwanda, South Africa, and Zimbabwe, (Ghana and Sierra Leone declaring their solemn commitment) with a Working Group constituted to facilitate the opening of African skies for African operators
2015	First Meeting of the Ministerial Working Group on Implementation of the Yamoussoukro Decision and Establishment of a Single Air Transport Market in Africa held in Addis Ababa, Ethiopia	Adopted Rules of Procedure and Road Map on the Implementation of the Yamoussoukro Decision and the Establishment of a Single African Air Transport Market within the context of the AU Agenda 2063
2016	AFCAC	Submission of the following documents to the AU for consideration and review for immediate implementation: Memorandum of Cooperation between AFCAC and Regional Economic Communities, proposal on collaboration in training relevant personnel, proposal for Rule Making on the YD and the Rule Making Procedure. All providing a framework for enhanced cooperation, collaboration and actualisation of the Single African Air Transport Market by 2017
2016	Signature of a Continental Open Sky Agreement	Was expected by June 2016 (not implemented)
2016	Establishment of an African Civil Aviation Arbitration Tribunal	Was envisaged to be finalised by December 2016 (not implemented)
2017	Single African Air Transport Market	Scheduled to be operational by June 2017

percent. The top five airlines in terms of number of aircraft in operation were Egypt Air, Ethiopian Airlines, South African Airways, Kenya Airways and Royal Air Maroc. Boeing (2015) forecasts that Africa will require 1,080 new airplanes over the next 20 years, approximately two-thirds of which will expand the region's fleet. Of this, about 4.9 percent will be medium-wide-body aircraft, 18.3 percent small wide body, 70.4 percent single aisle and 6.3 percent will be regional jets. The number of commercial aircraft forecasted to be in operations in Africa by 2034 will be 1,860.

The African aviation industry has experienced rapid growth over the past decade passing through a turbulent phase that came in the aftermath of the 2009 financial crisis. Intra-African air travel has also undergone continuous growth mainly driven by the expanding middle class, high population growth, emerging megacities, multitude of tourism spots, and recent increase in the rate of urbanisation, regional trade, and cross investments between African countries (Chingosho, 2015; Adeyeye, 2016). The following recent developments in the intra-African market can be observed.

The collapse of several airlines which have either been reorganised under bankruptcy protection or ceased operations. Over the last decade 37 airlines have launched in Africa and 37 have failed.[13]

Market consolidation accompanied by the building of the hubs by five major carriers (EgyptAir, Royal Air Maroc, South African Airways, Ethiopian Airlines and Kenya Airways), which in 2012 accounted for around 80 percent of all scheduled capacity within Africa. FlightStats (2013) highlights that since 1994 there has been route consolidation with a number of low frequency and small aircraft routes having been abandoned. The number of intra-African routes flown has decreased from 1088 in 1994 to 719 in 2013. This development led to uneven geographical distribution of intra-African air passenger traffic, primarily concentrated on a few key routes and predominantly linking large and medium cities to the five hubs. While Eastern and Southern Africa have successfully established a strong air transport industry, Central and Western African markets are characterised by a less developed hub system and in some cases negative growth (Njoya, 2016).

The low-cost sector has been rapidly developing in recent years,[14] Official Airline Guide (2012) states that the contribution of the low-cost carriers (LCCs) in market share to and within Africa grew by six percent over the last decade and African LCCs represented nine percent of the annual seats carried in Africa in 2013 (Boeing, 2015). These airlines address the traffic rights problems by setting up multiple subsidiaries. The extent of success and viability of the LCC model in Africa largely depends on addressing the challenges facing aviation operators on the Continent.

New market entry has accelerated over the past decade. Despite market consolidation by the major airlines and collapse of some airlines, the number of African-based carriers has doubled since 1994 to 70 in 2013 (FlightStats, 2013).

There has been an increasing private sector participation and the industry has seen a new breed of private carriers operating primarily in the domestic and regional markets. Countries, such as Botswana, Cote d'Ivoire, Ghana, Nigeria, and South Africa have successfully attracted private investors in their main airports (Njoya, 2016).

Large African carriers with expansive networks (South African Airways, Ethiopian Airlines, EgyptAir, and Kenya Airways) have entered into global alliances to open and secure new markets by interlining. The first three belong to Star Alliance, and Kenya Airways is a member of SkyTeam.

There has been an increase in intra-African airline network cooperation. In 2016, Ethiopian airlines and RwandAir announced a new alliance, which gives their respective flag carriers' fifth freedom rights to operate unhindered in each other's space. The alliance allows the use of one another as a hub for passenger traffic to a third country on the Continent. Ethiopian also partners with Malawi Airlines and Togo's ASKY. Another example of cooperation is the 2015 merger of Djibouti's privately-owned national carrier, Daalo Airlines and Kenya-registered Jubba Airways, operating out of Somalia (Adeyeye, 2016).

Notwithstanding Africa's growth drivers, the Continent's huge potential for air transport is underexplored.

Challenges impeding continued development of air transport in Africa

The heterogeneous and fragmented nature of African air transport market is linked to disparities in economic and political size of the countries. There are hubs in East, South, and North Africa, which account for most of the scheduled capacity in Africa, however they link only a limited number of key routes. West and Central Africa have not been so successful in establishing hubs and many state-owned carriers in these regions have collapsed[15] (Njoya, 2016).

Dependency of many countries on the former colonial powers: Africa's air transport integration efforts have failed to redress the continued focus upon colonial patterns of commerce, which paid little or no attention to the intra-African integration. The liberalisation progress achieved by several RECs has been primarily based on regional schemes introduced by former colonial powers and established according to common colonial and linguistic ties (Njoya, 2016).

Restrictions on ownership: the YD imposes limits on transnational ownership and control of airlines, which is a disincentive for any airline seeking to access foreign capital or countries in the region (Njoya, 2016). Approximately half of Africa's 54 countries have a national airline with at least 51 percent state ownership (Pirie, 2014). The absence of a mechanism to form or jointly own airlines on the Continent is a major impediment to liberalisation.

Nature and structure of African airlines: Over a quarter of routes in Africa are serviced by a monopoly carrier and of what is carried by African carriers, 80 percent is on 20 percent of the airlines. In some regions the monopolisation of markets is even greater, for example, in 2013, 53 percent of top routes in East Africa had a single carrier (Schlumberger and Weisskopf, 2014).

Lack of political commitment and unification: firm political commitment and actions are necessary to unify the liberalisation process at the national level, as well as to make it less heterogeneous in various sub-regions.

Non-physical barriers to liberalisation such as cumbersome immigration/customs restrictions and procedures, acute shortage of foreign exchange control, high taxes, fees, and charges, *inter alia*, that still exist, need to be relaxed for effective implementation of the liberalisation process. According to Africa Visa Openness Report (2016), Africans need visas to travel to 55 percent of other African countries and only 13 countries offer liberal access (visa free or visa on arrival). In some instances, such as in South Africa, a transit visa is required.

High Taxes, Fees, and Charges (TFCs): the cost of operations is high in Africa, with fuel prices almost twice higher than the world average in many airports and lack of transparency in the pricing system. Most of the service providers are monopoly providers, and without proper regulatory oversight of them coupled with lack of transparency and consultation, this has resulted in the setting of high TFCs. The effect of this is market distortion, damage to the commercial viability of carriers, limitation to growth, and diverted finance (Infrastructure Consortium for Africa, 2014).

Limited skilled manpower: many civil aviation and airport authorities do not have the appropriately skilled manpower due to lack of financial resources. Although African aviation is not new to the loss of skilled manpower, there has been a significant upward increase in the loss of professional and skilled manpower in the last five to six years, *inter alia*, pilots, safety inspectors, engineers, and aircraft technicians. The main factors contributing to the high rate of brain drain range from significant traffic growth in the last decade in certain markets, such as the Asia Pacific and the Middle East, resulting in an exodus of professionals and highly skilled employees from Africa; limited training capacity offered on the Continent; continued instability of African airlines to manpower poaching by large airlines, in particular from the Middle East (African Union, 2011).

Infrastructure, safety, and security concerns: the Continent's infrastructure is generally deficient, dilapidated and not coping with the growing airline industry. Other limitations include inadequate facilities to handle transit passengers, lack of equipment and human resources, and inadequate infrastructure to facilitate the use of cost-effective ICT tools (Kahonge, 2016). Although on average Africa's air transport infrastructure is very poor, a few countries have very good facilities. In particular, South Africa is ranked 15th in the world by the World Economic Forum in terms of its air transport infrastructure, while Tunisia, Mauritius, Ethiopia, Morocco, Seychelles, and Namibia are all in the top 60 globally (KPMG, 2014). The Continent has a poor safety record with the jet accident rate (measured in hull losses per 1 million flights) of 3.5 in 2015 compared to the global average of 0.32. As of the end of January 2016, only 21 African countries had complied with 60 percent or more ICAO Standards and Recommended Safety Practices (Pearce, 2016).

Excessive protection of national carriers: a number of countries continue to restrict market access under the pretext that their national airline is not ready to compete in a liberalised market. Furthermore, several countries insist that non-local airlines pay royalties for the privilege of using additional frequencies beyond what is allowed under the BASA (Chingosho, 2015).

Discriminatory practices against African carriers: some countries in Africa have refused to open their skies to each other, however they have opened up to carriers from other continents. This is particularly apparent in West Africa, where non-African airlines tend to be given more 3rd/4th and sometimes 5th freedom traffic rights while African carriers are denied. For instance, 17 foreign airlines are currently benefiting from 5th freedom rights between certain African cities compared to only 11 African airlines (Kuuchi, 2013). With limited market access it is very difficult for carriers in the region to grow and compete effectively, even if they have resources to expand their network. As a result it is often more convenient, cost-effective, and faster to fly from a city in West Africa via a European or a Middle Eastern hub to another city in West Africa than to travel direct (Inter*VISTAS*, 2014).

Lack of an effective enforcement mechanism: although there is a Monitoring Body that assesses and oversees the implementation of the YD, its role in enforcing the Decision has been ineffectual. However, it must be noted, that the Monitoring Body relies on the willingness of the states to cooperate as it does not have any enforcement rights on its own. Only in 2007 the AFCAC was entrusted with the functions of the Executing Agency and has been given the legal powers to police intra-African liberalisation, acting as an arbitrator between countries.

Competition policies and institutions: the vast majority of African countries do not regulate competition or have institutions that specialise in competition matters. Liberalisation has been further inhibited by the fact that no regional or AU competition rules and arbitration procedures have been implemented to support the implementation of the YD. No community treaty has been implemented in Africa that would ensure that competition in the African market is not distorted and that markets operate as efficiently as possible within a single economic market (Vermooten, 2008). Only in 2015, the African Union Executive Council adopted the four key regulatory and institutional YD instruments: Rules and Procedures Relating to Competition; Dispute Settlement Mechanism; Consumer Protection Regulations; Regulatory and Enforcement Powers of the Executing Agency (African Union, 2015).

Aged aircraft and operational inefficiencies: African carriers have some of the oldest fleets in the world, with 80 percent of all aircraft registering over an age of 10 years or older, which in turn triggers higher associated maintenance costs, increased fuel consumption, poor reliability, and increased downtime. Aircraft utilisation rates in Africa remain among the lowest in the world with rates averaging just 6.9 hours per day compared to Europe with 9.9 hours. This is attributable to poor scheduling, night flying restrictions, extended downtime of aging aircraft, and a shortage of flight and maintenance personnel (Heinz and O'Connel, 2013).

Connectivity: due to limited implementation of the YD and other issues discussed, connectivity on intra-African routes remains limited as depicted

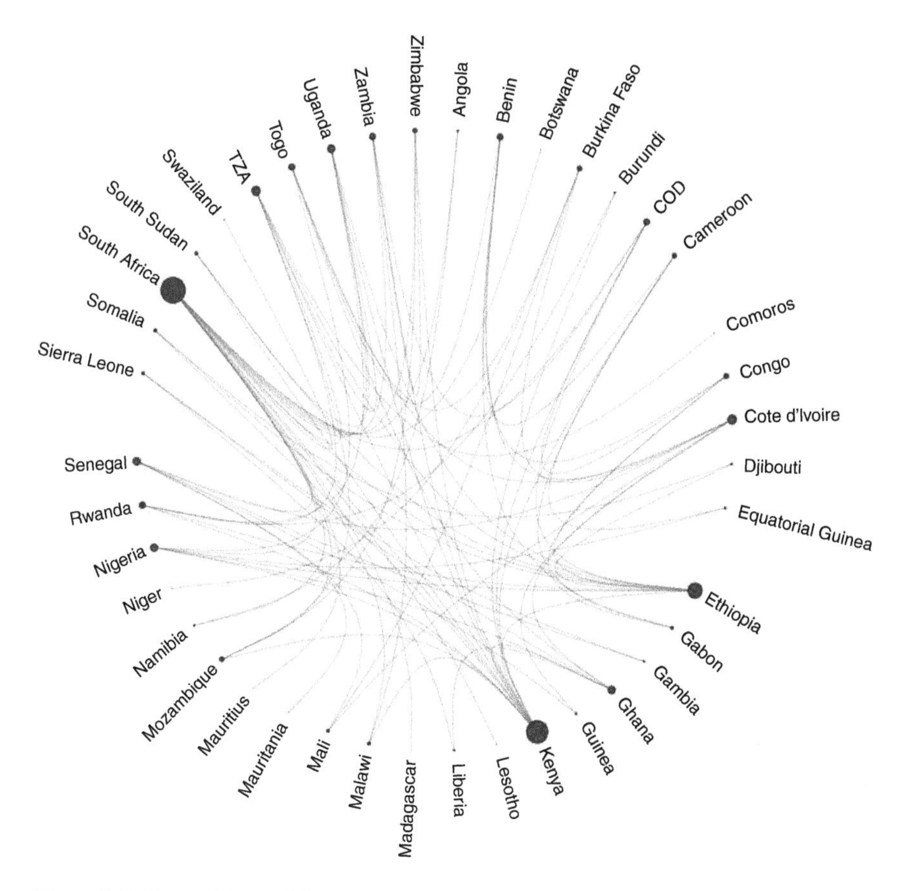

Figure 2.1 Limited intra-African connectivity.
Source: Boeing (2016).

in Figure 2.1. By the end of May 2016, only Ethiopia and Kenya had direct connections to more than half of the other countries in Africa (Pearce, 2016).

Conclusion

While the performance of the aviation industry in Africa still lags behind the rest of the world and it faces numerous challenges, growth in traffic has increased at a higher rate than the global average and this is expected to continue. Air travel plays a vital role in the continent's economic development. If Africa can overcome its numerous challenges and constraints, both from a political perspective and within its overall air transport system, growth in air travel will undoubtedly be accelerated. Air travel has the capacity to act as a catalyst for Africa's prosperity.

Notes

1 According to Button *et al.* (2015) North Africa, with its history and common religion, had a different tradition of colonisation going back much further with well-established trading ties with Europe. Their intra-regional economic linkages and integrated trade patterns were much more extensive than those between sub-Sahara nations.
2 This journey took four and a half days with 13 intermediate stops, two of which were overnight.
3 Pending the signing of a bilateral agreement with SAA Pan-Am (the American carrier) began a non-scheduled service linking New York, Kinshasha, and Johannesburg in 1947.
4 The British Airways Overseas Corporation (BOAC), a new public corporation, was created following in the footsteps of its European and South African competitors in forming a publicly-owned national airline.
5 Air Afrique declared bankruptcy in 2002, after years of financial crisis blamed on mismanagement e.g. many people with family links to government members and senior officials were allowed to travel free (Rhoades, 2004).
6 KLM acquired a 26 percent share in Kenya Airways in 1996.
7 The lifting of sanctions in the 1990s saw positive change and the resumption of flights. According to Pirie (in Budd, 2014) after being excluded from African skies during Apartheid, SAA was a conspicuous exponent of inward 'Africanisation' e.g. in 2002 it bought a 49 percent share in Tanzania's national carrier.
8 Examples include Botswana National Airlines (1966–69); Royal Air Burundi (1960–63); Air Congo-Brazzaville (1961–65); Gambia Airways (1964); Ghana Airways (1958); Air Malawi (1964); Nigeria Airways (1958–2003); Air Rwanda (1975–96); Zambia Airways (1963–94); and many others (Schlumberger, 2010: 7).
9 A World Bank Study (1998) states that the reasons for this are high operating and capital costs, which include 40 percent higher airline insurance premiums, 50 percent higher fuel costs, 15–30 percent higher lease rates for equipment and 100 percent higher air navigation fees (compared with South America); high handling and maintenance costs; and difficulties in obtaining necessary working capital.
10 The 10 non-signatory states can be grouped into three categories: (a) states that never signed the Abuja Treaty (Eritrea and Morocco); (b) states that signed but never ratified the treaty (Djibouti, Gabon, Madagascar, and Somalia); and (c) states that ratified and/or deposited the instruments of ratification after the African Union entered into force (Equatorial Guinea, Mauritania, South Africa, and Swaziland).
11 Ethiopian and Kenyan Airways.
12 Myburgh *et al.* (2006), Velia *et al.* (2008), Ndhlovu and Ricover (2009), Schlumberger (2010), Inter*VISTAS* (2014).
13 Examples include, *inter alia*, Air Afrique in 2002, Nigerian Airways and Ghana Airways in 2004, Cameroon Airlines in 2008, Velvet Sky in 2012, and Zambezi Airlines in 2012.
14 In 2015 four LCCs were launched in Africa: fastjet Zimbabwe, flyafrica.com Namibia, FlyEgypt, and Skywise.
15 Air Afrique in 2002, Nigerian and Ghana Airways in 2004, Cameroon Airlines in 2008.

References

Adeyeye, A. (2016) Understanding Africa's slow growth in intra-regional air transport. *Africa Business*. Accessed at: http://africabusiness.com/2016/06/01/africa-intra-regional-air-transport/.

African Development Bank Group (2016) Africa visa openness report 2016, African Union: Addis Ababa.

African Union (2011) *Capacity Building. Impact of Brain Drain on African Aviation.* African Union: Luanda.

African Union (2015) *Towards the Establishment of a Single African Air Transport Market in the Framework of the AU Agenda 2063.* African Union: Addis Ababa.

Akpoghomeh, O.S. (1999) The development of air transportation in Nigeria. *Journal of Transport Geography,* 7, 135–46.

Boeing (2015) *Current Market Outlook: 2015–2034.* Accessed at: www.boeing.com/resources/boeingdotcom/commercial/about-our-market/assets/downloads/Boeing_Current_Market_Outlook_2015.pdf.

Brooks, P.W. (1967) The development of air transport. *Journal of Transport Economics and Policy,* 1, 164–83.

Budd, L. (2014) Geographies of air transport in Africa: aviation's 'last frontier'. *Geographies of Air Transport.* Ashgate: Aldershot.

Button, K., Martini, G. and Scotti, D (2015) African decolonisation and air transportation. *Journal of Transport Economics and Policy,* 49, 626–39.

Chingosho, E. (2015) Report of the Secretary General. Document presented at the 47th AFRAA Annual General Assembly, Brazzaville.

Cumming, D. (1962) Aviation in Africa. *African Affairs,* 61, 29–39.

Doganis, R. 2001. *The Airline Business in the 21st Century.* London: Routledge.

FlightStats (2013) *Analysis: Evolution of the African Airline Market.* Accessed at: www.flightglobal.com/.

Florence, J.A.C. (1958) The growth of civil aviation in Nyasaland. *The Nyasaland Journal,* 11, 14–23.

Goldstein, A.E. (1999) *Infrastructure Development and Regulatory Reform in Sub-Saharan Africa: The Case of Air Transport.* OECD Development Centre: Paris.

Guttery, B.R. (1998) *Encyclopedia of African Airlines.* McFarland, Jefferson.

Heinz, S. and O'Connel, J.F. (2013) Air transport in Africa: toward sustainable business models for African airlines. *Journal of Transport Geography,* 31, 72–83.

Infrastructure Consortium for Africa (2014) *Opening Up Aviation Services in Africa: Implementing Air Transport Liberalization – Benefits and Opportunities.* ICA: London.

Inter*VISTAS*. 2014. *Transforming Intra-African Air Connectivity.* Inter*VISTAS*: London.

Irandu, E.M. and Rhoades, D.L. (2006) The development of Jomo Kenyatta International Airport as a regional aviation hub. *Journal of Air Transportation,* 11, 50–64.

Kahonge, M. (2016) Is Africa ripe for the low cost airline business model. *AFRAA Africa Wings.* Accessed at: www.afraa.org/index.php/media-center/publications/articles-a-research-papers/2016-articles-and-research-papers/602-is-africa-ripe-for-the-lcc-airline-business-model-maureen-kahonge/file.

KPMG (2014) *Transport in Africa.* KPMG: Johannesburg.

Kuuchi, R. (2013) *An Assessment of African Open Skies. AFRAA.* Accessed at: www.afraa.org/index.php/media-center/publications/articles-a-research-papers/2013-articles-and-research-papers/403-an-assessment-of-african-open-skies-by-mr-raphael-kuuchi/file.

McCormack, R.L. (1976) Airlines and empires: Great Britain and the scramble for Africa, 1919–1939. *Canadian Journal of African Studies,* 10, 87–105.

McCormack, R.L. (1989) Imperialism air transport and colonial development Kenya, 1920–1946. *Journal of Imperial and Commonwealth History,* 17, 374–95.

Meshela, B. (2006) *Implementation of the Yamoussoukro Decision: Progressing or Stalled?* Paper presented at the ICAO/ATAG/WB Development Forum, Montreal.

Myburgh, A., Sheik, F., Fiandeiro, F. and Hodge, J. (2006) *Clear Skies over Southern Africa: The Importance of Air Transport Liberalisation for Shared Economic Growth.* The ComMark Trust: Johannesburg.

Ndhlovu, R. and Ricover, A. (2009) *Assessment of Potential Impact of Implementation of the Yamoussoukro Decision on Open Skies Policy in the SADC Region.* (GS 10F-0277P). USAID Southern Africa: Gaborone.

Njoya, E.T. (2016) Africa's single aviation market: the progress so far. *Journal of Transport Geography,* 4–11, 50.

Official Airline Guide (2012) Africa aviation market analysis. Accessed at: www.oag.com/marketanalysis/.

Pearce, B (2016) *The Contribution of Aviation to the Growth of African Economies.* IATA: Abuja.

Pirie, G. (1990) Aviation, apartheid and sanctions: air transport to and from South Africa, 1945–1989. *Geojournal,* 22, 231–240.

Pirie, G. (2009) Incidental tourism: British Imperial air travel in the 1930s. *Journal of Tourism History,* 1, 49–66.

Pirie, G. (2011) Air Empire: British Imperial Civil Aviation, 1919–1939. *Journal of British Studies,* 50, 775–777.

Pirie, G. (2014) Geographies of air transport in Africa: aviation's "last frontier", in A.R. Goetz and L. Budd (eds.). *The Geographies of Air Transport.* Routledge: London, pp. 247–267.

Rhoades, D.L. (2004) Sustainable development in African civil vaiation: problems and policies. *International Journal of technology and Management,* 4, 28–43.

Schlumberger, C.E. (2010) *Open Skies for Africa. Implementing the Yamoussoukro Decision.* The World Bank: Washington, DC.

Schlumberger, C.E. and Weisskopf, N. (2014) *Ready for Takeoff? The Potential for Low-Cost Carriers in Developing Countries.* The World Bank: Washington, DC.

Sochor, E. (1988) International civil aviation and the Third World: how fair is the system? *Third World Quarterly,* 10, 1300–22.

Surovitskikh, S. and Lubbe, B. (2015) The Air Liberalisation Index as a tool in measuring the impact of South Africa's aviation policy in Africa on air passenger traffic flows. *Journal of Air Transport Management,* 42, 159–66.

United Nations Economic Commission for Africa (1988) *Declaration of Yamoussoukro on a New African Air Transport Policy.* ECA: Yamoussoukro.

United Nations Economic Commission for Africa (2001) *Liberalisation of Air Transport Markets Access in Africa: The Road Forward for the Implementation of the Yamoussoukro Decision.* ECA: Bamako.

United Nations Economic Commission for Africa (2005) *Compendium of Air Transport Integration and Cooperation Initiatives in Africa.* ECA: Addis Ababa.

Velia, M., van Bastern, C. and Dykes, A. 2008. Mozambican air transport liberalisation report: a discussion document (2008–03), Trade and Industrial Policy Strategies, Pretoria.

Vermooten, J. (2008) Competition rules within bi-lateral air service agreements (BASAs) for the purposes of developing a liberal regional transport policy within Africa, Paper to the Second Competition Commission, Tribunal and Institute Conference on Competition Law, Economics and Policy. Accessed at: www.econ-jobs.com/research/12684-Competition-rules-within-bi-lateral-air-service-agreements-for-the-purposes-of-developing-a-liberal-regional-air-transport-policy-within-Africa.pdf.

Weeks, G. (1965) Wings of Change. Africa Report February 1965, Africa-America Institute, New York.

3 The African air transport network

Davide Scotti, Gianmaria Martini, Stefano Leidi, and Kenneth J. Button

Introduction

The African aviation industry, according to aircraft suppliers such as Boeing and the UN's International Civil Aviation Organization, has considerable potential, albeit from a relatively low base. The African Continent has limited surface transport to serve its vast area, much of its terrain is hostile, and many of its constituent countries are land-locked limiting international maritime movement. Air transport, because of the relatively small amount of infrastructure it requires and its flexibility, provides a viable mode of transport for many types of both personal and freight movements (Button *et al.*, 2015a) However, it has typically been considered much more as a luxury good rather than as an instrument for economic growth. As a result, Africa has been traditionally seen as characterized by a lack of interconnectivity.

The recent economic and demographic growth of some countries and the joint emergence of a middle class have been changing the way in which aviation is viewed. This is confirmed by the several institutional efforts made over the last 15 years to improve connectivity. At one level, it has seen increased engagement by international agencies, such as the World Bank and, more recently, by institutions such as the China-Africa Development Fund, in financing investments. At the national, institutional level there have been efforts to remove many of the rigid bilateral constraints over capacity and fares. The Yamoussoukro Decision in 1999 was the most important agreement under the umbrella of the gradual liberalization process of African air transport markets (Button *et al.*, 2015b). The Yamoussoukro Decision aimed at liberalizing international air travel within Africa. As a result, many African countries have recently revised several of their bilateral agreements to incorporate the Yamoussoukro Decision's key principles into their national air transport policies (Njoya, 2016; Surovitskikh and Lubbe, 2015).

All these factors have led, albeit from a low base, to a rapid growth of the demand for air transport in Africa even if the promises to create a single air transport market are a long way from being kept and the infrastructure still of a very basic kind.

Here African airport network configuration is analysed in terms of capacity, spatial coverage, and connectivity with a look also at airports' dependency on their main airlines. Analysis is based on Official Airline Guide (OAG) databases for 1997 to 2013; a period starting a few years before the signature of the Yamoussoukro Decision and ending more than ten years later.[1] The study of scheduled direct flights allows us to examine the effects that relatively recent events, most notably, economic and demographic growth and partial market liberalization, have had on the structure of the African airport network.

Initially, however, we outline some of the general economic and technical features of airline networks and the forces that drive their pattern and viability.

The economics of airline networks

At the most basic level, networks can entail simple connectivity with a service along a link joining an origin and a destination.[2] In aviation terms this is often seen on longer routes where a plane provides a daily return trip. In many cases, however, there is sufficient traffic to justify such a service and in these cases either linear routes or hub-and-spoke operations become necessary. The former is essentially like a bus route with, in our case, a plane flying between a variety of airports dropping and picking up passengers so as to maximize its payload.

Hub-and-spoke networks replicate postal services by collecting passengers from a range of origins wishing to go to a diversity of destinations and delivering them at a hub, essentially the "sorting office" where they consolidate and transfer to planes heading to their various destinations. Economies are generated by airlines enjoying the economies of scope created by combining passengers from a diversity of origins and destinations on the same plane, economies of density emanating from the ability to fill larger planes, and, on the demand side, economies of market presence due to the much wider range of origin-destinations pairs they can serve.

There can also be radial networks where planes operate from a base servicing a set of radial routes with no simple, on-line interconnectivity between the services at the base. Here economies are mainly on the cost side resulting from such things as the ability to use standard aircraft, flexibility to change the routes served as demand patterns vary, and the quick turnaround times of planes that is possible.

In a free market context, the airlines will select the network format that generates the highest net revenue, and, indeed in those parts of the world where there are liberal regulatory regimes and no economic barriers to trade in airline services, we find a great diversity of airline network types. Market and policy imperfections of various types, however, are pervasive in the aviation context. Airports take a variety of forms in terms of runway length, radar coverage, terminal capacity, etc., which limit the aircraft that can use them and their number. Aircraft have limits on their range and their crew are constrained, for safety reasons, by legal limits on the hours that they can fly. Air traffic control is limited by its technical specifications, the availability of air traffic controllers, and the air space reserved for military use.

Perhaps of equal or more importance in the African context have been the policy constraints that have influenced the forms of network that are possible.

The Chicago Convention of 1944 gives countries sovereignty over their air space and many use this to extract economic rent from airlines entering from other countries. Many African countries have tried over the years to support a national flag carrier, usually a state-owned airline that has stymied the development of other carriers both within the country and those seeking to offer services to and from it. These are matters discussed elsewhere in the volume.

Also of some relevance here, there are historical inter-continental networks provided by the former colonial powers. These generally involve services from a European hub that collects traffic from not only the parent country but also in other nearby countries and flies it to major African airports where in some cases, such as South Africa, there are air links to other cities in the region, although this is not common elsewhere. Breaking into these sorts of routes to establish their own networks, even with the help of favourable regulations, is difficult for African carriers that lack economies of experience, large fleets, and large domestic markets. In some cases, membership of alliances can help solve this by adding shared routes to a network; e.g. Kenya Airways is a member of SkyTeam, while Egyptair and South African Airways belong to the Star Alliance.

Air transport traffic

Figure 3.1 shows that the number of seats offered by air services to and from African airports between 1997 and 2011 grew to 174.8 million seats in 2011, and by 2013 there were 185 million seats. The upward trend is largely driven by the economic growth of some of the continent's larger countries, by the general trend towards globalization, and by, the albeit often slow, implementation of the liberalization processes.[3]

As we see, available seats until 2006 increased at about the same rate on intra-Africa and inter-continental routes, but since then inter-continental capacity has grown slightly faster. One reason for this has been the commercially-driven move by many carriers as government financial aid has shrunk in many

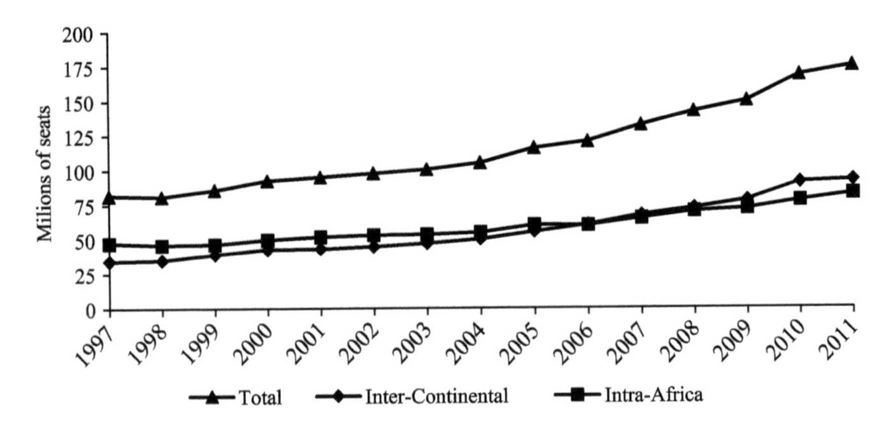

Figure 3.1 Available seats between 1997 and 2011.

countries, to use new capacity on the more profitable routes, especially those connecting African to European and Middle-East airports, with less going to pan-African routes. There has also been a similar pattern regarding existing capacity where it is suitable for inter-continental services. The latter trends have at least, in part, been stimulated by the liberalisation of markets taking place at the same time as the emergence of greater political stability in parts of Africa. As a result, African airports saw an increase of 170 percent in their traffic volumes involving non-African destinations, compared to a 74 percent increase between intra-African destinations. However, the largest increase between 1997 and 2011, over 230 percent, was seen on intra-Africa routes linking different African regions (e.g., Northern and Southern Africa), although this is in the context of an initially poorly developed Pan-African network. The Yamoussoukro Decision has boosted their expansion, from the three million seats offered in 1997 to 10.3 million in 2011.

Figure 3.2 provides details of the main internal and external routes involving Africa for both 1997 and 2011. As can be seen, east and west Africa have increased their connections thanks to the development of regional hubs such as the Kenya's Nairobi's Jomo Kenyatta International Airport, Ethiopia's Addis Ababa's Addis Ababa Bole International Airport and Nigeria's Lagos's

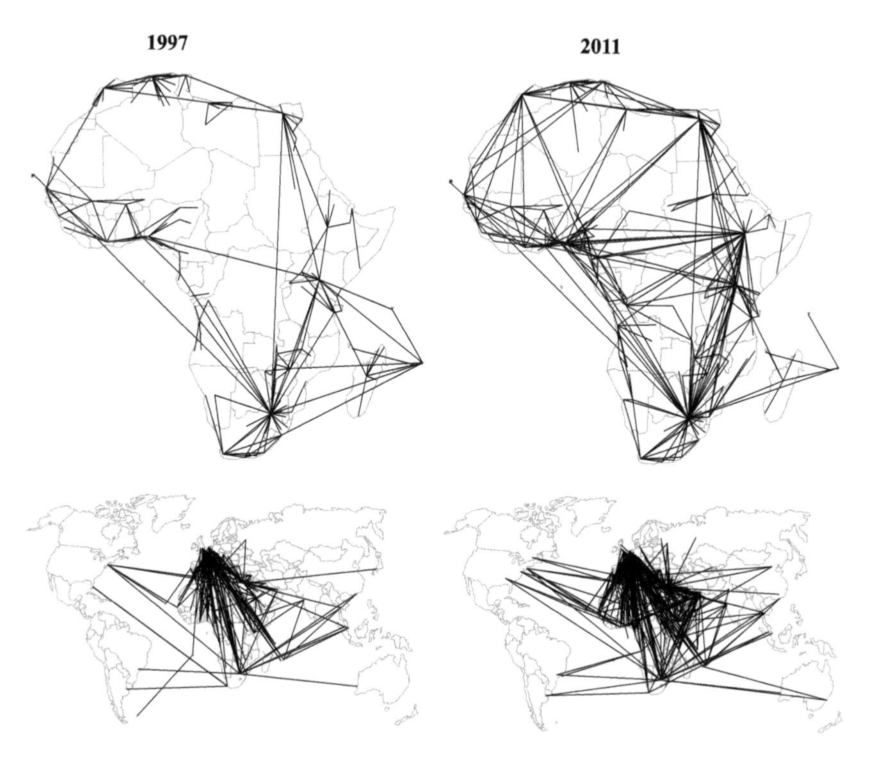

Figure 3.2 Air transport routes with more than 50 thousand seats, 1997 and 2011.
Note: Created using Philcarto (http/philcarto.free.fr).

Murtala Muhammed International Airport. South Africa's Johannesburg's OR Tambo International Airport, however, continues as the major hub, connecting the main African and non-African destinations. Inter-continental connections also exhibited a significant growth, and not only to the traditional hubs in Europe and the Middle East.

The available seat capacities at African airports in 2011 are seen in Figure 3.3. As Njoya (2016) argues the distribution of air capacity, and in turn of air traffic, is not balanced at the regional level. Regarding volume, the main airports are those located in south and North Africa, the two regions characterized by a high relative GDP per capita, supporting a correlation between air transport and economic growth, although not in itself suggesting any causal direction. However, while in the south, South Africa has strong ties with large regional airports of Johannesburg, offering 27.6 million seats, Cape Town with 11.3 million seats, and Durban with 6.5 million, in the north, the national capitals of Morocco, Algeria, Tunisia, Libya, and Egypt tend to be served by what used to be called their "flag carriers" with strong historical, political, and commercial relationships involving intercontinental links with Europe and the Middle East. The situation has recently been affected by the consequences of the Arab Spring and its aftermath that has inevitably impacted on the structure of these networks and the volumes of traffic (Button *et al.*, 2016).

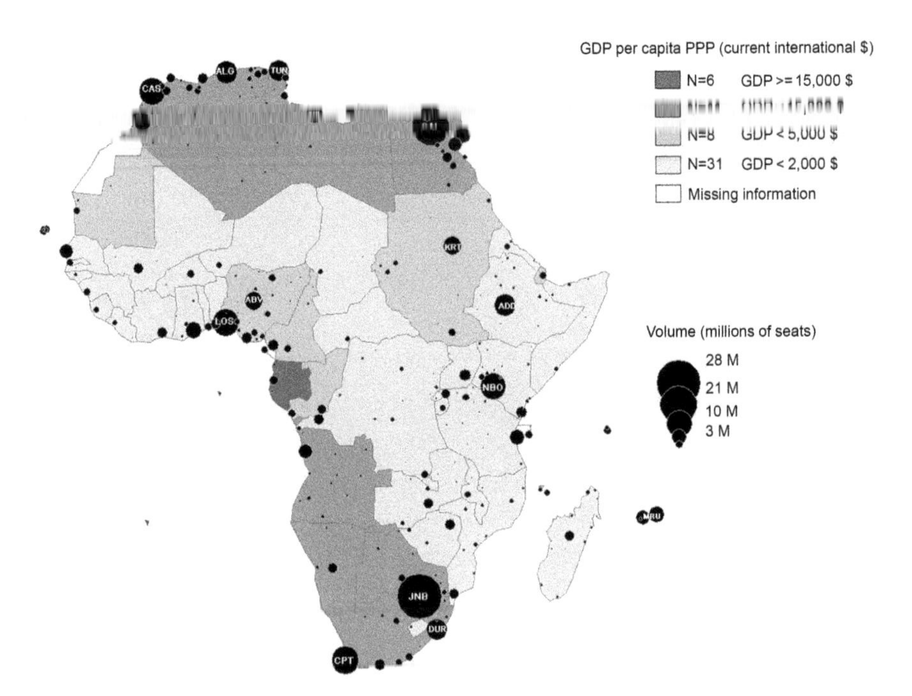

Figure 3.3 Capacity of African airports in 2011.
Note: Created using Philcarto (http/philcarto.free.fr).

In west/central Africa, we find again only one country with what might be termed a developed air transport industry, namely Nigeria with Lagos Airport having a capacity of 10.4 million seats and Abuja Airport (ABV) of 5.1 million. This level of activity has accompanied recent rapid economic growth of Nigeria and deregulation of much of its aviation activity (Ismaila *et al.*, 2014). It has also coincided with the demise of the national flag carrier and the emergence of more commercial driven airlines.[4] Other central/west African countries have much less dynamic air transport industries. Turning to east Africa, there has been considerable increases in activity based around the three international hubs of Nairobi with 9.9 million seats, Addis Ababa with 6.9 million, and Khartoum with 4.9 million.

Considering the evolution of airports' capacities, Figure 3.4 shows that the major African hubs highlighted are also those that have increased their capacity: available seats in 1997 is depicted by upper half-circles, while the geography of the current volumes is depicted by lower half-circles. Considering North Africa, Casablanca, and Cairo airports enjoyed expansions in traffic, taking advantage of the liberalization processes taking place and, in some cases, of the open-air agreements, including the open sky agreement between European Union and Morocco signed in

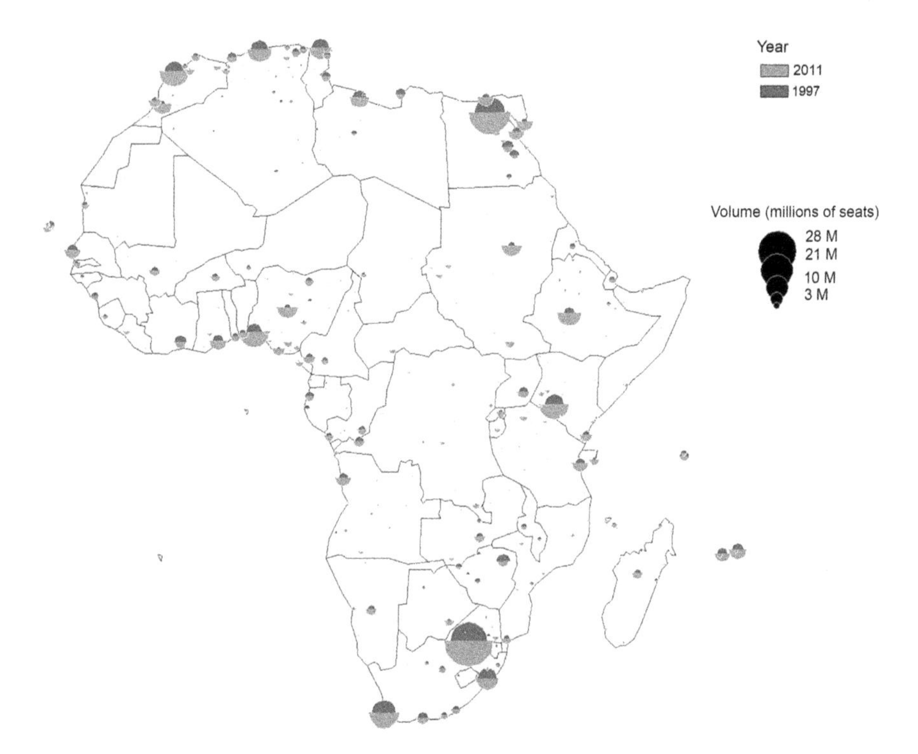

Figure 3.4 African airports' capacities; 1997 and 2011.
Note: Created using Philcarto (http/philcarto.free.fr).

2005 (Schlumberger, 2010). As a result, new connections toward Europe and the Middle East have been introduced. As far as South Africa, the main cities have followed the expansion at the country level, confirming themselves as leading hubs in the continent.[5] The development of the west African aviation network has been characterized by the significant increase in activity at Nigerian airports. Lagos and Abuja have outperformed other regional airports, exploiting the recent economic growth and establishing as the main hubs in the region. Similarly, Nairobi, Addis Ababa, and Khartoum airports in east Africa successfully exploited the growth of their respective flag carriers and increased their traffic volumes and their interconnectivity.

At the same time, many airlines at medium-size airports have maintained, or reduced, the scale of their operations.

This is the case, for example, with some Egyptian, Libyan, Gabonese, Ivorian and Zimbabwe airports. In Egypt, Egyptair has concentrated its network at its Cairo hub, thus reducing its operations at airports such as Luxor and Asyut. In Libya, internal conflicts have slowed the economic and air services growth, and significantly weakened the importance of Libyan Airlines in the northern Africa network. Côte d'Ivoire, Gabon and Zimbabwe have instead lost their relative importance in their respective regions mainly due to the decline of their national carriers. Air Afrique, which had its headquarters in Abidjan, Côte d'Ivoire, went bankrupt in 2002, Air Gabon ceased operations in 2006 and Air Zimbabwe only operates on a discontinuous basis, after having resumed operation in 2014 following a two-year gap.

Considering OAG data, these airlines were ranked in the top 20 in Africa in terms of seats offered in 1997, but a variety of factors, including mismanagement, corruption, and financial difficulties, led to crisis. As discussed in Bofinger (2009) when analysing the evolution of the African air transport markets between 2001 and 2007, despite the consequent short-term drop in capacity, such collapses stimulated a productive process of consolidation in the Sub-Saharan industry. The outcome was an expansion into western African markets by major carriers from the south, notably South African Airways, and the east, including Ethiopian Airlines and Kenya Airways.

Table 3.1 offers details of the top 10 African airports in terms of the sum of arriving and departing seats in 2011. Johannesburg's OR Tambo International Airport has almost doubled its volumes from 1997, confirming itself as the most important airport in Africa. South African Airways is the main airline operating at Johannesburg airport since it provides about 43 percent of the annual departing seats. Cairo International Airport has moved from 10.9 million in 1997 to 21.4 million in 2011. This airport is in a favourable position in the global network allowing it to act as a gate towards Europe and Asia. Consequently, Cairo is connected to 101 destinations, the highest value among African airports, 70 percent of which are located outside Africa. It is the home base of the Egyptian flag carrier Egyptair (its major carrier with 12.8 million seats). Casablanca's Mohammed V International Airport

Table 3.1 Ten largest hubs in Africa by seats (2011)

Airport	*City*	*Seats (millions)*	*Δ% from 1997*
OR Tambo International Airport	Johannesburg	27.642	59
Cairo International Airport	Cairo	21.389	96
Cape Town International Airport	Cape Town	11.273	66
Mohammed V International Airport	Casablanca	10.786	148
Murtala Muhammed International Airport	Lagos	10.430	241
Jomo Kenyatta International Airport	Nairobi	9.583	134
Houari Boumediene Airport	Algiers	7.304	104
Addis Ababa Bole International Airport	Addis Ababa	6.940	391
King Shaka International Airport	Durban	6.471	57
Tunis–Carthage Airport	Tunis	6.303	58

has even exceeded the relative growth of Cairo, becoming the most relevant African airport for the Europe-Africa connection, thanks to its proximity and the capacity provided by low-cost airlines such as EasyJet and Jet4You. Casablanca airport's focus on Europe and west Africa is confirmed by the fact that 68 out of 88 destinations are located outside North Africa. The three major carriers operating at Casablanca airport are Royal Air Maroc, Air Arabia, and Jet4You. In the west/central Africa, Lagos' Murtala Muhammed International Airport experienced a significant growth (i.e., from 3 to 10.4 million seats offered) in line with the country economic development of the last few years, while in the east Africa two major airports – namely, Nairobi's Jomo Kenyatta International airport and the Addis Ababa Bole International Airport – dominate the market.

Spatial coverage

The number of cities served and the number of city-pairs routes operated offers guidance to the spatial coverage of a network.[6] The number of cities involved in the African air transport network is seen in Figure 3.5. Looking at the internal network, it is evident that a slight contraction occurred between 1997 and 2011 mainly due the route consolidation process induced by the liberalisation. As a result, African airlines abandoned some less profitable and lower frequency routes and allocated most of their scheduled capacity to airports acting as new hubs. Hence, the increase in volumes noted earlier resulted mainly from concentrations of traffic at major airports and on a small number of key routes. Additionally, the number of non-African cities connected with the African continent increased.[7] African airlines opened new inter-continental routes from their hubs, exploiting their released capacity and exploiting the gradual deregulation of markets as these occurred. Moreover, non-African carriers entered the African market, connecting the continent

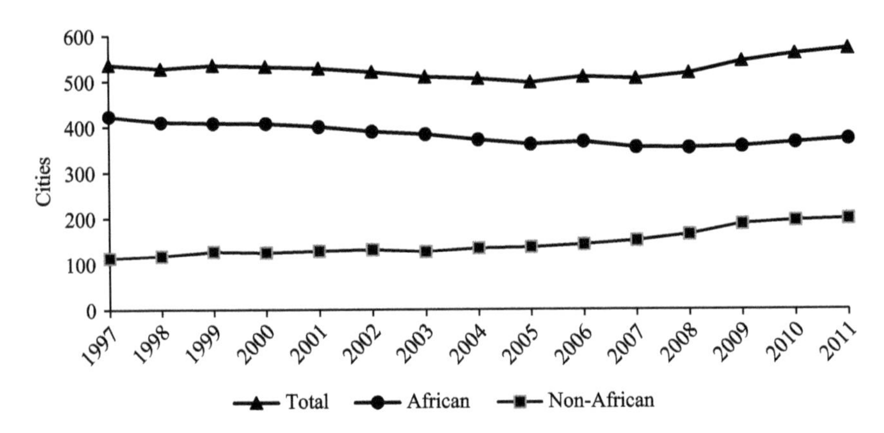

Figure 3.5 Cities connected by airline origin (1997–2011).

with their home country. Middle East and European airlines are trying to leverage their developed network and their strict country relationships to exploit the potential of African market. Also, low-cost carriers, both European, such as Ryanair and EasyJet, and African, such as Jet4You, aggressively entered the North Africa market, especially in Morocco, which entered into an Open Air Agreement with the European Union in 2005. Other African regions do not have anything like a developed LCC market yet.

Focusing on African destinations, it is possible to identify which regions contribute most to the contraction observed in terms of internal spatial coverage. Figure 3.6 illustrates the evolution of the number of cities served by major airports within Africa.[8] The former shows that west/central Africa (AF3), which was the region with the highest number of operating airports served in 1997, has consistently reduced the number of cities connected to the network. East Africa (AF4) has reduced its connections as well, but still exhibits the highest number of airports with scheduled services. The absence of main hubs and the contemporary existence of bilateral agreements between countries contributed to the development of a network in which small airports with low demand were unprofitable. The deregulation process, coupled with the growth of national airlines and the concentration of their network at operating hubs, contributed to the elimination from the network of many airports with scarce demand. South Africa (AF2) shows, for similar reasons, a decreasing trend in the period under analysis. North Africa (AF1) is the only region exhibiting an increase in the number of cities served. This is mainly due to the increasing attention that low-cost carriers are directing to the North African market.

Concerning the evolution of connections with other continents, Europe is the predominant market for Africa and the number of airports directly connected to Africa is more than doubled, from 66 to 125, between 1997 and 2011. Airlines in the Middle East also increased their connections with Africa from 22 to 34, largely due to the Middle East's central position in the

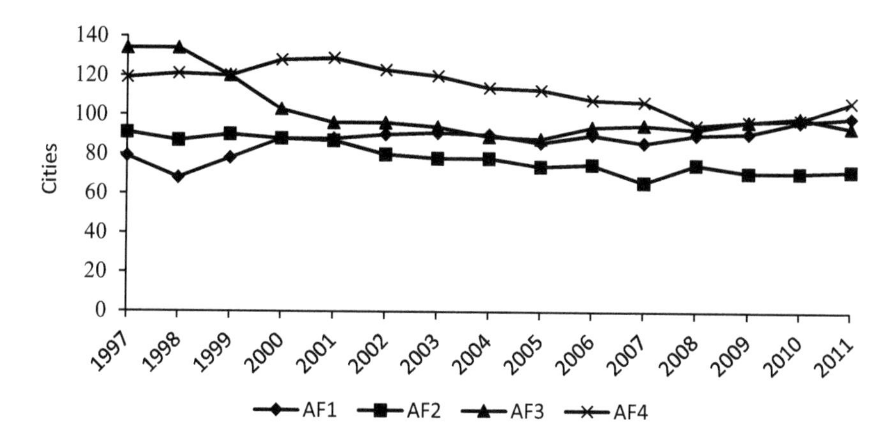

Figure 3.6 African cities connected by African region (1997–2011).

global air transport network and the rise of the Gulf carriers in line with the national priorities of these states. Other regions have fewer relevant direct connections with Africa according to the 2011 data, although China has recently shown an increasing interest in securing more direct passenger and freight links to support its wider supply chains involving the continent.

The evolution of routes served confirms the increase in inter-continental connections in the larger African air transport network from 1997 to 2011. The number of routes in which non-African airlines operate within this period almost doubled from 485 to 913, while African airlines have reduced the number of routes they serve from 1,595 to 1,587, abandoning secondary airports and reallocating capacity to more profitable inter-regional and inter-continental services.

After having quantified the spatial coverage of the African air transport network, we try now to (1) qualify it from the geographical point of view and (2) weight it in terms of traffic volumes. This is done both at the regional and at the city level. Table 3.2 shows the main regional connections to, from and within Africa. North Africa-Europe is by far the most important linkage, with more than 37 million seats yearly offered. It exhibits a dramatic increase given that the 1997 capacity was equal to 12.3 million seats. This was mostly stimulated by European full-service and low-cost carriers, which contributed to more than 50 percent of such capacity increase. Agreements between North African countries (e.g. Morocco) and Europe, the development of Cairo International Airport, and the strong commercial and historical relationships between these regions generate a consistent demand for travel that is being exploited by airlines.

The connection between North Africa and the Middle East exhibits a similar pattern, with many of the latter's carriers exploiting their central position in the global air transport network. At the same time, connections within North Africa have registered a limited growth. The intra-south African

Table 3.2 Top regional connections within and outside of Africa (seats offered in 2011)

Connections between regions	*Seats (million)*	*Δ% from 1997*
North Africa – west Europe	37.540	+204
Intra-south Africa	26.691	+51
Intra-central/west Africa	18.957	+109
North Africa – Middle East	17.980	+200
Intra-north Africa	14.214	+29
Intra-east Africa	12.346	+85
Central/west Africa – west Europe	8.003	+115
East Africa – west Europe	6.653	+127
Southern Africa – west Europe	5.244	+40
East Africa – Middle East	4.409	+288
Central/west Africa – east Africa	2.518	+524
South Africa – east Africa	2.486	+100
North Africa – central/west Africa	2.387	+524
North Africa – east Africa	1.325	+460
South Africa – central/west Africa	1.321	+93
North Africa – South Africa	235	+94

market is the second market in terms of seats. This is mainly due to the developed South African domestic market. Durban is focused on connecting South Africa with other regional airports, Cape Town focuses on inter-continental routes, and Johannesburg uses regional connections as feeding services for their inter-continental flights. Other considerable increases have been reported by both inter-west Africa and east Africa-Middle East connections. The growth of regional hubs has boosted the growth of these markets.

Finally, the more profitable inter-continental markets are dominated by non-African airlines, which are seeking to exploit the emerging potential of the African air transport market. Furthermore, many African airlines are limited to flying within Africa, due to their inclusion on European Union and United States blacklists because of their poor security standards. As a result, they cannot compete on these routes. Moreover, no linkages between African regions are present in the top 10 connections. Despite the market deregulation process, inter-regional markets are still under-developed, and greater connections between the different regions in Africa is almost certainly needed to stimulate and sustain the growth of the African economy. However, it is important to stress that connections between African regions exhibit considerable variations between 1997 and 2011 of around 500 percent: this is the case of central/west-east Africa, north-central/west Africa, and north-east Africa with the 2011 volumes ranging between 1.3 and 2.5 million seats. This suggests that, even if more slowly than hoped, liberalisation is progressing despite the economic heterogeneity of African countries.

Considering available seats on the major routes to, from, and within Africa, South Africa domestic market represents the major network in Africa. Connections between Cape Town, Durban, and Johannesburg and, albeit to a lesser extent, Port Elizabeth, involve more than 10 million seats every year with an increase in 2011 of over 50 percent compared to 1997.[9] The more developed

South African domestic market of 18 million of annual seats, reflects most the fact that the country's economy of the most prosperous in the sub-Sahara region. Nigerian internal market of 7.8 million seats has also shown considerable growth, with routes like Abuja–Lagos and Lagos–Port Harcourt routes increasing from about 0.2 million seats to 2.4 and 1.2 million respectively. This is a further confirmation of the positive impact of the significant economic growth of Nigeria associated with the reformed air transport market. Arik Air (private Nigerian full-service carrier) provides most of the capacity on these routes.[10] Cairo–Jeddah (Saudi Arabia) route is the third one in Africa, and confirms the focus of Cairo airport on Middle East, due to its favourable geographical position. Most other major African network routes are inter-continental connecting European destinations such as Paris and London, to northern African and Johannesburg airports. Currently, most African countries have still strong commercial relationships with their colonizing countries.[11] The African economic growth, combined with African suppliers penetrating European markets, has strengthened this later relationship, as confirmed by the consistent growth of traffic.

Connectivity and network structure at African airports

Between 1997 and 2011, a number of environmental and economic regulatory changes have affected airport networks and strategies. As a result, airports have increased both their connectivity – the number of destinations served – and the number of long-haul connections (i.e., outside the airport region). The significant increase in longer-haul activity markets offers some supports to the idea that connectivity has increased in line with trend towards a continental network with fewer airports, but more connections involving regional hubs. More weight, in this context, is being given to long-haul connections both in terms of volume and in terms of terms of destinations. Such a trend is confirmed by an increase in the number of destinations served at the main regional African airports: Johannesburg from 86 to 87, Cape Town from 24 to 26, Cairo from 89 to 101, Casablanca from 58 to 88, Algiers from 54 to 71, Lagos from 35 to 47, Nairobi from 53 to 82, Addis Ababa from 39 to 68. Two exceptions are Durban and Libreville, but for divergent reasons. Libreville lost its centrality due to the bankruptcy of the national carrier Air Gabon, while Durban modified its portfolio of destinations.

Examination of the evolution of network concentration at these airports reveals a number of different trends. The Network Concentration (NC) Index used – a sort of normalized Gini index of the traffic allocated on each route – is a measure of traffic distribution at airports. The higher the index, the greater its level of concentration of the traffic on a few routes. Despite a lack of a uniform trend among major African airports when comparing 1997 to 2011, most of the airports' networks are concentrated with some airports exhibiting values exceeding 7.1 – the lower bound of what is considered a highly concentrated network. This may be due to the intra-African passenger traffic distribution that, is mainly concentrated on a limited number of primary routes, especially regarding intra-African air travel markets.

However, the entrance into the market of many non-European carriers serving African airports has also contributed to the spread of capacity over routes, often resulting in a lower concentration level (e.g. at Casablanca airport).

In Figure 3.7, 1997 and 2011 network connections are compared for each of the selected airports. All the connections from these origins are included. Most of the airports show an increasing number of routes being served, especially regarding inter-regional services linking airports to different African regions, and inter-continental destinations. Addis Ababa Bole International Airport, for example, clearly reflects such trends, with routes directed to west and south Africa, Europe, the Middle East, and Asia. Other airports focus on specific routes: e.g. west African airports have increased the connections to North America, south African airports connect Africa with South America, and east African airports focused on Asia.

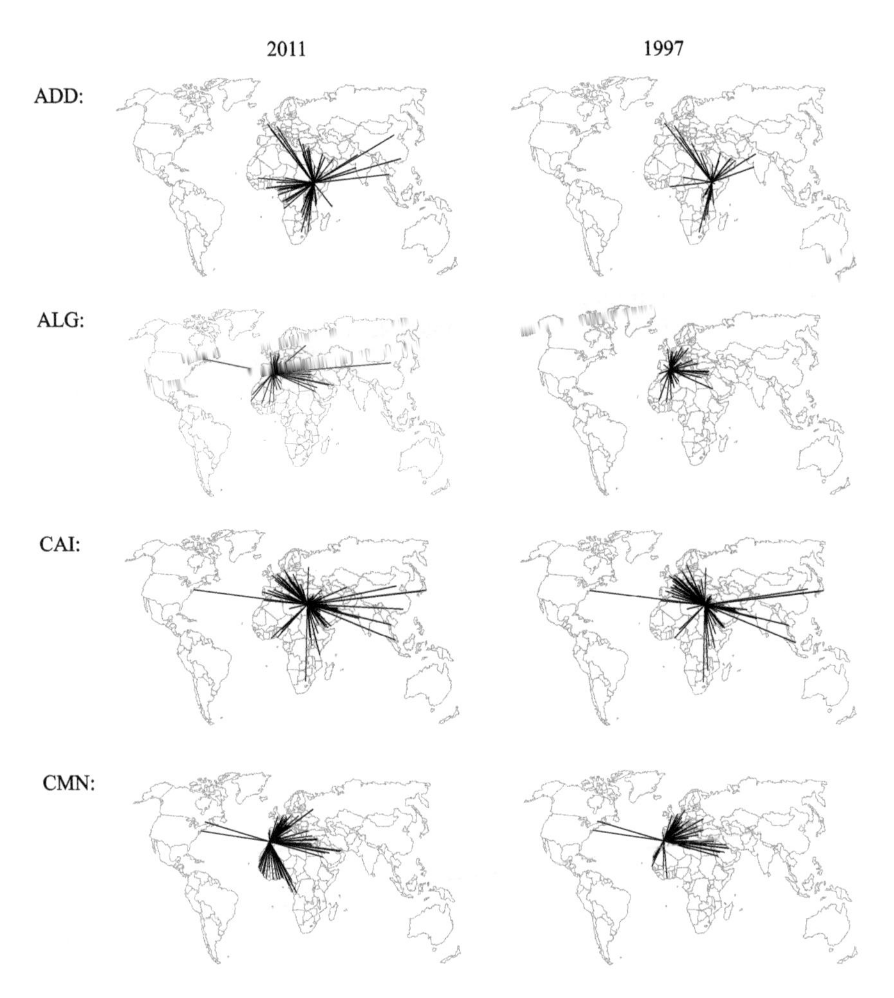

Figure 3.7 Spatial configuration at African main airports.

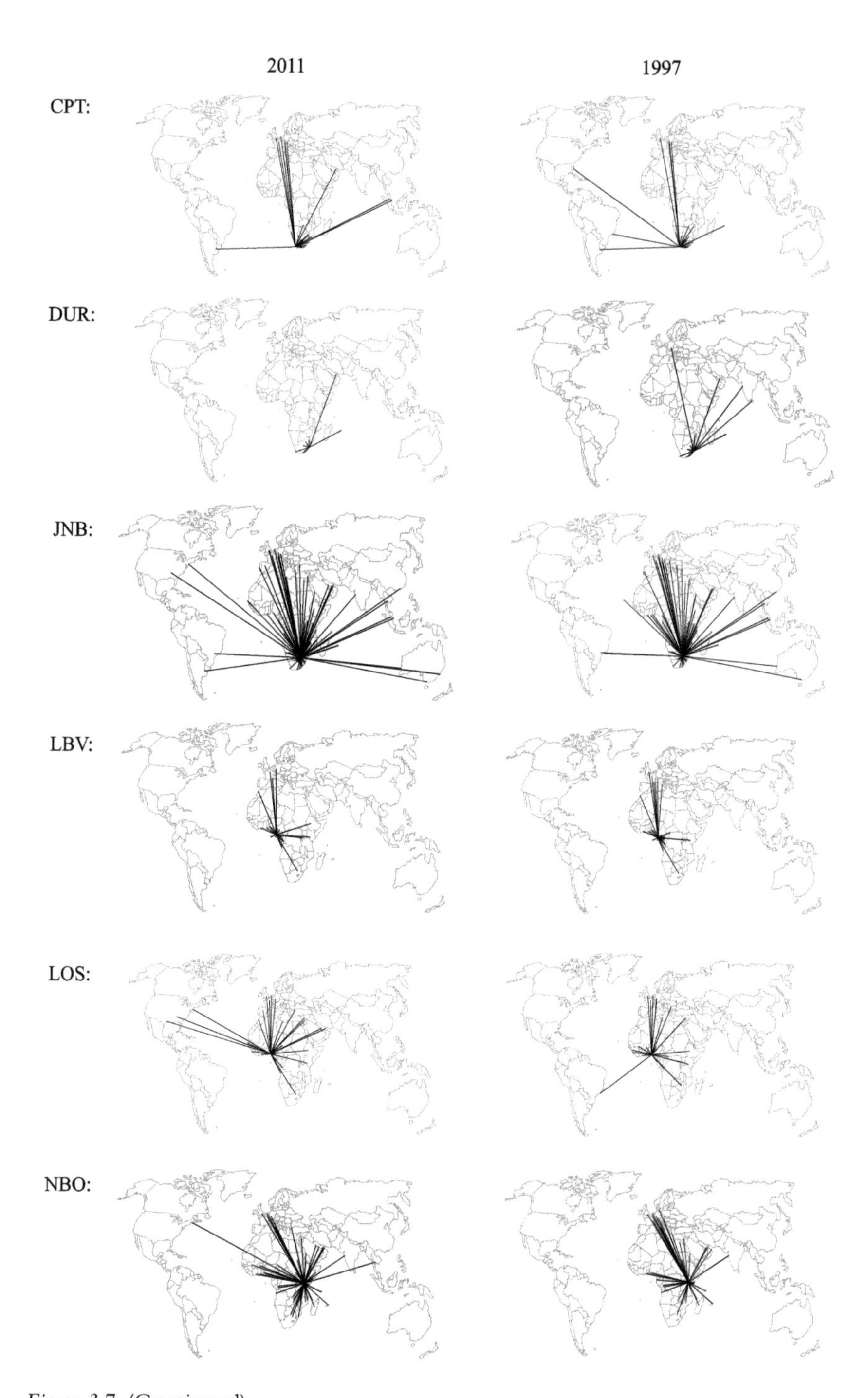

Figure 3.7 (Continued)

This strategic differentiation is possible thanks to the post-liberalization entrance of new airlines in the African air transport market. In this sense, South Africa is a particular case where the three main airports have specialized their network during the period analysed. Most of the capacity is provided by South African Airways, whose base is in Johannesburg's OR Tambo International Airport. Cape Town network has shifted mainly on domestic and European destinations, abandoning North America destinations. Instead, Durban airport changed its strategy focusing on the domestic network. Johannesburg airport has instead greatly increased its spatial network by including destinations in all the continents and African regions and establishing itself as the main African hub.

Airport dependency

When only a few carriers are responsible for providing a large proportion of the movements at any airport, any changes in the carriers' operations considerably affect the performance of that airport (Jimenez *et al.*, 2012). Moreover, such airlines, because of their quasi monopoly power, can exert considerable influence regarding an airport's operations (Scotti *et al.*, 2012). This is especially true for Africa where the ongoing liberalization process coupled with the traditional internal market instability led to airline failures and route withdrawals and most of the main continental hubs have developed, as already discussed, thanks to the rise of the reference flag carrier. Hence, a look at the airline market shares at the main African airports is relevant.

Firstly, we look at the proportion between African and non-African airlines at African airports: Figure 3.8 compares 2011 to 1997 and shows that the way in which dependency on African airlines has changed is not homogeneous across African regions. While in south, central/west and east Africa the proportion of traffic operated by African airlines seems on average increased, the situation in the northern Africa is less clear.

This mainly because many North African airports, and especially those in Morocco and Egypt, have seen a significant increase of traffic due to non-African carriers, especially European and Middle East airlines.

To better quantify the role of African airlines in the continent's airports, Figure 3.9 shows the changes in their capacities between 1997 and 2011. Most airports, 162 out of 256, and most notably the small and medium ones, enjoyed increased traffic volumes determined almost exclusively by growth in African airlines services. Furthermore, the major airports of Cairo, Casablanca, Lagos, Nairobi, Addis Ababa, and Johannesburg became increasingly dominated by African carriers, whereas, North African secondary airports are increasingly characterized by dependencies on non-African carriers, and especially European and Middle East airlines.

Most of the airports are dominated by a national, typically state-owned carrier. At the North Africa airports of Alger, Cairo, and Casablanca, the flag carriers (Air Algerie, Egyptair and Royal Air Maroc) provided between 60 percent and 62 percent of the seats, with second-tier airlines having market shares less than a quarter of those of the main carriers. Many foreign carriers,

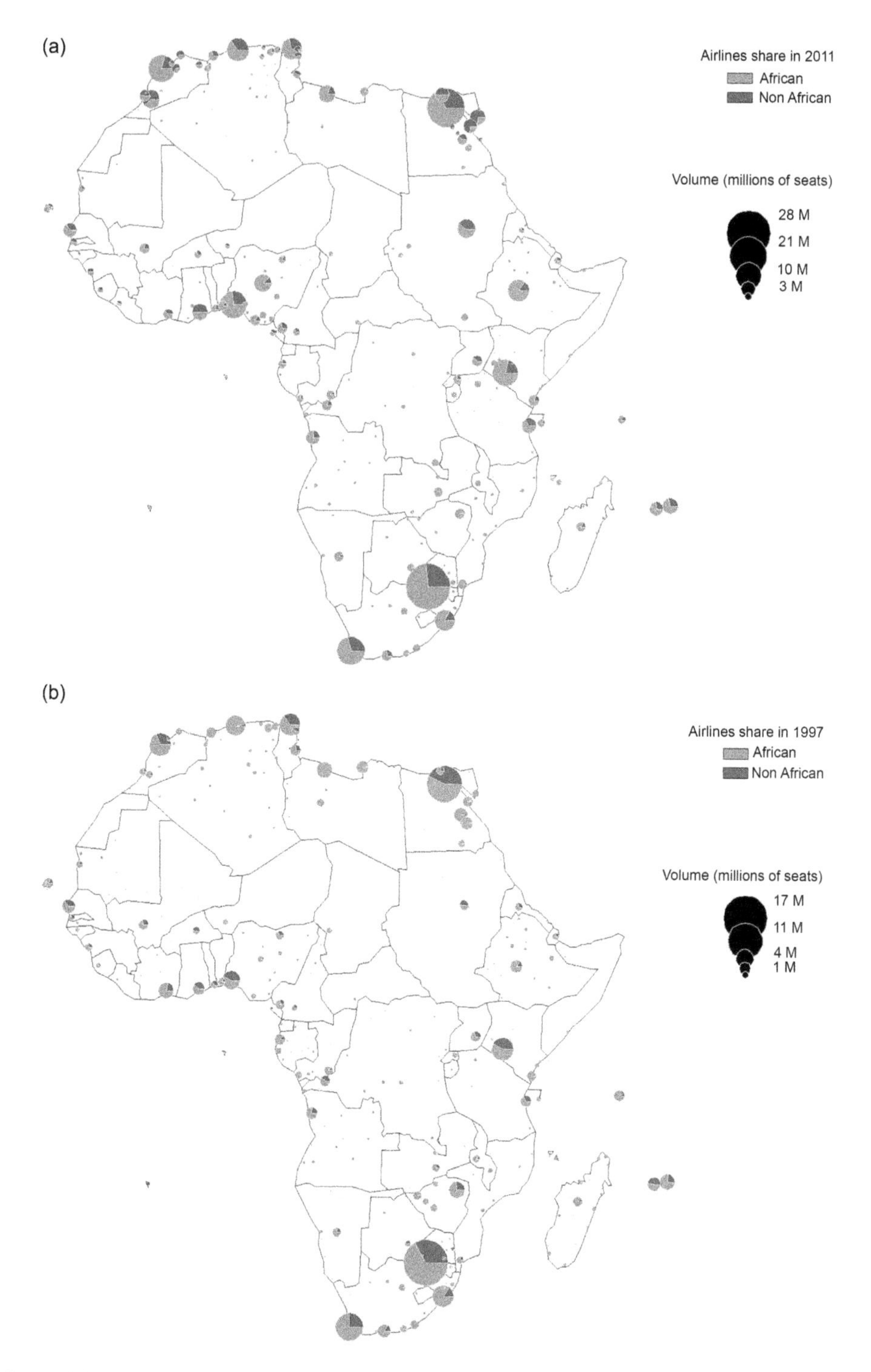

Figure 3.8 Airports' airline dependency by airline registration, 1997 (top) and 2011 (bottom).
Note: Created using Philcarto (http/philcarto.free.fr).

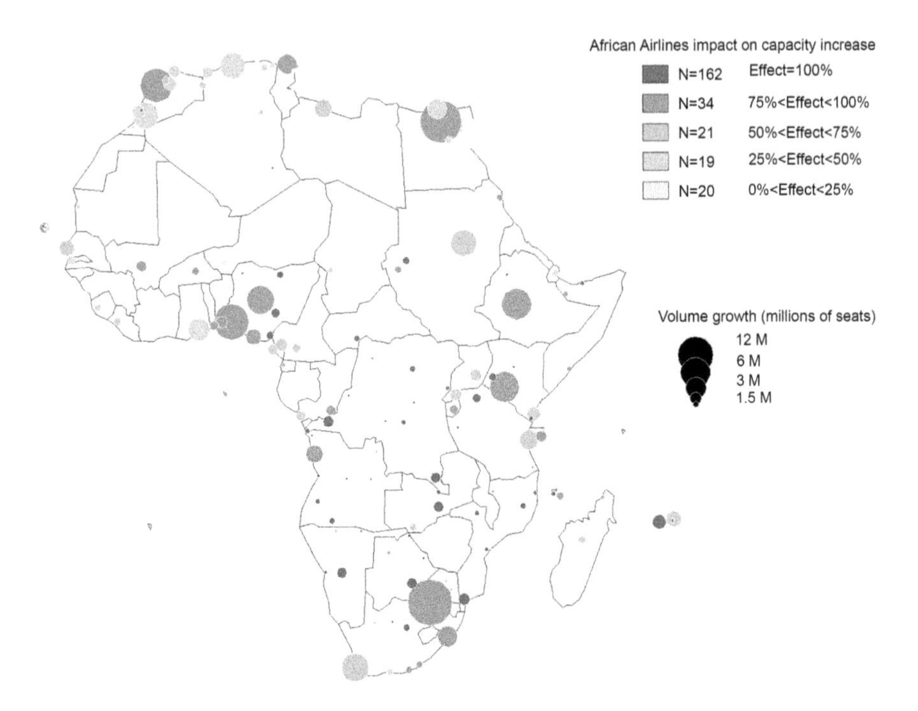

Figure 3.9 African effect on airports capacity growth.
Note: Created using Philcarto (http/philcarto.free.fr).

generally under bilateral air service agreements, including European and Middle East carriers, usually provide the remaining capacity. In east Africa, national full-service flag carriers provide most of capacity in Addis Ababa (80 percent) and Nairobi (52 percent) with the secondary players having market shares of between five and six percent.

West African airports, such as Lagos and Libreville, are in a different situation with no established national carriers but rather a fragmentation of services across several airlines. For example, most of Lagos' capacity was, until 2011, provided by the privately-owned Nigerian airline, Arik Air with 24 percent of the seats, the state-owned Aerocontractors with 21 percent, Air Nigeria, failed in September 2012, with 11 percent and Dana Air, which suspended operations between 2012 and 2014, with 6 percent. Libreville experienced the bankruptcy of Air Gabon in 2006, with capacity now spread across several non-Gabonese operators including Ethiopian Airlines (17 percent), Lufthansa (15 percent), and Air France (11 percent).[12] Finally, South Africa's airports are dominated by South African Airways, providing 43 percent of capacity at Johannesburg, 31 percent at Cape Town and 30 percent at Durban, supplemented by some other South African carriers such as Comair (subsidiary of British Airways), Mango, and 1Time (a subsidiary of South African Airways). Some foreign carriers, such as Emirates and British Airways, provide services on both domestic and intercontinental routes at Johannesburg and Cape Town.

Air freight

As with other markets for air cargo around the world, those involving Africa have, with some volatility and local variations, grown and evolved in recent years. Air cargo transport can be particularly important for moving high-value, low-density products, and perishable goods, and its value often increases for the land-locked countries of the Continent that otherwise would have to rely entirely on the surface transport networks of other nations when conducting international trade. Having said that, the Africa market only accounts for about 1.7 percent of the world tonnage of air cargo moved.

The gradual liberalization of passenger airline markets in Africa has also seen institutional reforms for air freight, and a significant increase in specialized air freighter capacity. Along with this, belly-hold capacity has risen with passenger traffic flows. In addition, the increase in passenger services provides more z for the movement of the extremely precious cargoes, such as diamonds, in the hand baggage of security personnel. This is not to say that there are no restrictions to the use of air cargo services, either belly-hold or dedicated freighters, but restrictions have been reduced as markets have liberalized.[13] Where institutional impediments remain, these are often more due to general trade restrictions, both tariff and non-tariff, *per se* than those specific to air transport regulation.

The freight market tends to be geographically focused in Africa and Figure 3.10 provides the breakdown of the tons loaded and unloaded at the main airports of the countries involved. Europe is the main destination for African originating cargoes, with cut flowers and other perishables, such as fish, being the main export. Narrowing things further, and just taking a single supply chain as an example, the Dutch Aalsmeer Flower Auction is the main destination for African grown flowers. Kenya and Ethiopia are the main exporter of these products, accounting for about 18 percent of the world's production.

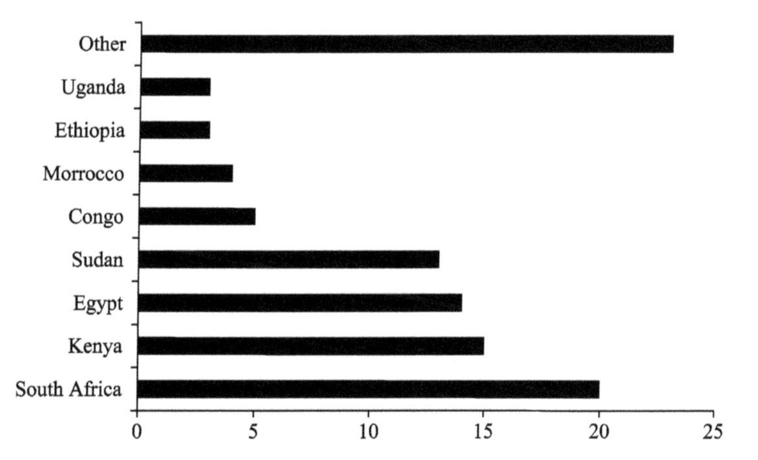

Figure 3.10 The distribution of cargo by African countries in tons loaded/unloaded.
Source: World Bank (2009).

Return air freight movements to Kenya are, however, small reflecting the back-haul problems in many of the African air cargo networks. South African, another of the main users of air cargo, exports are mainly of manufacturing goods with inflows of capital equipment, intermediate products, and transport equipment.

In terms of network configurations, the two main African cargo hubs are Johannesburg and Nairobi, with Lagos and Khartoum being somewhat smaller, and with much of their activity involving aid imports. Other countries, such as Uganda and Ghana, have sought to increase their presence in the cargo market but suffer from poor landside facilities and access, and especially regarding the "cold-chains" needed to handle perishables that are important exports for parts of the continent. Regarding airlines, while there is some capacity provided by African carriers, there is still a reliance on the legacy European airlines, although the growth of the Gulf carriers involvement in African routes may change this.

A major problem in developing a larger explicit air cargo network in Africa is the lack of demand and the inadequacies of infrastructure to handle specialized cargoes. For example, even for sectors such as flowers, vegetables, and fruit the cold aviation supply chain is often constrained by inadequate refrigerated warehousing. Deregulation of the airline market in general has been a spur to stimulating more use of air cargo, but the increased availability of belly-hold capacity of passenger places means that, like many other air cargo markets in the world, there is pressure on the pure freight carriers.

Conclusions

The African aviation industry experienced a period of significant growth between 1997 and 2011 largely driven by economic and population growth in many African countries, and by the liberalization process of many air transport markets. The Yamoussoukro Decision since 1999 has stimulated many African countries to reform their national air transport policies, even if its implementation is still not complete and have been slower than expected.

As a result, the African network evolved and it is possible to identify a group of main gateways located in the different African regions. More specifically, Casablanca and Cairo airports in North Africa, Lagos in the west/central Africa, Nairobi and Addis Ababa in east Africa, and Johannesburg in South Africa. It is evident that there is an asymmetric distribution in terms of regional air traffic given that in north and east Africa different countries have successfully developed their own air transport hubs, while west/central Africa and south Africa are mainly dominated by single country aviation systems, those of Nigeria and South Africa. South African and Nigerian markets are also the two most developed domestic markets in part because of the relative efficiency of the aviation policies of South Africa and Nigeria.

Volumes growth has been registered mainly (1) on intercontinental routes (also due to a greater and greater relevance of non-African airlines) and (2) on inter-regional African routes, even if the capacity allocated on these last ones is still much lower in terms of volumes. Furthermore, an analysis of the spatial coverage has shown that while the intercontinental market has experienced an increase in the number of routes supplied (mainly towards Europe and Middle East), the African internal market has experienced route consolidation practices leading to the withdrawal of many secondary routes. Furthermore, we also provide evidence that the level of concentration of the traffic flows at the main hub is relevant.

Most of the growth in Africa's main hubs has been driven by African airlines, while the influence of non-African carriers has dominated many small and medium airports in North Africa.

Finally, in most of the main hubs major national flag carrier enjoy a strong position in terms of their numbers of flight and passengers, leading to a significant degree of dependency on them by the airports: Royal Air Maroc in Casablanca, Air Algerie in Algiers, Egyptair in Cairo, Ethiopian Airlines in Addis Ababa, and Kenya Airways in Nairobi have a market share in terms of available seats exceeding 50 percent. South African Airways has about 40 percent of the seats in Johannesburg, although the main carrier at Lagos airport in Nigeria, Arik Air, provides less than 24 percent of the capacity.

Despite its economic growth, it is evident that a considerable portion of the aviation potential of Africa is still unexploited. The continent still only accounts just over two percent of global air transport traffic in terms of revenue passenger kilometres (African Airlines Association, 2015) and many bilateral agreements still incorporate significant restrictive clauses. There are, however, indications that more stable networks are emerging and that the market is gradually becoming more efficient as competition between carriers is being allowed to develop, and as infrastructure is gradually being better maintained, upgraded and expanded.

Notes

1 Figures and tables relate mainly to the period 1997 to 2011, although the text, where possible, updates this to 2013.
2 Shy (2001) and Economides (1996) provide introductions to the basics of network economics.
3 Several authors agree that liberalisation, and especially the Yamoussoukro Decision, has stimulated the growth of air traffic, albeit in a rather limited way (e.g. Njoya, 2016).
4 Air Nigeria, which had subsumed both Virgin Nigeria Airways and Nigeria Eagle Airlines, ceased operations in September 2012 with the privately-owned Arik Air taking over its operations.
5 Pirie (2006) speaks about "Africanisation" of South Africa's international air connections when comparing 1994 with 2003, emphasising that the proportion of African flights in the overall market increased more significantly.
6 The number of cities and of airports is similar, especially within Africa where only few cities have more than one airport.
7 The trends are also confirmed for 2013, when the number of African airports connected was 352, while that of non-African airports was 240. Notice again that looking at airports or cities is supposed to provide similar results especially for Africa, where the number of cities with more than one airport is limited.
8 OAG codes are used for regions – "AF1" is north Africa, "AF2" is south Africa, "AF3" is central/west Africa, and "AF4" is east Africa.

9 South African Airways (the national airline) provides about 30 percent of the capacity and Comair (a British Airways franchisee) around 25 percent. The Cape Town-Durban route is operated mainly by Mango (a South African public low-cost carrier) with 37 percent of yearly seats, and British Airways, with 22 percent.
10 Other African domestic markets are less significant in terms of size (e.g., Egypt with 3.8 million seats and Algeria with 2.4 million).
11 See Button *et al.* (2015) for an analysis about the residual effects of colonialism on airline network development in Africa.
12 Gabon Airways, with 15 percent of the seats, has been the only exception, but it ceased operations in 2012.
13 Dettmer *et al.* (2014) offer some estimates of where further gains would be possible.

References

African Airlines Association (2015) AFRAA Annual Report 2015, www.afraa.org/index.php/media-center/publications/annual-reports/644-afraa-annual-report-2015.

Bofinger, H. C. (2009) An Unsteady Course: Growth and Challenges in Africa's Air Transport Industry, AICD Background Paper, 16. World Bank, Washington, DC.

Button, K.J., Brugnoli, A., Martini, G. and Scotti, D. (2015a) Connecting African urban areas: airline networks and intra-Sub-Saharan trade. *Journal of Transport Geography*, 42, 84–9.

Button, K.J., Martini, G. and Scotti, D. (2015b) African decolonisation and air transportation. *Journal of Transport Economics and Policy*, 49, 626–39.

Button, K.J., Martini, G. and Scotti, D. (2016) Impacts of the Arab Spring on trade in airline services. *Applied Economics Letters*, 23, 532–5.

Dettmer, B., Frytag, A. and Draper, P. (2014) Air cargo beyond trade barriers in Africa. *Journal of Economic Integration*, 29, 95–138.

Economides, N. (1996) The economics of networks. *International Journal of Industrial Organization*, 14, 673–99.

Ismaila, D. A., Warnock-Smith, D. and Hubbard, N. (2014) The impact of air service agreement liberalisation: the case of Nigeria. *Journal of Air Transport Management*, 37, 69–75.

Jimenez, E., Claro, J. and de Sousa, J.P. (2012) Spatial and commercial evolution of aviation networks: a case study in mainland Portugal. *Journal of Transport Geography*, 24, 383–95.

Njoya, E.T. (2016) Africa's single aviation market: the progress so far. *Journal of Transport Geography*, 50, 4–11.

Pirie, G. (2006) 'Africanisation' of South Africa's international air links, 1994–2003. *Journal of Transport Geography*, 14, 3–14.

Schlumberger, C. E. (2010) *Open Skies for Africa: Implementing the Yamoussoukro Decision*. World Bank, Washington, DC.

Scotti, D., Malighetti, P., Martini, G. and Volta, N. (2012) The impact of airport competition on technical efficiency: a stochastic frontier analysis applied to Italian airport. *Journal of Air Transport Management*, 22, 9–15.

Shy, O. (2001) *The Economics of Network Industries*. Cambridge University Press, Cambridge.

Surovitskikh, S. and Lubbe, B. (2015) The air liberalisation index as a tool in measuring the impact of South Africa's aviation policy in Africa on air passenger traffic flows. *Journal of Air Transport Management*, 42, 159–66.

World Bank (2009) *Air Freight: A Market Study with Implications for Landlocked Countries*. World Bank, Washington, DC.

4 The development of air service agreements in Africa

David Warnock-Smith and Eric Tchouamou Njoya

Introduction

> There is ample evidence that African countries stand to reap substantial economic benefits as a result of liberalising and unifying their air transport markets. On the other hand, the status quo which is characterised by market fragmentation, inadequate and inefficient air services, declining share of African airlines in both the African and international markets, chart the way for Africa to become the biggest loser in this field.
>
> (African Union Commission Statement, Kenya, October 2014)

This chapter provides an historical account of developments in bilateral and multilateral Air Service Agreements (ASAs) in Africa. Most accounts of the air transport liberalisation process and commercial air transport policy reforms in general have focussed on North America, Europe, and, more recently, the Asia-Pacific region. The few accounts that do exist on ASA developments in Africa have been partial in terms of either the time-period of analysis or the sub-regions/countries analysed.

It is easy to overstate the role of commercial ASAs in stimulating demand for air services and as such the focus of this chapter is to provide a more complete historical account of ASAs in Africa spanning a 55-year period starting from the post-independence period of the 1960s to the modern age and covering all the continent's sub-regions to facilitate more informed judgements on the role, speed, and importance of the air transport liberalisation process in Africa.

It should be noted as the following historical account is read, that ASAs in Africa are still very much a 'work-in-progress', and that any ground work seemingly failing to produce desired market outcomes should be taken in the context of high growth but very low volumes and underlying socio-economic/cultural ties that are counter-intuitively stronger with more distant non-African partners than with fellow African states in the same or neighbouring sub-regions.

The account covers both intra-African and inter-continental markets involving African states and is broken down into six sections. Section 2 deals with the early post-colonial period, Section 3 details the first efforts towards more liberal air policies, Section 4 provides an account of the Yamoussoukro Decision and sub-regional fragmentation, Section 5 reviews ASA developments during the first decade of the 21st century, a period of sustained economic growth, and the final section comments on the latest ASA developments and proposes several possible future air policy trajectories.

Early developments: the post-colonial period (1960s–1980s)

During the colonial period and the early years after independence, international air transport was concentrated on routes between Africa and the North with international air services primarily based on European relationships and agreements (Guttery, 1998). Africa provided raw material and imported manufactured products. Most African countries gained independence in the 1960s. The newly independent nations became owners of their air space and proclaimed their desire to establish their own airlines, especially for reasons of prestige. In 1960, five African nations, namely Cameroon, Cote d'Ivoire, Mali, Nigeria, and Senegal became members of the International Civil Aviation Organization (ICAO). Between 1960 and 1980 African countries had signed a total of only 78 bilateral air services agreements (BASAs) among themselves and 172 BASAs with Europe (Figure 4.1). The lack of domestic capital and know-how meant that the newly independent African countries were highly dependent on the west for the development of their air transport sectors (Peltre, 1963). Schlumberger (2010) argues that instead of developing an intra-African or domestic network, many countries aimed at building international networks. African countries were focused on international routes to and from their former colonisers. Likewise, Economic Commission for

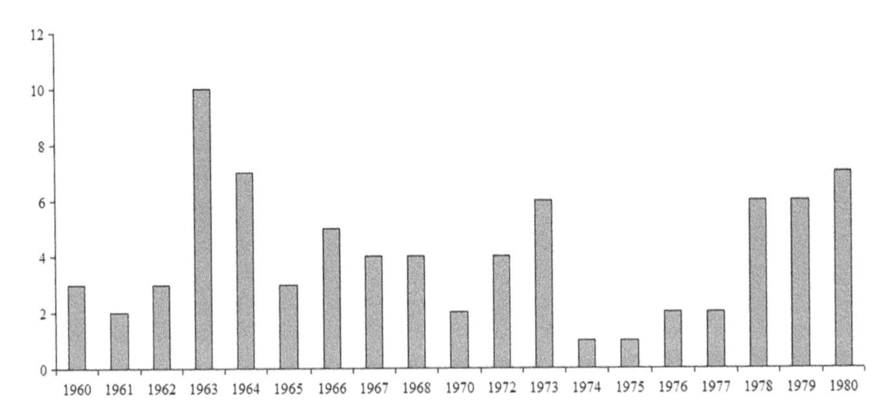

Figure 4.1 Bilateral air services agreements concluded between African states from 1960 to 1980.

Source: World Trade Organization (2016).

Africa (2005) outlines that it was not until the 1970s that due importance was given to the intra-African route network.

In the early stages of development, air transport was highly protected and air infrastructure was not seen as a road to economic development (Schlumberger, 2010). Africa's independent states pursed nationalistic economic policies in the first decades following independence. Protection was justified with the infant industry argument. Moreover, African governments in the 1960s favoured import-substitution industrialisation as their principal method to achieve economic growth. Guttery (1998) argues that with few exceptions, the African air transport environment encompassed common traits and elements that are important to the understanding of the development of BASAs on the continent. These include:

- Every nation formed its own flag carrier following independence;
- Lack of know-how and resources to attain minimum efficient scale by the time African countries gained their independence;
- Airline managers were in many circumstances political appointees;
- Airlines were organised as a division of government;
- Airlines were seen as places of employment for many people far beyond what is needed for efficient operations;
- Poor management in some carriers led to the collapse of airlines;
- Several governments pooled resources to set up a joint airline;
- Strong influence of European airlines;
- Lack of reliability and safety for many airline companies.

The lack of data is one of the primary challenges to analysing the provisions of BASAs in Africa. The World Trade Organization (WTO) QUASAR analysis represents one of the most comprehensive sources of information on the regulatory features of BASAs on the continent. Drawing from information contained in the World Air Services Agreement (WASA) database published by ICAO in 2005, the WTO QUASAR covers the following types of regulatory measures: freedoms of the air, routes, designation, ownership and control, tariffs, capacity, cooperative agreements, and charter services. On the basis of these provisions the review identifies seven types of "standard" ASAs (see Table 4.1).

An analysis of intra-African ASAs reveals that airlines faced restrictive access in Africa in the first decades after independence. Despite the granting of 5th freedom rights in many agreements (e.g. 55 percent between 1960 and 1980) in addition to 3rd and 4th freedom rights, those rights were restrictive (Table 4.1). Moreover, restrictions on capacity, ownership rules, and tariff requirements were maintained in almost all ASAs. Schlumberger (2010) outlines that restrictions on capacities enabled stakeholders to drive up prices and create an expensive air sector.

The 1960s and 1970s witnessed the creation of many regional institutions and joint facilities that impacted the aviation industry. African governments

Table 4.1 Features of Air Services Agreements between African Countries 1960–2000

Type	*Freedoms*	*Designation*	*Withholding-ownership*	*Tariffs*	*Capacity*	*ASAs 1960–1980*	*ASAs 1981–2000*
A	3, 4	Single	SOEC	2 appr.	Pre-det.	13 (17%)	8 (22%)
B	3, 4	Multiple	SOEC	2 appr.	Pre-det.	6 (8%)	4 (11%)
C	3, 4, 5	Single		2 appr.	Pre-det.	14 (18%)	12 (33%)
D	3, 4, 5	Single	SOEC	2 appr.	Bermuda I	1 (1%)	1 (3%)
E	3, 4, 5	Multiple	SOEC	2 appr.	Pre-det.	17 (22%)	5 (14%)
F	3, 4, 5	Multiple	SOEC	2 appr.	Bermuda I	11 (14%)	0 (0%)
G	5>	Multiple	SOEC *or* COI *or* PPOB	Free *or* 2 appr.	Free det.	0 (0%)	0 (0%)
N/A						15 (19%)	2 (6%)
Other						1 (1%)	4 (11%)

Notation: SOEC = Substantive ownership and effective control; 2 appr. = Double approval; Pre-det. = Predetermination; COI = Community of interest; PPOB = Principal place of business.

Source: WTO ASAP Database (2016).

saw inter-governmental arrangements and regional cooperation as essential to reduce their external dependence and facilitate trade. Between 1960 and 1980, African nations created various regional institutions addressing air transport, which were mostly targeted at coordinating the activities of their respective member states or pooling resources to expand the sector. Many African countries did not have the financial resources and the know-how to create and maintain a national airline (USAID, 1988). For instance, Egypt signed bilateral air services agreements in 1964 with the East African Community States of Kenya, Uganda, and Tanzania, which had together established East African Airways (ICAO, 2013).

Of tremendous importance to the expansion of international air transport in West and Central Africa was the signing of the Yaoundé Treaty in 1961. Abeyratne (1998) argues that one major milestone in the history of African Civil Aviation was in 1961 when 11 African nations signed the Treaty on Air Transport in Africa, which established Air Afrique, regionally owned and operated by its member states. The airline's network comprised regional air services connecting cities of countries that co-owned it and intercontinental air services between those countries and beyond by jointly exploiting the traffic rights of all members (USAID, 1988). Profitable intercontinental routes were used to cross-subsidise unprofitable domestic and regional routes (Schlumberger, 2010). While Air Afrique constituted cooperation at the industry level, it had an impact on regulatory initiatives in the respective regions. Air Afrique, for example, enjoyed preferential treatment regarding regional traffic through 5th freedom rights. The company suffered several severe problems during the 1980s and 1990s and ceased operations in 2002, mainly due to the political interference and conflicting interests of the carrier's many government owners (Amankwah-Amoah and Debrah, 2013).

Another important regional organisation dealing with air transport includes ASECNA (Agency for Air Navigation Safety in Africa and Madagascar). Created in 1959 and replaced by a new agreement signed in Dakar in 1974, the multi-state governmental agency is the air space manager for 18 African countries. Air Afrique and ASECNA, to overcome the problems associated with the small size of African airlines and low demand, embarked on activities such as joint purchasing of telecommunications equipment and maintenance of aircraft, and pilot, ATC controller and crew member training. As such, they benefited from decreasing costs by exploiting economies of scale.

Other regional attempts to regulate international commercial aviation in Africa include councils, commissions, and trade bodies. All regional groupings followed a policy of restricting 5th freedom rights within the region by granting such freedoms freely to states from within but restricting them to states from outside the region (Stadlmeier, 1998). These are:

- *Civil Aviation Council of Arab States* – created in 1961 with the goal of coordinating the international air transport activities of the members of the

League of Arab States. Its functions were later transferred to the Arab Civil Aviation Council. Its main achievement was a major harmonisation of internal civil aviation legislation among its member states (Stadlmeier, 1998).

- *Arab Air Carriers Organization (AACO)* – Established in 1965, AACO is the regional association of the Arab Airlines that have their home base in member countries of the Arab League, namely the Middle East and North Africa (Stadlmeier, 1998).
- *African Civil Aviation Commission (AFCAC)* – created by the Constitutive Conference convened by ICAO and the Organisation of African Unity (OAU), now the African Union, in Addis Ababa, and began functioning in 1969. On May 11, 1978 it became an OAU Specialised Agency in the field of Civil Aviation. AFCAC operates at the policy level, examining issues such as the development of appropriate rate structures, the feasibility of equipment standardisation, and the meeting of African aviation training needs (USAID, 1988).
- *African Airlines Association (AFRAA)* – Established in 1968, the Association's primary focus is with promoting safe, regular, economical, and efficient air transport and cooperation among airlines themselves to further their joint interests (Stadlmeier, 1998).

Moves towards more liberal air policies in the 1980s and 1990s

In contrast to the 1960s and 1970s, the last two decades of the 20th century represented mainly externally driven pushes towards economic trade liberalisation as championed by the International Monetary Fund and the World Bank *inter alia* and as reflected by the Washington Consensus and the United States Department of Transportation with the creation of its Open Skies Agreements framework to be signed with as many bilateral partner jurisdictions as possible starting in 1992.

In the case of the Washington Consensus a set of ten pre-conditions known as Williamson's ten points, were imposed on African countries seeking loans and loan guarantees from international banks and lending institutions. This had a tangible impact on the aviation sector whenever external lending was sought for new or improved airports, capital injections for national carriers, or for general aviation infrastructure improvements, given that monies were only released upon receiving government commitments for further privatisation and trade liberalisation. An example of this was a $13 million World Bank IDA loan to Zambia in 1994, part of which was to be used to restructure Zambia Airways, but with the second tranche of the loan only to be released upon receiving a solid financial plan that would avoid further public subsidy for the airline (World Bank, 1994).

The Open Skies Agreements were the US Aviation Sector's response to global drives for trade liberalisation and by the end of the 1990s it had already signed agreements with 37 countries. Notably among those 37 was Tanzania that had provisionally signed up to the more liberal policy in 1999, which is in stark contrast to the 26 African states that are signed up to the policy today (US Department of State, 2016). This initial reticence on the part of African states partly reflected the lack of air transport demand between the US and some African countries but it also reflected the protectionist tendencies of many African states at the time, despite global pressure for change, in addition to a preferred conformance to the Chicago Convention model of bilateral Air Service Agreements.

Though the terms of the US Open Skies initiative did not represent truly open skies they did, on paper, represent a significant leap forward for most African states when set against the status quo of no or restricted Air Service Agreement based on dual designation and the granting of traffic rights only up to 3rd and 4th freedoms. Of course, even for those states willing to quickly liberalise through the signing of Open Skies Agreements, market opportunities both within Africa and to other world regions were still stifled by a highly fragmented and disjointed regulatory framework.

Parallel developments in multilateral cooperation at the time are also important precursors to later developments in intra-Africa traffic freedoms. The precursor to the Yamoussoukro Decision was the Yamoussoukro Declaration, which was announced jointly in October 1998 by 40 African states. It pledged a new African Air Transport Policy focussing primarily on airline integration and cooperation to be implemented within eight years in three separate phases (Schlumberger, 2010). These commitments were clearly not implemented as intended but the Declaration set the foundations for later efforts towards air policy liberalisation across the continent. The Abuja treaty signed in 1991 created the African Economic Community (AEC), which set its sights on implementing a pan African common market by 2023. The idea of the AEC was to finish off some of the overlapping regional integration efforts as started in 1975 with the Economic Community of West African States (ECOWAS) and followed by the Southern African Development Community (SADC) in 1980, the Common Market for Eastern and Southern Africa (COMESA) in 1994 and later the East African Community in 2001. Substantive progress in terms of the creation of a free trade area and customs union have been observed in the EAC, ECOWAS and SADC, although this has not translated into visa-free or borderless travel in any of the regional blocs. An exception being some member states in ECOWAS – the eight members of the sub-regional West African Economic and Monetary Union – WAEMU set up in Senegal in 1994.

One notable absentee country from the AEC or any of the regional trading blocs aside from the Arab Maghreb Region (UMA) is Morocco. Morocco represents an extreme version of the conflicting interests and often divided loyalties of many African states. Morocco's political and cultural ties have been more focussed on other Arab speaking states in North Africa and the Middle East as well as on Europe than the rest of Africa. This has had a tangible knock-on effect on its approach to air policy with Morocco stalling on many regional integration efforts (e.g. with AEC) yet being the first African state to later sign a horizontal agreement with the European Union (in 2006).

Concurrent bilateral and multilateral moves towards air transport liberalisation went hand in hand with efforts to remove government ownership of airlines in some states, especially those that were more serious about stimulating the market and attracting private investment. Nigeria is a case in point with progressive moves to deregulate its domestic and some international markets in the 1990s with the privatisation of airlines and handling companies (InterVISTAS, 2014). Many other countries also attempted to privatise their national carriers with various calls for investment, but most proved to be fruitless (e.g. Cameroon's successive attempts to privatise ailing carrier Cameroon Airlines). Exceptions to this were observed in Kenya, for instance, where the Kenyan Government succeeded in attracting a mix of foreign and domestic investors to take over struggling Kenya Airways in 1995 (IFC International, 2008).

Some African states, however, pursued continued state involvement in national carriers while simultaneously pursuing liberalisation of Air Service Agreements, at least to some extent. An example would be South Africa, a country which was quite prepared to negotiate liberal bilateral agreements with states such as Kenya (2000),[1] while failing to consider any form of privatisation of its national carrier South African Airways. By extension, the policy of direct government involvement in the running of air carriers can be epitomised through the signing of the African Joint Air Services (AJAS) accord in 1994, which paved the way for the creation of Alliance Air, a now-defunct Uganda-based airline with joint ownership from South African Airways, itself government owned, along with the governments of Uganda and Tanzania. Later efforts to offload 30 percent of the company to private investors in Uganda and Tanzania never materialised (Flightglobal, 1998). That said, the AJAS, based in Tanzania from 1997, later evolved into more of an international merger and management company (i.e. facilitating moves towards airline privatisation) than an international organisation of national airlines as originally envisioned in 1980s (Mays, 2015).

During this time, rather less attention was directed towards the continent's airports with a sustained period of direct government involvement and underinvestment in facilities with a few notable exceptions such as the Airport Company of South Africa selling a 20% stake to Aeroporti de Roma in 1998 (Organisation for Economic Co-operation and Development, 2006). Inconsistent government restrictions on access to airport gateways, as was the case, for instance, in Nairobi and Mombasa, Kenya, whereby international charter operators were only allowed to use Mombasa, presenting artificial barriers to entry and demonstrating the impact individual ASA policies can have on levels of airport traffic and the potential for airport competition for airline business (World Bank, 2005).[2]

The Yamoussoukro Decision and continued fragmentation

Despite internally (1960s) and externally (1980s) driven efforts to harmonise the continent's air transport industry, the aviation industry was still very fragmented in the 1990s and intraregional connectivity was largely undeveloped. This led to the adoption by the African ministers responsible for civil aviation, of the Yamoussoukro Decision in 1999, considered a significant milestone in African aviation cooperation.

The Yamoussoukro Decision came into force in August 2000 with a two-year transitional period, and it became fully binding on 12 August 2002. The Decision is a multilateral agreement among 44 African states to liberalise the internal market, promote fair competition of the air transport sector, and provide safe, efficient, reliable, and affordable air services to consumers (Table 4.2).

Responsibility for the effective implementation of the Yamoussoukro Decision has rested with regional blocs including the Abuja Treaty of 1994 and the African Union (2001), established to serve as a key instrument for achieving socio-economic development in Africa. Regional economic organisations have therefore had to play a determining role in ensuring that the fully binding terms of the Yamoussoukro Decision were delivered. An analysis of liberalization in the different regions indicates the following:

AMU – The Arab Maghreb Union

Founded in 1989 by a treaty signed in Marrakesh, Morocco, the AMU is a pan-Arab trade agreement aiming to achieve economic and political unity in North Africa. Member states include Algeria, Libya, Mauritania, Morocco, and Tunisia. Schlumberger (2010) pointed out that the AMU did not consider the liberalisation of air services among member states. Morocco, which never signed the Yamoussoukro Decision, and Mauritania, which deposited its ratification instruments too late, are not parties to the Yamoussoukro Decision. Though no liberalisation in the region has been initiated, AMU ministers seem to have recognised the need for opening-up of aviation services within member states (Schlumberger, 2010).

CEMAC – Central African Economic and Monetary Community

Created in 1994, CEMAC is made up of six states. It is based on two main institutions: the Economic Community of Central African States and the Monetary Union. There are many texts that govern civil aviation within the community, some of which took effect before the Yamoussoukro Decision, such as the Agreement on Air Transport, the Civil Aviation Code, and the Joint Competition Regulation. According to Schlumberger (2010), all major provisions of the Agreement on Air Transport developed for the CEMAC member states are identical to those of the Yamoussoukro Decision. CEMAC

Table 4.2 Progress towards liberalisation of air transport in Africa at a regional and continental level since 1988

Policy	*Signature year*	*Members*	*Salient features*
Yamoussoukro Declaration	1988	40	Airline cooperation and integration
	1994	41	Establishing the African Economic Community and creating a multilateral free trade area in air transport services; constituting the legal basis for the Yamoussoukro Decision
Mauritius Decision	1994	—	Speeding up the implementation of the Declaration
Banjul Accord	1997	6	Agreements covering infrastructure, airline operations, traffic rights, safety and security
ACAC agreement[a]	1998	6	Agreement on the Liberalisation of Air Transport of the Arab League States
Yamoussoukro Decision	1999	44	Gradually elimination of non-physical barriers and restrictions on: • The granting of 5th freedom traffic rights for passengers and freight air services by eligible airlines • African airlines' aircraft capacity • Tariff regulations • Designation • Ensuring fair competition on a non-discriminatory basis and compliance with international safety standards
CEMAC	1999	6	Agreement on Air Transport of the Economic and Monetary Community of Central Africa
COMESA	1999	12	Regulations for the implementation of Liberalisation of Air Transport Services of the Common Market for Eastern and Southern Africa
SADC/EAC/ COMESA	2007	26	Competition regulation specifically applied to air transport
WAEMU	2002	8	Common air transport programme 2009 Horizontal agreement with European Union

Source: Adapted from Schlumberger (2010).

a Algeria, Egypt, Libya, Morocco, Sudan, and Tunisia are affiliate members of ACAC and signatories to the Yamoussoukro Decision.

has made significant progress towards implementation of the Yamoussoukro Decision. The region is among the most liberalised in Africa, though some restrictions remain in areas such as limited frequency and capacity (Economic Commission for Africa, 2005; Ranganathan and Foster, 2011).

COMESA – The Common Market for Eastern and Southern Africa

East Africa has two regional economic communities, COMESA, which is made up of 20 countries, and EAC (the East African Community founded in 1999), which currently includes five countries. Common Market for Eastern and Southern Africa (2013) was established in 1994 to promote economic integration among countries. The COMESA Air Transport Liberalisation programme is based on the Yamoussoukro Decision. The road map to the liberalisation of air services in Eastern Africa included two phases. Phase I, which has been implemented, aims to provide free movement of intra-regional scheduled passenger services, with some limitations on the number of daily frequencies to a maximum of two frequencies between city-pairs, and to grant 5th freedoms on specific routes. Phase II, which is yet to be implemented, provides for full granting of 5th freedoms and makes no restrictions in terms of daily frequencies between city pairs (Common Market for Eastern and Southern Africa, 2013). Although significant changes had also occurred in the quality and quantity of air transport services that could be attributed to the liberalisation process, traffic rights between member states are still bilaterally exchanged.

ECOWAS – Economic Community of West African States

Founded in 1975, ECOWAS is a regional group of 15 West African countries. Its Department of Transport and Telecommunications is responsible for the development of common transport and telecommunications policies, laws and regulations in conformity with Articles 32 and 33 of the ECOWAS Revised Treaty (www.ecowas.int/wp-content/uploads/2015/01/Revised-treaty.pdf). With respect to air transport policy and implementation of the Yamoussoukro Decision, the West African states split early into two distinct groups: the African Economic and Monetary Union (WAEMU), which consists of eight French-speaking West African states, and the Banjul Accord Group (BAG) (Table 4.2), which comprises seven predominantly English-speaking countries.

Unlike WAEMU and BAG, ECOWAS has not adopted any legally binding legislation or regulations that could considered steps towards implementation of the Yamoussoukro Decision. However, the regional organisation has achieved the most progress in lifting capacity and frequency constraints, instituting free pricing and granting of 5th freedom traffic rights (Ranganathan and Foster, 2011). In the WAEMU, the Yamoussoukro Decision has been fully implemented and all freedoms, including cabotage rights, have been granted (Gwilliam, 2011). Within BAG the principles of Yamoussoukro Decision have been agreed upon in a multilateral air service rights agreement.

SADC – The Southern African Development Community

Founded in 1992, SADC is an organisation of 15 independent states in Southern Africa. In 1996, SADC member states signed the Protocol on Transport, Communications and Meteorology, whose main objective was to establish transport and communications systems which are efficient, cost effective, predictable, environmentally sustainable, and able to meet the needs of users (SADC.int). Though SADC never formally agreed on intra-regional liberalisation of air services, it worked continuously to implement the Yamoussoukro Decision, to which all SADC member states, except Madagascar, South Africa, and Swaziland, are bound (Department of Transport, Republic of South Africa, 2006). The SADC member states have not liberalised air transport in the spirit of the Yamoussoukro Decision, although nearly all the states have liberalised domestic air transport markets, and private airlines have been established (Ndhlovu and Ricover, 2009). The COMESA-EAC-SADC tripartite adopted in 2007 guides provisions and procedures for the implementation of regulations for competition in air transport services within a much larger region.

Bofinger (2008) assesses the status of implementation of Yamoussoukro Decision in the various RECs and concludes that CEMAC and WAEMU carry the highest implementation score of 5, followed by BAG (4), COMESA and EAC (3) and SADC (2). AMU was rated as having an overall implementation score of only 1 out of 5.

The overall status quo by the early 2000s was therefore that the Yamoussoukro Decision was only implemented to varying degrees of success at the sub-regional level with no continent-wide or between sub-region implementation. In such cases, individual states were still free to develop ASAs bilaterally up to a level either more or less restrictive than Yamoussoukro Decision.

Sustained economic growth and further piece-meal liberalisation

The first decade of the 21st century is largely seen as a decade of sustained economic growth in Africa. Some countries including Angola, Ethiopia, Ghana, Kenya, Morocco, and Nigeria have been leading African economic growth tables in recent years. The continent's annual growth rate was more than 5 percent, doubling the annual average for the previous decade. GDP growth encouraged air passenger traffic in Africa to grow annually at 6% between 2000 and 2010 (Official Airline Guide, 2012). The reasons for this significant growth are most likely:

- Increased demand for natural resources and tourism products
- Improved macroeconomic and political stability
- Increased urbanisation and a growing middle class
- Further liberalisation of air services.

Between 2000 and 2010, the most significant expansion in growth in passenger traffic took place in Western Africa, which saw its share of African seats rise from around 13% to 19 percent (ICF International SH&E, 2010). This was driven among others by an increase in capacity with the entry of new airlines such as Arik Air (founded in 2002), Air Mali (2005) and ASKY (founded in 2008) and, in some cases, the concurrent liberalisation of markets with Western Africa having been recognised as having the most liberal air transport environment (Ranganathan and Foster, 2011).

Moreover, the 2000s brought important reforms such the horizontal agreement concluded between the European Commission (EC) and the West African Economic and Monetary Union in 2009, and the signing of a Memorandum of Understanding in late 2006 between ECOWAS and SPCAR (the banking group Societé de Promotion d'Une Compagnie Aérienne Regionale) to set up a multi-national carrier in West and Central Africa. This airline was to be modelled on Air Afrique but with private finance rather than a regional government ownership structure (*Flightglobal*, 2006).

Various organisations such as the International Air Transport Association and ICAO demonstrated increasing commitment during the 2000s to support government aviation activity at national, regional, and intercontinental levels and to work closely with African organisations such as AFCAC in co-ordinating the development of air transport in Africa. Frustrated by the varied progress from the sub-regional economic blocs, the role of AFCAC was to facilitate the implementation of the Yamoussoukro Decision and the improvement of supporting infrastructure. In 2007, AFCAC was entrusted by the African Union with the responsibility of being the executing agency for the coordination and implementation of the Yamoussoukro Decision. These initiatives helped to improve African connectivity and to facilitate the growth of the aviation industry.

AFRAA has in recent years also played an important role in speeding up the implementation of the Yamoussoukro Decision, pushing for a higher level of liberalisation within Africa and more cooperation between African airlines. The organisation proposed in 2006 the formation of a 'Club of the ready and willing states', which would take the lead in implementing the Yamoussoukro Decision on a bigger scale. States that are reluctant to remove 5th freedom restrictions tend to be those with weak airlines for fear of the stronger positions of the region's larger carriers such as South African Airways, Kenya Airways, Ethiopian Airlines, and EgyptAir. According to Schlumberger (2010), Ethiopia had until 2006 concluded a total of 84 BASAs, of which 46 had been concluded with African states, 13 with European states, and 25 with other states. Of the 46 BASAs with African states, 19 can be considered in line with Yamoussoukro Decision, six being concluded before the Yamoussoukro Decision came into force in 2002 and 13 afterwards.

Likewise, Kenya bilaterally liberalised air services with several African countries where existing BASAs were reviewed based on key components of the Yamoussoukro Decision. For instance, in 2003, Kenya and South Africa agreed on liberalisation of the Nairobi–Johannesburg route, resulting in an increase in passenger volumes of 69% between 2003 and 2005 (Myburgh *et al.*, 2006).

South Africa liberalised its domestic market in the early 2000s. The country had 45 BASAs with African states in 2010 of which 22 were in line with the key principles of the Yamoussoukro Decision (Department of Transport, Republic of South Africa, 2014; Surovitskikh and Lubbe, 2015). Egypt agreed to harmonise aviation policies and regulations and to extend full privileges to each other's airlines in the Economic Commission for Africa countries in 2005 and Burundi in 2007 (ICA, 2014). It can be argued that much of the growth achieved between 2000 and 2010 can be linked to a relaxation of restrictions on designation, code-sharing, and enhanced market access through increased 3rd and 4th freedom capacity, new routes, and flexibility in granting 5th freedom rights. The liberalisation initiative has resulted in the emergence of new private carriers operating largely in domestic and regional markets. The Official Airline Guide (2012) states that the contribution of low-cost carriers in terms of market share to/from and within Africa grew by 6% between 2000 and 2010. Using 5th freedom as a proxy for liberalisation, Kuuchi (2012) shows that Cote d'Ivoire has also adopted a liberal approach to trade in air transport. An analysis of BASAs concluded between Cote d'Ivoire and the rest of the world shows that the country is relatively liberal with a score of 5.3 out of seven (Table 4.3).

Unlike the progressive liberalisation regimes, other states such as Zambia have continued to protect their markets and have not fully liberalised in the spirit of the Yamoussoukro Decision. The country scores 4.4 out of seven in its BASAs with the rest of the world. Ndhlovu and Ricover (2009) argue that the country's BASAs are still quite restrictive and are not in line with Yamoussoukro Decision principles. The country maintains a single designation regime and is very reluctant to grant 5th freedom traffic rights. Table 4.3 compares the cases of Zambia with Cote d'Ivoire, a member state of the more liberal WAEMU group and party to a greater number of liberal bilateral agreements than Zambia to see if these developments have led to any differences in traffic/capacity growth between 2005 and 2014.

The data show that, though total traffic levels have been higher in Cote d'Ivoire, recent traffic growth in Zambia has been more prolific despite the lower level of liberalness in its ASAs. On the flip side, growth in the more liberal Cote d'Ivoire has still be quite healthy and by the year 2015 is now served by a larger number of home and foreign carriers, offering routes to a larger range of destinations than Zambia. Absolute volumes both in Zambia and Cote d'Ivoire show that their air transport industries are still very much in their infancy stages, indicating that underlying income levels and economic activity is having more of an impact on demand and supply of air transport than the level of policy liberalisation. That said, previous evidence has suggested that having the regulatory ground work in place has helped states to take full advantage of such freedoms when the economic environment

Table 4.3 Liberalisation status and traffic development in Cote d'Ivoire and Zambia

Cote d'Ivoire			*Zambia*		
Year	*Partners*	*Score out of 7*[a]	*Year*	*Partners*	*Score out of 7*[a]
1962	France	7	1968	United Kingdom	3
	Israel	1			
1963	Guinea	7	1971	Cyprus	1
	Lebanon	5			
	Belgium	7	1972	Malawi	7
	Netherland	7		Botswana	7
1964	Ghana	7	1977	Russia	3
	Mali	7			
1966	Denmark	7	1983	Netherlands	3
	Norway	5			
	Sweden	7	1984	Lesotho	7
1967	Tunisia	2			
	Algeria	3	1992	South Africa	7
1969	Switzerland	3			
1976	Italy	7	1993	India	1
	United Kingdom	7			
	Spain	7	2007	Mauritius	7
1978	Germany	7		China	2
	United States	3			
1979	Romania	7	2008	UK (reviewed)	3
	Morocco	1			
1987	Canada	3	2010	United States	7
Average liberalness score		5.3	Average liberalness score		4.5
Traffic volumes 2014[b]		1,267,579	Traffic volumes 2014[b]		1,080,836
% traffic growth 2005–2014[b]		63	% traffic growth 2005–2014[b]		143
Average annual growth % 2004–2014[b]		7.6	Average annual growth % 2004–2014[b]		11.2
Number of airlines serving		19	Number of airlines serving		10
Number of destinations		22	Number of destinations		10

Source: WTO ASAP Database and Flightglobal (2016).

a This scale was transposed from the WTO A-G classification of ASAs with A (1) representing most restrictive and G (7) most liberal.

b Traffic/supply data from ABJ and LUN airports only.

becomes more favourable for air travel. This is especially so for discretionary leisure travel, which has been shown in regions like the EU to benefit most from the lower fares that come with increased supply and competition in more open markets. The difference in the level of liberalness between the two countries may also not be big enough to have a real tangible impact on traffic growth in infancy markets.

Post 2010 and the longer term

Continued frustrations relating to the piece-meal approach towards true, all-encompassing liberalisation in the first decade of the 21st century have led to renewed calls for the implementation of the Yamoussoukro Decision at the continental level over the past few years. AFRAA and 11 of the 53 member states of the African Union have led the way, with an intense lobbying campaign in the case of the former and a joint declaration at the January 2015 African Union Summit in Addis Ababa in the case of the latter, committing to the full and immediate implementation of the Yamoussoukro Decision by 2017. The signatory states to the renewed declaration were Benin, Cape Verde, Congo Republic, Cote d'Ivoire, Egypt, Ethiopia, Kenya, Nigeria, Rwanda, South Africa, and Zimbabwe with a further statement of commitment by Morocco.

Additional government level, multi-lateral ground work for complete, unfettered open-skies across the continent and the establishment of a single African aviation market was made in the form of further African Union Executive Council Decisions in June 2014 and January 2015 in lieu of conclusions made in the Africa-wide meeting on air transport jointly organised by AFRAA, AFCAC and African Union Commission held in Nairobi in October 2014 (AFRAA, 2014). Despite the best intentions of such joint government declarations, it is difficult to determine that they will lead to any substantive change given that identical declarations have been made in the past, with a prime example being the July 2000 Executive Council Decision for full Yamoussoukro Decision implementation by the year 2002. The Pretoria Communiqué, delivered by members of the African Union Ministerial Working Group in January 2015, gave a further showing of support for the full implementation of open-skies within Africa by January 2017 (African Union, 2015). By March 2017, the 11 signatory states of the African Union had increased to 15 to include Botswana, Gabon, Ghana, and Sierra Leone, with Elijah Chingosho, CEO of AFRAA urging the 15 states to enact the agreement between them rather than waiting fruitlessly for the rest to join (AIN Online, 2017).

Despite this long list of joint declarations and statements, to date there is still limited evidence that these verbal commitments will translate into fully implemented multi-lateral policy, which can be respected and adhered to within the air transport industry. In the absence of such a policy, there have been some initial signs of forward-looking states, 'breaking ranks' and implementing the tenements of the Yamoussoukro Decision on a bilateral rather than a multilateral basis. The recent signing of an 'open-skies' agreement between Rwanda and Ethiopia in February 2016 is a case in point. The agreement gives the two designated carriers of the respective states, RwandAir and Ethiopian Airlines, full 5th freedom traffic rights, access to airports/airspace and tax benefits, giving RwandAir the ability, for instance, to operate freely into Addis Ababa with point-to-point or connecting flights. While designation of only two carriers within the agreement still appears quite restrictive, overall it is a clear sign of progress towards liberalisation, and a signal that if any game changing moves towards open-skies within Africa can be made, then perhaps the first moves will be observed on a bilateral basis by similar forward-looking states (e.g. the now 15 signatory states to the African Union Summit Statement) thus easing the way for further multi-lateral implementation later on, especially between African sub-regions and at the continent wide level.

Further signs of progress relate to the continued entry and early expansion of low-cost carriers in parts of Africa, though the financial sustainability of these ventures remain unproven. Foreign carriers such as Emirates, Qatar, Etihad and Turkish Airlines from the Middle East and European carriers have also found it easier of late to receive traffic and operative rights to lay on additional capacity and frequencies on a 3rd, 4th, 5th, and 6th, freedom basis. In the absence of strong home-based carriers, many African policymakers have been willing to attract such services to stimulate traffic and additional trading activity due to the more favourable long-haul fares being offered to/from Africa by these carriers.

The success of African airlines rests on greater collaboration at a pan-African level, which has been difficult to achieve under the current regulatory framework. It is most likely that market trends will exert further pressure on African governments and strengthen the move towards liberalisation at the pan-African level. It is also likely that, due to the fragmented nature of African countries and airlines and the fact that the Yamoussoukro Decision does not enjoy full acceptance from member countries, that liberalisation will continue at least in the short run to be negotiated on a bilateral basis.

Notes

1 Refer to Section 5 for more detail.
2 The policy has since been liberalised but the traffic pattern in Mombasa and Nairobi has not changed highlighting the potentially lasting effects of previously restrictive air policies.

References

Abeyratne, R.I.R. (1998) The future of African civil aviation. *Journal of Air Transportation World Wide*, 3, 30–49.

AFRAA (2014) Report of Africa wide air transport conference, Nairobi, Kenya, 29–31 October. Accessed at: http://afraa.org/index.php/media-center/publications/conferences/africa-wide-air-transport-conference.

African Union (2015) Assembly of the Union, 24th Ordinary Session: Decisions, Declarations and Resolutions. Assembly/AU/Dec. 563(XXIV), 30–31 January, Addis Ababa.

African Union Commission Statement (2014) At the opening of the Africa wide air transport conference. Nairobi, Kenya, 29–31 October, Accessed at: www.afraa.org/index.php/media-center/publications/conferences.

AIN Online (2017) AFRAA demand progress on African Open Skies liberalisation, Shaw-Smith, Peter, March 6th 2017, Accessed at: http://www.ainonline.com/aviation-news/air-transport/2017-03-06/afraa-demands-progress-african-open-skies-liberalization

Amankwah-Amoah, J. and Debrah, Y.A. (2013) Air Afrique: the demise of a continental icon. *Business History*, 55, 1–30.

Bofinger, H.C. (2008) Air transport; challenges to growth, African Infrastructure Country Diagnostic, Summary of Background Paper 16, World Bank, Washington, DC.

Common Market for Eastern and Southern Africa (2013) Progress Report on The Status of Implementation of COMESA Air Transport Programmes. Accessed at: http://programmes.comesa.int/.

Department of Transport, Republic of South Africa (2014) Airlift Strategy, Presentation to Industry Growth & Safety Conference. Date: 04–06 November 2014. Accessed at: www.caa.co.za/.

Economic Commission for Africa (2005) *Compendium of Air Transport Integration and Cooperation Initiatives in Africa*. Economic Commission for Africa, Addis Ababa.

Flightglobal (1998) African turf fight. Accessed at: www.flightglobal.com/news/articles/african-turf-fight-31005/.

Flightglobal (2006) Africa report: Survival test. Accessed at: www.flightglobal.com/news/articles/africa-report-survival-test-210613/.

Guttery, B. (1998) *Encyclopedia of African Airlines*. McFarland & Company, Jefferson.

Gwilliam, K. (2011) *Africa's Transport Infrastructure Mainstreaming Maintenance and Management*. World Bank, Washington DC.

International Civil Aviation Organization (2013) Worldwide Air Transport Conference (ATCONF), Sixth Meeting Montréal, 18 to 22 March, Montreal. Accessed at: www.icao.int/Meetings/atconf6/Documents/WorkingPapers/ATConf6-wp041_en.pdf.

IFC International (2008) Public-private partnership stories: Kenya – Kenya Airways privatisation. Accessed at: www.ifc.org/wps/wcm/connect/a0db52004983907882 3cd2336b93d75f/PPPStories_Kenya_KenyaAirways.pdf?MOD=AJPERES.

ICF International SH&E (2010) *Competitive Africa: Tourism Industry Research Phase II Air Transport Sector Study*. World Bank, Washington, DC.

InterVISTAS (2014) Transforming Intra African Air Connectivity: The Economic Benefits of Implementing the Yamoussoukro Decision. Prepared for International Air Transport Association in Partnership with AFCAC and AFRAA by InterVISTAS, Geneva.

Kuuchi, R. (2012) Africa is slowly opening-up its market. Accessed at: www.afraa.org/index.php/media-center/publications/articles-a-research-papers/2012-articles-and-research-papers/.

Mays, T.M (2015) *Historical Dictionary of International Organisation in Africa and the Middle-East*. Rowman and Littlefield, London.

Myburgh, A., Fathima, S., Fatima, F. and James, H., 2006. *Clear Skies over Southern Africa*. ComMark Trust, Woodmead.

Ndhlovu, R. and Ricover, A. (2009) *Assessment of Potential Impact of Implementation of the Yamoussoukro Decision on Open Skies Policy in the SADC Region*. Accessed at: http://pdf.usaid.gov/pdf_docs/PNADU389.pdf.

Official Airline Guide (2012) Africa Aviation Market Analysis. Accessed at: www.oag.com/marketanalysis.

Organisation for Economic Co-operation and Development (2006) African Economic Outlook 2006. Accessed at: www.oecd.org/dev/emea/africaneconomicoutlook 20052006.htm.

Peltre, J. (1963) L'evolution du transport aerien en Afrique. *L'Information Géographique*, 27, 196–206.

Ranganathan, R. and Foster, V. (2011) *The SADC's Infrastructure: A Regional Perspective. AICD.* World Bank, Washington, DC.

Schlumberger, C.E. (2010) *Open Skies for Africa: Implementing the Yamoussoukro Decision.* World Bank, Washington, DC.

Stadlmeier, S. (1998) *International Commercial Aviation: From Foreign Policy to Trade in Services: Vol. 5.* Atlantica Seguier Frontieres, Paris.

Surovitskikh, S. and Lubbe, B. (2015) The Air Liberalisation Index as a tool in measuring the impact of South Africa's aviation policy in Africa on air passenger traffic flows. *Journal of Air Transport Management*, 42, 159–66.

USAID (1988) *Regionalism and Economic Development in Sub-Saharan Africa. Volume I: Regional Cooperation in Africa.* Accessed at: http://pdf.usaid.gov/pdf_docs/PNABE880.pdf.

US Department of State (2016) Accessed at: www.state.gov/e/eb/rls/othr/ata/114805.htm.

World Bank (1994) Memorandum and recommendation of the president of the International Development Association to the Executive Directors on a proposed credit in the amount equivalent to SDR 19.1 million to Zambia for a second social recovery project, Report No. P-6591-ZA, June 5, 1995, Washington, DC.

World Bank (2005) East Africa air transport survey, Revision 2, June. Accessed at: http://siteresources.worldbank.org/INTAIRTRANSPORT/Resources/514573-1117230543314/050617-East_Africa_Air_Transport_Survey_Revision_2.pdf.

World Trade Organization (2016) *ASAP Database, 2016.* Accessed at: www.wto.org/asap/index.html.

5 Persian Gulf and Turkish airlines in Africa

Gordon Pirie

Belying its title, the May 2015 'Aviation Africa' summit was not held on the continent, but in Dubai. The patron, Sheikh Ahmed Bin Saeed al Maktoum, is president of Dubai's Civil Aviation Authority. He also chairs both Dubai Airports and Emirates airlines, the 30-year-old Persian Gulf giant.[1] The hosting expressed the influence and convening power of these inter-locked aviation entities.

The Dubai event highlighted ongoing commercial interest in Africa as "the last frontier" of world commercial aviation. The Dubai venue, rather than, say, London or Paris, signified dilution of European presence in African skies. The locale confirmed the magnetism of Gulf airports as offshore airway hubs serving Africa. The 'Who's Who' gathering was a novelty in the continent's aeronautical regime recently dominated by peripatetic, but home-soil, meetings of the African Airlines Association and the African Civil Aviation Commission.

The rocketing growth of Gulf aviation has attracted considerable public and journalistic interest, and some scientific analysis (e.g. see, Hooper *et al.*, 2011; Murel and O'Connell, 2011; O'Connell, 2006, 2011; Alkaabi, 2014). Simply put, the tale is about three 'sheikdom' airlines capitalizing on a natural asset of oil plus the locational asset of centrality to intercontinental air transport markets. Airline development at the crossroads of Africa, Asia, and Europe was, first, a way of spending oil revenues. Second, it was a way of diversifying from single-export resource-based economies into global tourism and business, complemented by a thriving aerospace service industry. Three Gulf 'petro-states' are becoming 'aerostates': aviation will soon account for almost a third of both Dubai's Gross Domestic Product and its employment (Gerchick, 2016).

The Dubai-based airline, Emirates, founded in 1985, is barely one-third the age of some of the world's oldest, biggest and best-known airlines, but it has caught up with and outstripped them: it is bigger than Air France, KLM and Lufthansa combined (El Gazzar, 2015). Likewise, Qatar Airways (1994) and Etihad Airways (2003; growing out of Gulf Air) have leveraged territorial wealth and geography to grow apace. Based on large fleets of new and fuel-efficient aircraft, Gulf airliners are conspicuous on airport aprons around the world.

The Gulf's 'Big Three' carriers operate from airports that have expanded proportionately in extent and activity: in 2014 Dubai International Airport became the world's busiest international airport in terms of international passenger numbers. In 2015 it handled 78 million passengers, making it also third busiest in the world behind Atlanta (101 million) and Beijing (90 million), where considerable traffic is domestic. Dubai International is not, however, the exclusive domain of Emirates airline: some 100 airlines landing there connect with more than 240 global destinations. In May 2015, 13 African airlines operated to Dubai from 29 origins in 20 countries. Part of the attraction is landing fees which are kept low ($4.05 per ton in January 2015). In a very particular inflection of 'aero-regionalism' (Addie, 2014), the home airports of the 'Big Three' handled 124 million passengers in 2014.

The significance of the Gulf aviation powerhouse for Africa arises precisely because of geography: countries in North East Africa and the Middle East are near neighbours. Regional flights have served Arabic religious, cultural, social, and economic ties in the Middle East for decades, and major international airlines have long passed through the "hour-glass waist of the Arab states" (Williams, 1957; Butt, 2011).

In the last 25 years, however, war and economic sanctions in the Middle East, and new geographies of flying, have transformed relatively obscure Gulf sheikdoms into focal staging posts for long-distance air transport. In this new aeronautical mosaic, far-flung African countries feature for the first time. The 'Big Three' Gulf airlines deploy their ever-growing capacity to deflect and funnel passengers flying to and from Africa through their hubs at Abu Dhabi (Etihad), Doha (Qatar), and Dubai (Emirates). They also woo inbound tourism and business traffic. For transit traffic, they compete on price and service to counteract more circuitous air routes and longer flying times. In waves of carefully dovetailed flights, aircraft arrive at and depart from the three hubs open around the clock to enable the quickest possible transit connections.

African air traffic is increasingly voluminous, but most global air traffic passing through the Persian Gulf remains East-West. Relatively little capacity is offered in a North-South direction: by 2005, approximately 11 percent of traffic transiting through Dubai on Emirates was connecting onwards to Africa (O'Connell, 2006). In that year, Africa accounted for 5.5 percent of available seat kilometres outbound weekly from Abu Dhabi, Doha and Dubai together; by 2009 that proportion had increased to 8.1 percent. The longer route distances to Latin American destinations than to African ones were not outweighed by higher passenger totals, so Latin America continued to account for fewer seat kilometres than Africa (Hooper *et al.*, 2011). Gulf airports are between 10 and 11 hours flying time from the furthest African airports (Cape Town and Dakar), whereas flights between the Gulf and one of the closest South American cities (Sao Paulo) take 15 hours.

Middle East airlines' growing share of African markets

According to data from the African Airlines Association, of the 26,886 inter-continental flights (direct and indirect) serving Africa in July 2015, 32 percent linked Africa to Middle East countries, including those in the

Persian Gulf. Almost twice as many flights (63 percent of the total) served the Africa–Europe market. The ratios do not show Middle East airlines engulfing Africa, but they do register a significant shift in past African air route geographies, and in carrier nationalities. The July 2015 Middle East market share jumped by two percentage points on the previous year's flights which numbered some 1,500 fewer. Between July 2014 and July 2015 the rate of increase in flights (14 percent) and seats (15 percent) on Africa–Middle East routes substantially outstripped those (4 percent and 6 percent) on the Africa–Europe routes.

Taking successive months of July traffic as indicative, the absolute increases in airline capacity between Africa and the Middle East were not shared equally between continental and other airlines. From 2013 to 2015 African airlines had a minority share of both flights and seats; their share of flight totals increased by just less than a percentage point, but their share of seat capacity declined by a little more (Table 5.1). Non-African carriers have been deploying bigger aircraft offering more seats.

Between 2006 and 2012, Middle East carriers more than doubled their share of inter-continental seat capacity to and from Africa (from less than 10–20 percent). In the same period, African airlines lost about 12 percent of their seat capacity share of all intercontinental air traffic to and from Africa. European carriers maintained a steady share at a little more than one third of capacity; African airlines' share of seat capacity offered dropped from approximately 57–44 percent (Getachew, 2014).

Due to the centrality of the Persian Gulf to global air transport markets, especially those experiencing traffic growth, the region's airlines were estimated to have a 12 percent share of global revenue passenger kilometres (rpk) in 1995; that share is forecast to increase to 16 percent in 2027. The common perception that transiting through the Gulf is a feasible option mostly for Europe–South East Asia traffic needs balancing against the very real options it presents as a hub for Africa–Europe traffic: in 1995 this North–South transit market (2.3 percent of global rpk) was only marginally smaller than the East–West catchment (2.57 percent). By 2027 the ranking of the Gulf's two biggest air traffic transit markets in the global total is expected to have reversed such

Table 5.1 Flights and seats in July months offered by African and other airlines on Africa–Middle East routes and shares in the traffic

	African airlines				*Other airlines*			
Year	*flights*	*% of all flights*	*seats*	*% of all seats*	*flights*	*% of all flights*	*seats*	*% of all seats*
2013	3,288	43.4	627,563	40.7	4,287	56.6	912,481	59.3
2014	3,283	43.6	627,767	40.0	4,246	56.4	940,313	60.0
2015	3,798	44.1	708,350	39.4	4,817	55.9	1,088,251	60.6

Source: African Airlines Association Newsletters.

that Africa–Europe transit traffic (2.92 percent of global rpk) will exceed the Europe–South East Asia share (2.78 percent) (Hooper *et al.*, 2011).

Not all Middle East countries have participated equally in the growth of services into Africa. The United Arab Emirates and Qatar now outperform all others courtesy of the services established by the 'Big Three' Gulf airlines on medium-and long-haul Africa services. It is tempting to single out the novelty and success of their brand and degree of market capture, but the innovative and energetic Africa services of Emirates, Etihad, and Qatar should not be regarded as uniquely Middle Eastern. The 'Big Three' are not the only new mega-airlines whose home base is the geographical knot between Europe, Asia, and Africa, and they have not had African skies to themselves as new entrants. They have had to contend with a rival which, in the past, might have been labelled as the national airline of a non-Arab Middle East country.

From its home base in Istanbul, four hours flying time from the Gulf, Turkish Airlines has been developing its own Africa network aggressively in the past decade. It too has seized on its extremely favourable location as a transit hub between Africa and Europe. The part-privatised Turkish flagship airline belongs to the Association of European Airlines and is considered a European carrier, but from an African perspective its growth strategies and outsize Africa footprint render it more-or-less indistinguishable from the Gulf carriers (Figure 5.1).

Crucially, Africa was not an afterthought but a strategic piece in each of the four airlines' integrated global networks. In 2014, these had the four 'super-connectors' handling 115 million passengers at their hubs in the Gulf or Istanbul, compared with 50 million in 2008. Their combined fleet comprised more than 700 aircraft; 900 more were on order (*Economist*, 2015).

The 'Big Four' in Africa

In a continent renowned for wildlife safaris, phrases such as 'big three' and 'big five' generally refer to beasts renowned for their power and speed. Here, the coinage 'Big Four' refers collectively to the three thrusting and fleet-footed Gulf airlines, plus Turkish Airlines, their near neighbour. With its (non-colonial) history dating back to 1933 the Turkish national carrier is a recent entrant into African skies. It now competes with the 'Big Three' on numbers of aircraft, youthful fleet, flight frequencies, numbers of African destinations, and centrality to major global air travel markets. Toward the end of 2012 the combined capacity of the 'Big Four' to sub-Saharan Africa was equivalent to nearly 80 percent of the capacity offered to the region by the three big European airline groups, Air France-KLM, BA-Iberia, and Lufthansa-Swiss-Brussels (anna.aero, 2 August 2012) whose historical presence in Africa stretches back far longer.

In the history of civil aviation in Africa, the incursion of the four 'super-connectors' into continental airspace has been explosive. The unprecedented rate and range of penetration has been made possible by rapid growth of large fleets at each home base, by long-haul technologies that protect home

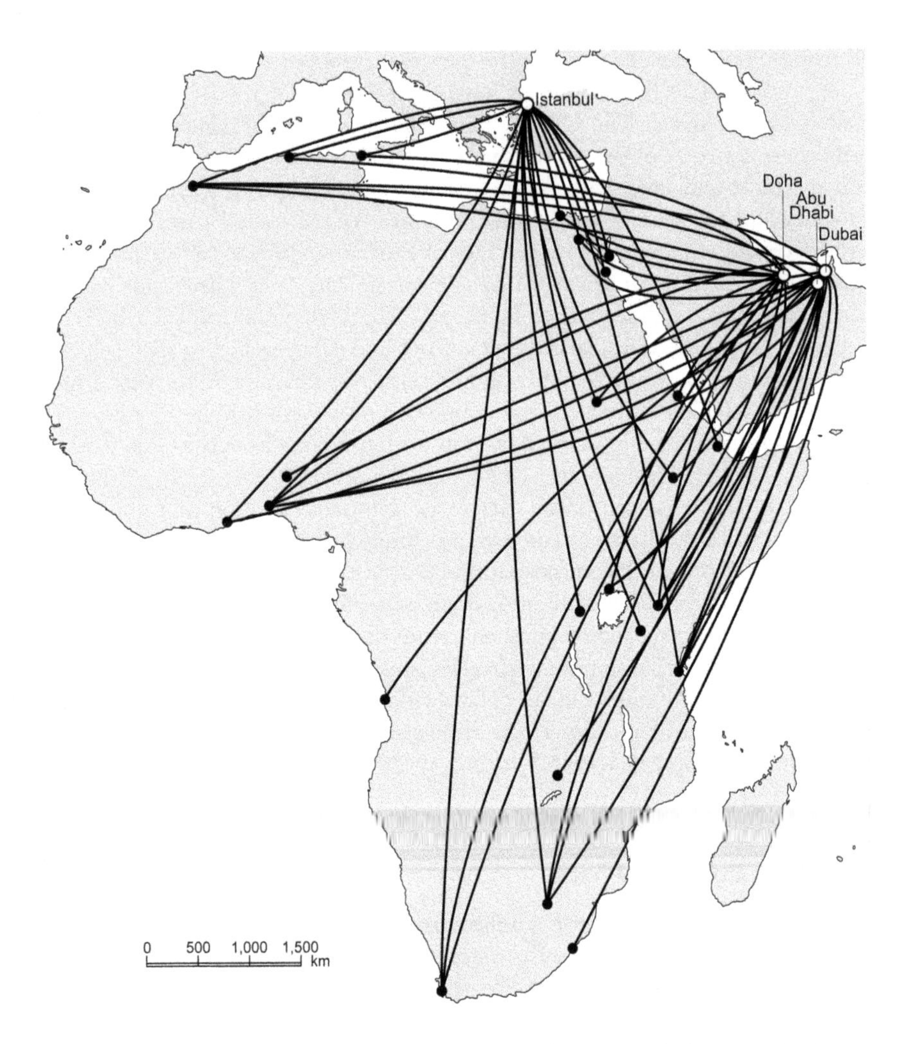

Figure 5.1 Africa mainland destinations served at least once daily on 57 Emirates, Etihad, Qatar and Turkish airlines' non-stop passenger routes, February 2016. Cartography: Phil Stickler.

Note: The 'Big Four' carriers served 18 (unmapped) cities on 25 African routes flown less often than daily.

hubs, and by a pre-existing route network beyond Africa that feeds and disperses traffic widely. In 2013 nearly three-quarters of passengers from sub-Saharan Africa headed to Dubai, Doha, and Abu Dhabi were connecting onward onto other flights (Jacobs, 2013). India is the biggest 'beyond' market for Gulf carriers generally (Britton, 2015), but not for Africans transiting through the Gulf. Africa–Asia traffic accounted for 3 percent of flights and 4 percent of seats on all intercontinental services to and from Africa in July 2015.

Inbound into Africa, the 'Big Four' have diverted significant volumes of traffic away from airlines (African airlines among them) flying out of major European hubs such as London and Amsterdam. In 2012, for example, Qatar Airways started serving Kilimanjaro in competition with KLM, which serves the Tanzanian airport from Schiphol. London is by far the most common one-stop destination for the 'Big Four'. Emirates alone has about a 20 percent share of the South Africa–London market, in which it competes with non-stop service by entrenched legacy carriers, primarily British Airways and South African Airways (Centre for Aviation, 2015b). Data on air traffic deflection are hard to come by, but regarding even just the relatively small numbers of passengers flying between Chicago and Johannesburg, one calculation is that the 'Big Three' airlines' share of passenger bookings between those major cities soared from less than 1 percent in 2008 to 23 percent in 2014 (Britton, 2015). Generation of new traffic may have been as important as displacement of existing traffic.

Emirates was the quickest of the three Gulf airlines into Africa. In 2004, it operated 56 weekly flights to the continent; in 2011 that number was 142 (Heinz and O'Connell, 2013). By 2012 Emirates was flying to 22 destinations on the continent. Being first gave Emirates considerable advantage: in 2006 it had a 55 percent share of air traffic between the Gulf and South Africa: Qatar had 20 percent, Bahrein's Gulf Air had 13 percent, and Etihad 12 percent (Surovitskikh and Lubbe, 2008). In the years since, Emirates has branched out further. As of November 2015, it flew to 27 destinations in 21 African countries, including one-stop services such as Lilongwe (the Malawian capital) via Dar-es-Salaam five times a week. Emirates connected to 35 destinations in Africa in January 2016, offering some 70,000 seats weekly. Plans to add about ten destinations in the next decade suggest a slowing of activity, in part owing to competition.

Among the various measures of Emirates' penetration of Africa is its position in South Africa's comparatively mature long-haul civil air market. Based on seat capacity, in 2015 it ranked as the largest airline in South Africa's long-haul market, offering 36,358 seats, slightly ahead of the national flag carrier. Qatar Airways was in the top ten ranking, together with British Airways and Virgin Atlantic. Turkish Airlines was forecast to break into the top ten in November 2015; Etihad ranked 14th (Centre for Aviation, 2015b). Yet another index of and perspective on Emirates' and Qatar's inroads into Africa emerges from statistics about their growing share of regional air passenger capacity. In 2013 there were 33 million seats available on domestic and international flights in the southern African market (the region south of Angola, Zambia, Malawi, and Tanzania). Emirates' (3.5 percent) and Qatar's (1 percent) share leapt by 20 and 30 percent respectively over the previous year (Maslen, 2014). Significantly, Emirates' share of scheduled capacity was larger than the combined share of Kenya Airways and Ethiopian Airlines in the region adjacent to their East African home market.

The development of its Africa services has been important for Emirates, but the continent is its smallest geographical revenue source, generating approximately 8 percent of $23 billion in 2014–2015, and a similar share of 49 million passengers (Emirates Annual Report 2014–2015). This was, however, a 15 percent jump on the previous year (Hanafusa and Kumon, 2015). The contribution may be a disappointment in another "scramble for Africa" in which airlines were said to be chasing the last and best possible pickings for "sky-high" per-mile passenger revenues (Jacobs, 2013). In the financial year ending 31 March 2015, Emirates transported over five million passengers to and from Africa, on more than 21,000 flights (Douglas, 2015).

Between 2008 and 2013 Emirates increased the number of seats to Africa by 62 percent; in the same five-year period, Qatar increased its seat capacity to Africa by 44 percent (Jacobs, 2013). The Doha-based carrier served 16 African cities by the end of 2011. In 2016 the airline was advertising service to 21 cities in 17 African countries. The carrier's African ambitions attest to its muscle: neither aircraft and crew numbers, nor slot and gate capacity at Doha, are restricting planning of a three-times-weekly service to Marrakesh (Morocco) in July 2016, a daily service to the Seychelles from December 2016, three flights a week from Doha to Douala (Cameroon) and Libreville (Gabon) from January 2017, and a thrice weekly service to Lusaka, the Zambian capital, by mid-2017 (Hamill, 2016). A bi-lateral air services agreement signed between the governments of Nigeria and Qatar in February 2016 after a year's negotiations clears the way for air services between the two countries, and for assisting Nigeria to re-establish a national airline.

Etihad is the youngest and smallest of the 'Big Three'. Its African coverage is correspondingly less dense. When it added Dar-es-Salaam to its African network late in 2015, the East African coastal city was its ninth destination on the continent; Emirates and Qatar serve double that number. The three Gulf carriers do share the tarmac at eight African airports, with Etihad alone flying to Rabat (Morocco). The overlap features the eight African cities, which account for 58 percent of the 580 weekly African flights undertaken by the 'Big Four' in early 2016. Cairo, Johannesburg and Nairobi stand out as the most frequently served.[2] All four airlines fly non-stop from their home bases to all eight cities, except for Etihad, which, for three years, used its codeshare partner, South African Airways, to serve Cape Town from Johannesburg. No other African cities are connected by all four carriers: five cities share three airlines, four share two. The majority, 21 cities, are served by just one of the 'Big Four'. In the absence of any collusion around traffic division in thin markets, solitary landings at so many African airports could signal either inspired or tentative ventures.

Turkish Airlines can capitalize even better than Gulf airlines on an intermediate location between Europe and Africa; Turkey is less of an obvious pivot for Asian traffic connecting with Africa. From its home at 24-hour Atatürk airport in Istanbul (and with a large hinterland of potential passengers), the Turkish carrier operates narrow body airliners on relatively short-haul routes to and from Europe's dense markets. Not least, this gives the Turkish airline the ability to fill its aircraft, and to service multiple smaller cities in Europe. Beyond Europe too, the airline has been growing swiftly. Even better connected than the 'Big Three' (more than 230 destinations across the globe), Istanbul funnels considerable traffic into and out of Africa – this may soon help to propel Atatürk past Frankfurt into third spot in the ranking of Europe's busiest airports, behind Heathrow (London) and Charles de Gaulle (Paris).

The growth of Turkish Airlines activity in Africa is no less striking than its Gulf rivals, and will have contributed to successive years of profitability, peaking in 2015 at $1 billion. The carrier's Africa services will have deflected considerable traffic away from the Gulf, including transit traffic, outbound Turkish tourists, and inbound tourists exploring Istanbul's and Turkey's cosmopolitanism and cultural history. Between 2008 and 2013 Turkish tripled the number of seats to Africa and doubled the number of its destinations there (Jacobs, 2013). The following year, 2014, Turkish launched new flights to six African cities. Its number of weekly Africa-bound flights rose to 200, up nearly 200 percent from four years earlier (Hanafusa and Kumon, 2015). In the course of 2014 the airline transported two million passengers on its African network and completed nearly 25,000 flights on African routes. Many of its destinations are in North Africa, and include coastal resorts in Algeria and Egypt. These could be served by a Turkish low-cost carrier; the airline's much touted 50 Africa destinations need qualification (and comparison with, for example, Emirates and FlyDubai together). Nevertheless, the sub-Saharan reach of Turkish Airlines is considerable, with direct services to, for example, Cotonou (Benin) and Bamako (Mali) which none of the 'Big Three' offer.

Africa is the Turkish carrier's smallest, but fastest-growing, market. Similar to Emirates, in 2014 the continent accounted for 8 percent of the carrier's international passenger loads and revenues. By the end of that year, when Turkish flew to 32 Africa destinations, traffic in Egypt and South Africa contributed more than a fifth of the airline's Africa total. Over the previous decade, from 2003 when it had only five African destinations, Turkish increased its weekly departures from Istanbul to Africa by over 1000 percent, nearly twice as fast as to the Americas and to Asia (Dursun *et al.*, 2014).

In terms of the number of weekly flights and destinations flown to in Africa, one source ranked Turkish the dominant overseas airline in Africa in July 2014 (30 destinations, 229 weekly flights), edging out even the historic giant, Air France (29 destinations, 217 weekly flights). The same source registered 140 Emirates weekly flights to 19 African destinations, and 124 Qatar flights to 13 continental destinations (Dursun *et al.*, 2014). All such comparisons need to be treated carefully, allowing for inconsistencies with other news and reports: counts are not always clear about the precise dating of information, on whether flight tallies enumerate just passenger, non-stop, and non-codeshare services, and on whether destination counts enumerate countries or cities. For example, through its SkyTeam alliance with Kenya Airways, Air France effectively flies to more than 45 African cities (Mwiti, 2015). Turkish provided 37,514 weekly seats to and from Africa in August 2015, less than Ethiopian (42,571) but similar to the combined capacity of legacy carriers British Airways and South African Airways (39,842 seats).

Despite the vigorous growth of the Turkish airline, planners have not yet detected market saturation. Toward the end of 2015 it opened a service to Durban, South Africa's third largest city (Ozbeck, 2015). More or less concurrently it grafted a three-times-weekly branch service to and from Maputo, the Mozambican capital, onto its daily Istanbul–Johannesburg link. That trunk service itself began in 2007 as a thrice-weekly operation. Maputo became the 45th stop in the Turkish Africa network. The airline is tapping yields on African routes which management reckons are two to three times higher than on European routes. And, it sees "10 times more opportunity in Africa than in the rest of the world" (anna.aero, 7 October 2015).

As with the 'Big Three' Gulf airlines, service upgrades are another marker of market penetration by Turkish Airlines. A recent case is the introduction in October 2015 of a daily non-stop 11-hour flight between Cape Town and Istanbul in place of longer journeys stopping daily in Johannesburg. In June of 2015, the 'Big Four' operated 83 weekly flights to South Africa. In comparison, the entire long-haul operation of the South African national airline amounted to only 73 weekly flights (Centre for Aviation, 2015b). Diversion of traffic to the 'Big Four' carriers may explain some of the persistent losses on all South African Airways' ten or so intercontinental routes: in 2014 the flag-carrier halved its previously lucrative London–Johannesburg service from four to two flights daily (the route was reportedly losing $28 million per annum), and cut its thrice weekly Beijing and Mumbai flights out of Johannesburg (Centre for Aviation, 2015a).

For all the 'Big Four' operations in Africa, increased market penetration is discernible in new routes, bigger aircraft, and more frequent flights. For instance, in December 2015 Qatar started four-times-weekly service to Durban, and increased its services to Johannesburg from 10 to 14 weekly flights. Starting non-stop flights from Durban to Doha captures sizeable traffic otherwise routed via the South African domestic hub at Johannesburg.

Air lifting cargo is another strategy and dimension of airline penetration into Africa by the 'Big Four'. They face a spatially concentrated market: in 2013, 60 percent of the continent's still undeveloped air freight volume was handled by just five countries (Campbell, 2015).[3] All four airlines routinely carry belly-hold freight on their passenger aircraft serving Africa, but dedicated freighters enhance cargo capacity. Emirates' cargo-only service, 'SkyCargo', flew to five African cities in 2015. Its import capacity to Abuja and Kano (Nigeria), Djibouti, Eldoret (Kenya) and Lilongwe (Malawi) was 3,700 metric tons per week in 2015 (*Aircargonews*, 28 January 2015; Campbell, 2015).

Imbalances between inbound and outbound cargo volumes at all but major African hubs make dedicated freighter service risky; limited fifth freedom rights worsen the risk. Emirates' weekly inbound service to Lilongwe is freighted with merchandise and pharmaceuticals, but is very lightly loaded outbound, and calls at Nairobi to load cargo for Europe. Electronic items dominate Emirates' air cargo into Kenya; mobile phones, equipment spare parts, industrial spare parts, and garments. These are often for onward regional distribution. Freight traffic outbound from Kenya comprises mainly fresh flowers and fish. Exports from Kano and Abuja include leather, kola nuts, spices, and fresh meat. Into Johannesburg, Emirates flies pharmaceuticals from India, automotive parts from Germany and general cargo from China. Outbound loads from Johannesburg are 40 percent manufactured goods and 60 percent fresh produce (Campbell, 2015).

In August 2015 when Qatar Airways launched a specialized freighter service into Djibouti (Dron, 2015), it was already operating dedicated freighters to six African destinations.[4] In mid-2014 Etihad started a weekly maindeck freighter service between Abu Dhabi and Entebbe, Uganda's capital, and freight-only flights to and from Dar-es-Salaam via Nairobi. Expected outbound cargos include heavy electronics, medical equipment, food, and textiles, with inbound loads primarily perishable goods destined for the Gulf and Europe. Etihad Cargo flies directly from Abu Dhabi to eight destinations in Africa, and this is extended to over 30 destinations across the continent through codeshare partnerships. In mid-2015, Etihad Cargo increased its freighter links to Africa with the launch of a twice-weekly service between Abu Dhabi and Brazzaville (Republic of Congo), via Lagos. At that time Turkish had ten dedicated freight destinations in Africa.

Proliferating their own route networks has been the most obvious way in which the four 'super-connnectors' have developed their services to Africa. Less apparent are the partnerships and servicing arrangements struck en route. One expression of this is the membership of global airline alliances that two of the 'Big Four' have secured. Turkish (Star Alliance) and Qatar (OneWorld) use their membership to offer convenience and loyalty privileges to African travellers.

Flight codesharing is another device used to build traffic on African routes. It has occurred between, for example, South African Airways and Emirates (from 2001) and between South African and Etihad. Etihad also codeshares with Royal Air Maroc, Kenya Airways, and Air Seychelles. The codeshare agreement on the Johannesburg–Abu Dhabi route lasted less than one year in practice before the troubled South African airline cut its monthly losses of $3 million at the end of February 2016 and left the route open to Etihad alone (Smith, 2016). This happened despite the Etihad president and chief executive claiming a "resounding commercial success" just a month earlier: in the six months since codeshare flights went on sale, the two partner airlines fed more than 20,000 passengers onto each other's flights (du Venage, 2015).

Qatar will be hoping for a more lasting partnership from its February 2016 signing of a codeshare agreement with Comair, a franchise of British Airways operating in South Africa and Zimbabwe. The agreement adds three new African destinations to the Qatar Airways route map, and provides additional flight options to travellers in Cape Town and Durban. Other developments feature Emirates expanding its codeshare with Air Mauritius from just the Mauritius route to ones serving six other cities.[5] Indian Ocean island air traffic is often counted as being part of the African air passenger market, and on that basis, Etihad's 2013 purchase of a 40 percent equity stake in Air Seychelles rates as the deepest linkage between a Gulf and an African carrier.

Emirates has ruled out acquisitions of "struggling African airlines", and has not taken equity shares or started joint ventures. Its Chairman noted in 2015 that Emirates' anticipated purchase of 35 new aircraft in 2016 was itself equivalent to launching a new airline (*African Cargo News*, 2015). Emirates' preferred mode of collaboration has been via formal memoranda of understanding, such as the August 2014 agreement with Arik Air, the West African airline, to develop and expand their existing commercial relationship and explore areas for cooperation. The following month Emirates signed an agreement with the government of Angola to advise and help manage TAAG Angola Airlines, and to co-operate in codesharing, passenger and cargo handling, and a frequent flyer programme (Hanafusa and Kumon, 2015). The TAAG code-share agreement bolsters Emirates' daily non-stop 14.5-hour link with Brazil (Rio de Janeiro) by a four-times weekly TAAG feed via Sao Paulo.

In multiple ways, the new 'Big Four' overseas airlines in African skies wield huge influence. Their size, reach, and ambition eclipses the Africa services flown by 16 smaller Middle East carriers for varying lengths of time (Alkaabi, 2014). By way of example, at the start of 2016 Saudia, the national airline of Saudi Arabia, operated to seven African countries, with its strongest presence in s16 North African cities (in Egypt, Algeria, Tunisia, and Morocco). It has a smaller presence in the Sudan, Ethiopia, Kenya, and South Africa. It operated three weekly flights on the Jeddah–Johannesburg route, with a fourth planned. Gulf Air's only remaining African service in 2016 was to Addis Ababa.

The Gulf's low-cost airlines operate mainly on short-haul holiday routes into North and East African resorts. FlyDubai (an Emirates subsidiary, started in 2003) launched its first African route to Djibouti in 2009, followed by destinations in Egypt and then Ethiopia (Addis Ababa) in 2011. In 2014 the airline added six East African destinations to its network.[6] FlyDubai registered a 14 percent increase in passenger numbers over the two-year period 2013–2014 in Africa. By 2015 the airline was operating 60 weekly flights to 13 destinations in North and East Africa.[7] Air Arabia, the United Arab Emirates' low-cost airline based at Sharjah, has been flying daily to Nairobi from Sharjah since 2012. Since then it has added seven African destinations.[8] The African portfolio of Kuwait's Jazeera Airways only includes Egyptian destinations.

African responses to offshore hubbing

The scale of incursion of the 'Big Four' airlines into Africa could not possibly have gone unnoticed. Of course, African airlines that have tied up with Gulf carriers have welcomed their new partnerships with fanfare, emphasizing access to additional destinations. But some aviation commentators have been less than enthusiastic, writing, for example, about the "onslaught of Gulf-based airlines" (Thome, 2012) and cursing "buzzing Middle East carriers that have pummelled African competitors" (Mwiti, 2015). African carriers, it has been said, are "bleeding" in the face of competition from airlines from the Gulf and Turkey that have been "stealing" African passengers (Mungai, 2015).

Several explanations have been given for the success of at least the 'Big Three' in Africa. The head of Africa and Middle East sales at Airbus, the aircraft manufacturer, said bluntly on one occasion that African nations' failure to manage their air transport properly had opened the door to Gulf airlines (Furlonger, 2014). The allusion here is to African governments having conceded air traffic rights too readily while at the same time not giving tax breaks that would have placed the cost structures of African airlines on par, and not investing in local airports sufficiently to enable growth of African airline fleets and maintenance facilities (Thome, 2012). The criticism cuts both ways: Gulf carriers have also echoed frustrations about poor airport infrastructure in Africa (Douglas, 2015).

Pointing fingers at African governments has stopped short of accusations of corruption and improperly awarded concessions to wealthy and powerful outsiders. More often it is the Gulf airlines that get criticized for having unfair advantages. The most commonly cited among these are the low fuel price in the Gulf (from which African airlines also benefit when refuelling there), low wages paid to non-unionized labour, and the seemingly unlimited finance available in its oil economies, as a senior member of Ethiopian Airlines put it in 2014 (cited in Getachew, 2014) before the oil price plunged. Airline subsidies are prominent in Africa so they would be a weak plank in any argument about unfair competition. The *modus operandi* of Turkish Airlines has attracted least attention, possibly because the airline is 83 years old and its expansion is regarded as an organic element of wider Turkish-African diplomacy. The airline management has spoken of Turkey as an 'Afro-Eurasian state'; Turkey is the fourth largest global donor to Africa; the Africa Union has designated it a "ground breaking strategic partner" (anna.aero, 7 October 2015).

Public commentary makes repeated reference to the Gulf airlines being able to offer cheaper fares than their African counterparts, and these for flights in bigger and newer aircraft. On routes where they compete with African airlines, the Gulf airlines have also faced terrorist threats, Ebola outbreaks, and tourism curbed by foreign government advisories against travel. But they have not had to contend with crew protest or with weak currencies that nullify oil price decreases (Mungai, 2015). These phenomena (but not autocratic governance in the home states of the 'Big Four') are cited as evidence of the uneven playing field on which airline competition in Africa is played out. Add charges of Gulf airlines poaching African airline pilots and cabin and engineering staff (at higher and tax-free salaries), and the retreat into protectionism becomes palpable. Gulf carriers themselves have remarked on the levels of protection which African governments give to their national airlines (Douglas, 2015).

Indeed, in 2012 the suggestion was made that Africa's strongest airlines (Ethiopian, Kenyan, and South African) should band together to create a mega-carrier which could protect and project African aviation, and whose economies of scale could counter external threats (Pirie, 2014; Mwiti, 2015). The idea foundered because of airline selfishness, membership of different global airline alliances, the very different economic health of the three African airlines, and a simmering spirit of aviation deregulation across the continent. In practice, even a giant African airline would have been a global minnow. In 2012 the combined seat capacity of the three airlines would have been 650,000 weekly, making it only the 30th largest airline globally. The combined revenue of the three African airlines would have amounted to little more than one-third that of Emirates', and the three would have carried only half the passenger numbers logged by Emirates at the time (Getachew, 2014). Other defensive measures taken by a few African airlines against market share loss have included joining global airline alliances, and, occasionally, contracting out some management and servicing.

'Super-connector' airline service has certainly taken some of the shine off African airline offerings. Two carriers, Kenyan and South African, have been reporting crippling financial losses while the four overseas carriers have been expanding their services into Africa. Reputations are dented and the force of own-marketing has been diminished. It is hard now for South African Airways to uphold its slogan 'Bringing the World to Africa, Taking Africa to the World'; it is moot whether embattled Kenya Airways remains 'The Pride of Africa'. Ethiopian Airlines, meanwhile, is posting healthy profits ($96 million in 2014) and better deserves its branding as 'The New Spirit of Africa'.

Twenty-first century Africa is indeed more than a curiosity and a safari destination: it is an important originator of mobile workers and tourists. In 2014 there were more than 500,000 African nationals living and working in Dubai; an additional 800,000 Africans visited (*Aircargonews*, 23 October 2014). Serving other African needs, Ethiopian Airlines transferred about 296,000 passengers in 2012 from all of Africa to Europe through its Addis Ababa hub, up from 103,000 in 2006. Similar traffic spurts occurred on its Asian services (including the Indian subcontinent) to which Ethiopian transferred 502,000 passengers from across Africa in 2012, up from 166,000 in 2006. In similar tripling of passenger traffic over six years, at its Dubai hub Emirates switched 1.25 million passengers from its Africa routes onto its Asian routes in 2012 (Heinz and O'Connell, 2013).

In July 2015, Kenya Airways cited competition from the Gulf carriers as one reason for annual net losses that spiralled from $33 million in 2013–2014 to $275 million for 2014–2015 (Dron, 2015). At approximately the same time, South African Airways posted a net loss of $200 million, more than double its losses during the 2013 financial year. Gulf airlines have simply stepped into a vacuum created by corrosion of executive and management morale and leadership in South African Airways, by innuendo and political meddling in the airline, by overstaffing, and by reliance on old and fuel inefficient aircraft. The weak local currency means that the real cost of fuel to South African Airways has soared by 77 percent since 2011. An incorrect hedge against fuel price rises cost the carrier dearly (Mungai, 2015; Smith, 2016).

South African Airways has not made a profit since 2011. It needed – and hoped for – mutually beneficial relationships with the 'Big Four'. South Africa and the United Arab Emirates entered into their 2007 bilateral air service agreement in that spirit. By 2015 Emirates was operating 49 flights a week into

Johannesburg, Cape Town, and Durban, and was second only to the domestic flag carrier as the largest international carrier in South Africa (El Gazzar, 2015).

Despite formal agreements, misunderstandings – or trials of strength – do occur. In November 2014, when Emirates was ten days away from inaugurating its fourth daily service between Dubai and Johannesburg, the South African Department of Transport declined to approve the additional flight, ostensibly because of a domestic dispute about authorization powers in the Department. Three days ahead of the planned launch, Emirates successfully petitioned a South African High Court to force the South Africans to allow the flight in accordance with the 2007 agreement. Before the court edict, rumours surfaced that the South Africans might impound an Emirates aircraft. Denials and backtracking followed in swift succession.

Later, in June 2015, on the verge of an agreement with Emirates to extend a $160 million lifeline to South African Airways, the acting head of the beleaguered airline was apparently instructed not to sign. Never made public, the deal might have created a partnership similar to the successful 2013 tie-up between Emirates and the Australian airline Qantas. This excluded equity investment, and was confined to revenue sharing and corporate co-operation in scheduling, marketing, pricing, and frequent flyer programmes. Qantas did agree to switch its regional hub to Dubai from Singapore.

An authoritative but exasperated commentator remarked of yet another South African Airways debacle that there were always political overtones in anything to do with South African aviation, and that those "continue to divert logic and sound policy" (quoted in El Gazzar, 2015). The politics in this case appear to have been associated with a struggle for control over government departments, budgets, and ministries.

African responses to overtures from Gulf airlines have ranged from eager embrace to hesitancy and obstruction. The mix of gratitude for service, fear of eclipse, and submission to superiority would be difficult to articulate publicly. So too would treating aviation as developmental regardless of who provides it under which flag. The temptation is still to nationalize the leverage which air transportation provides in terms of mobility and in terms of direct and indirect jobs (*Economist*, 2016).

The principles, protocols, protectionism, and progressivism sought and practiced in Africa's dealings with the 'Big Four' are being tested as Chinese and Asian airlines seek traffic rights in Africa. China is Africa's biggest trading partner, and its interest extends to serving tourism and the considerable Chinese investments in African agriculture, mining, industry, and infrastructure (including airports). Guangzhou-based China Southern airline inaugurated services to Nairobi in 2015, having abandoned its four-year Beijing–Dubai–Lagos experiment in 2010. Also in 2015, Air China started three-times-weekly non-stop flights from Beijing into Addis Ababa and, further still, into Johannesburg (14.66 hours; 11,772 km).

Unlike the Gulf aerostates, whose aeronautical links with Africa are mostly in the form of air services, China is also investing directly in African airport construction and upgrading, in aircraft sales, and in regional aviation. It may have to contend with competition from Turkey's state-owned airport organisation, which will bid to upgrade additional airport infrastructure in Africa based on its successful build-operate model at the new international terminal at Mogadishu, Somalia (anna.aero, 7 October 2015).

An early instance of Chinese aero-industrial activity in Africa was Hainan Airlines' parent group 2012 purchase of a controlling stake in Africa World Airlines based in Ghana, a country without its own airline since 2010. The investment was a joint venture with the China-Africa Development Fund (Dron, 2015). The initiative complements the 2014 China-Africa Regional Aviation Cooperation Forum, and keys into China's massive "strategic co-operative partnership" endorsed at the second summit of the Forum on China-Africa Cooperation, held in Johannesburg in December 2015.

Direct air services between Africa and cities in Asia and China will test the adaptability and resolve of the Gulf airlines in Africa, and the centrality of the Persian Gulf to new long-haul geographies. The literally diversionary tactic by Gulf carriers will be to promote an intermediate leisure or business stop-over in wealthy Abu Dhabi, Doha, or Dubai on a long cross-hemispheres flight. Retaining a share of growing Africa–China traffic is important for the Gulf airlines. In respect of airfreight, Emirates carried over 40,000 tons of cargo between Africa and China between 2009 and 2014 (Aircargonews, 23 October 2014). In respect of passengers, between 2009 and 2014, the number of Chinese visitors to Africa increased eight-fold from 380,000 to three million. In 2013, more than half (1.9 millions) of Chinese passengers flew from China directly to Africa, and about 5[illegible]3,000 Africans arrived in China (Liqiang, 2016). In 2009, four million passengers transited through Dubai between China and Africa; in 2014 the number had reached 6.5 million.

Apart from South African Airways' expensive miscalculation about the viability of its Johannesburg–Beijing service (it relinquished its 2012 route codeshare with Air China in 2015), initial indications are that some non-stop Africa–China services can compete with those routed along the Gulf boomerang. In 2014 Ethiopian Airlines had a 45 percent share of *direct* Africa–China traffic, carrying 318,000 one-way passengers, up from 149,000 in 2012. Emirates and Qatar had 87 percent of the 400,000 passengers flown *indirectly* between Africa and China in 2014 (up from 275,000 in 2012), but neither they nor Etihad nor Turkish ranked Addis Ababa in their top ten Africa destinations for this connecting traffic. Effectively, Ethiopian Airlines had a 25 percent share of all Africa–China traffic, direct and one-stop, with Qatar having 20 percent and Emirates 14 percent (Grant, 2015).

Conclusion

The location of and patronage behind the May 2015 'Aviation Africa' summit in Dubai were powerful signals of 21st-century nodes and axes of influence in African skies. A second 'Aviation Africa' summit scheduled for 2017 will return the event to another small state, but this time in Africa, in Rwanda.

The country has significantly less wealth and influence than the United Arab Emirates, but it has championed Africa-centric activities. In May 2016 it hosted the Africa regional meeting of the World Economic Forum. In August 2015 Rwanda hosted a symposium on 'The African Democratic Developmental State' backed by the African Development Bank. The Rwandan national airline, started almost at the same time as Etihad, was at that time in talks with Ethiopian Airlines about a strategic partnership, but with a tiny fleet of eight aircraft it does not begin to match either rival's profile or potential. RwandAir's sole overseas stop was Dubai until September 2016 when flights to Mumbai started. Aerial inequalities with the 'Big Four' could hardly be starker, feeding narratives and practices of domination.

The ascent into African airspace of big airlines from the Gulf and from Turkey has been very striking. They have not emerged as part of any strategic decolonizing policy in Africa to replace European legacy airlines, which dominated Africa's overseas civil air transport for more than 60 years. Rather, they have pushed themselves to the fore by trading smartly on their pivotal location and by buying and working large fleets of modern aircraft. Depending partly on time and pace of entry into African skies, each of the 'Big Four' has adopted different operational tactics and each has a different size and footprint. At one extreme is Turkish, rapidly offering the highest number of weekly flights non-stop to the greatest number of African destinations using mostly single-aisle aircraft; at the other extreme is Emirates, longest in the market, using wide-body aircraft to offer most seats and most freight capacity to and from fewer African cities. In Africa, Qatar is most like Emirates, but like Etihad, has more distinctive business arrangements with African airlines.

The precise impacts of realigned air transport in Africa on air travel and on the fortunes of African and other airlines need more detailed analysis than the data used in this chapter can support. For one, net global connectivity gains need careful reckoning. Initial indications are that the four 'super-connectors' offer extremely competitive services that have diverted some traffic and generated yet other new traffic. There is no way of gauging yet what their long-term influence will be: it will depend on persistence of the geographical advantage of their home bases as global air transport markets evolve, on any outflanking manoeuvres by Asian carriers, on the robustness and agility of African airlines, and on geopolitics.

In the absence of better information and perfect foresight, it is tempting to suggest that after European airlines' lengthy prevalence in Africa's colonial skies, a new, second-generation civil aviation hegemony may be in the making in post-colonial Africa. There is certainly concern among African airlines about being out-muscled and losing "unreasonable amounts" of traffic to airlines based outside the continent. The growing influence of offshore airlines sits uneasily with the notion and slogan of 'Africa rising' in the 21st century. In addition, the externally directed capital-to-hub flights operated by non-African carriers contradicts the African wish to use aviation as an instrument of development and regional integration in the vast and poorly inter-connected continent. With few exceptions, African airlines may once again be confined to flying as subordinate local and regional carriers feeding traffic into and collecting it from trunk services operated by non-African mega-airlines. The spirited notion of 'Driving African Economies through the Power of Aviation' (the International Air Transport Association's theme for its May 2016 'Aviation Day Africa' meeting in Abuja, Nigeria), is silent about the driver, the driven, and the power transmission.

Although their rank order varies on different units of measurement (number of destinations served, number of flights, seats and cargo space offered, airline partnerships, service agreements, codesharing, equity stakes), by every yardstick Emirates, Etihad, Qatar, and Turkish are turning heads in Africa. Yet the 'Big Four' have not entirely engulfed the continent from peripheral offshore hubs. Presently, there is one more shooting star in African skies. Operating out of its (onshore) Addis Ababa hub, one indigenous African carrier, Ethiopian Airlines, is a significant countervailing force. For the moment, Kenya's and South Africa's national airlines are engulfed by troubles of their own making. And, West Africa's geographical position offers little to the Gulf carriers whose preferred model does not involve stop-over flights at hubs they don't control, in this case on putative Caribbean and South American routes.

The much heralded 21st-century 'African renaissance' is not much evident overhead the continent or at many of its airports. The 'Big Four' airlines are increasingly visible. Their presence spells resurgent overseas airline penetration and dependency. The suitability of this configuration of 21st-century aviation to African tourism and business may not be problematic initially. Its longer term match to aspirations of regional integration, to job creation, capacity building, nation building and cultivating national pride is more contentious. Questions about partnerships and profiteering hang in the air. Matters of appropriation versus sharing need clarification. The direction and weight of advantage need disentangling. Risk needs reckoning. Responsibility is required. Critics will seize on deep memories: Africa has once before been trafficked greedily; once before it had its future piloted remotely; once before it has flattered the prestige and served the business interests of (small) foreign polities. Conversely, 'Big Four' proponents will deny megalomania, will refer to irresistible globalisation and to de-territorialisation of economic activity and identity, and will welcome non-African entities shouldering the burden of the often-bankrupting business of running airlines.

Notes

1 The nomenclature 'Persian Gulf' or just 'Gulf' is used here instead of the less conventional term 'Arabian Gulf' preferred by some regional parties and used strategically by others.

2 Cairo (71 weekly flights = 12 percent of weekly 'Big Four' Africa flights), Johannesburg (56 weekly flights = 10 percent), Nairobi (42 weekly flights = 7 percent), Casablanca, Dar-es-Salaam, Khartoum, Lagos, and Cape Town (between 31 and

35 weekly flights each = 5 percent to 6 percent each). Source: calculations from airline websites and flightconnections.com.

3 South Africa (16.7 percent), Egypt (14 percent), Kenya (13.1 percent), Nigeria (9.4 percent), and Ethiopia (9.1 percent).
4 Accra, Entebbe, Johannesburg, Khartoum, Lagos, Nairobi.
5 Cairo, Colombo, Dammam, Jeddah, Karachi, Riyadh.
6 Bujumbura (Burundi), Dar-es-Salaam, Entebbe, Kigali (Rwanda), Kilimanjaro, Zanzibar (Tanzania).
7 Addis Ababa, Asmara (Eritrea), Dar-es-Salaam, Djibouti, Entebbe, Hargeisa (Somaliland), Juba (South Sudan), Khartoum, Port Sudan, Zanzibar.
8 Dar-es-Salaam, Entebbe, Juba, Khartoum, Kilimanjaro, Port Sudan, Zanzibar.

References

Addie, J-P.D. (2014) Flying high (in the competitive sky): conceptualizing the role of airports in global city-regions through 'aero-regionalism'. *Geoforum* 55, 87–99.

African Cargo News (2015) Emirates not interested in buying struggling African airlines, 17 November. http://www.africancargonews.com/?p=4380.

Alkaabi, K. (2014) Geographies of Middle Eastern air transportation, in A.R. Goetz and L. Budd (eds), *The Geographies of Air Transport*. Ashgate, Aldershot, pp. 231–246.

Britton, R. (2015) The Big Three: U.S. airlines versus Persian Gulf carriers. *Forbes Opinion*, 12 May.

Butt, G. (2011) *History in the Arab Skies: Aviation's Impact on the Middle East*. Rimal, Limassol.

Campbell, K. (2015) Air freight helping to change and grow Africa. *Engineering News*, 8 May.

Centre for Aviation, (2015a) South African Airways outlook brightens as recovery plan and partnership strategy roll out, 6 February. Accessed at: centreforaviation.com/insights/analysis/south-african-airways-outlook-brightens-as-recovery-plan-and-partnership-strategy-roll-out-208472.

Centre for Aviation, (2015b) SAA faces intense competition from Gulf airlines, 26 June. Accessed at: centreforaviation.com/insights/analysis/south-african-airways-long-haul-turnaround-continues-with-accra-washington-launch--a340-extensions-231902.

Douglas, K. (2015) Emirates' eyes fastened on Africa – an 'underserved' air transport market. *How we made it in Africa*, 20 October.

Dron, A. (2015) Africa's airlines face powerful incomers. *Airways News*, 28 October.

Dursun, M.E., O'Connell, J.F., Lei, Z. and Warnock-Smith, D. (2014) The transformation of a legacy carrier – a case study of Turkish Airlines. *Journal of Air Transport Management,* 40, 106–118.

du Venage, G. (2015) South African Airways spreads wings with help from UAE carriers. *The National* (Abu Dhabi), 20 July.

Economist (2015) Super-connecting the world, 25 April. Accessed at: www.economist.com/news/business/21649509-advance-emirates-etihad-and-qatar-latterly-joined-turkish-airlines-looks-set.

Economist (2016) Let Africans fly, 13 February. Accessed at: www.economist.com/news/leaders/21692882-air-travel-africa-needlessly-hard-and-costly-open-skies-would-make-it-cheaper-let-africans.

El Gazzar, S. (2015) Politics could scuttle Emirates tie-up with South African Airways. *The National* (Abu Dhabi), 25 June.

Furlonger, D. (2014) African failure opens the skies to Gulf airlines. *Business Day Live*, 29 May.

Gerchick, M.L. (2016) The rise of the aerostate: U.S. carriers scramble as Persian Gulf rivals emerge. *Washington Post*, 30 April.

Getachew, K. (2014) *Air Transport in Major Airlines in Africa: Challenges and Prospects*. MA Thesis, Centre for African and Oriental Studies, Addis Ababa University, Addis Ababa.

Grant, J., (2015) The Africa, China and Hong Kong market. *Africa Wings*, August–October.

Hamill, L. (2016) Qatar Airways announces network expansion. *RoutesOnline*, 10 March.

Hanafusa, R. and Kumon, T. (2015) Flying to Africa: well-situated carriers scurry to connect world with continent. *Nikkei Asian Review*, 17 January.

Heinz, S., and O'Connell, J.F. (2013) Air transport in Africa: toward sustainable business models for African airlines. *Journal of Transport Geography*, 31, 72–83.

Hooper, P., Walker, S., Moore, C. and Al Zubaidi, Z. (2011) The development of the Gulf region's air transport networks – the first century. *Journal of Air Transport Management*, 17, 325–32.

Jacobs, R. (2013) Airlines race to conquer the last bastion of sky-high yields. *Financial Times*, 26 November.

Liqiang, H. (2015) Chinese airlines open new routes to Africa. *China Daily Africa*, 24 April.

Maslen, R. (2014) Air transport capacity in Southern Africa – a market snapshot. *routesonline.com*, 28 May.

Mungai, C. (2015) Airlines in Africa, and the tale of democracy: Kenya and South African carriers bleed, while Ethiopian flies high. *Mail and Guardian Africa*, 3 August.

Murel, M. and O'Connell J.F. (2011) Potential for Abu Dhabi, Doha and Dubai Airports to reach their traffic objectives. *Research in Transportation Business and Management*, 1, 36–46.

Mwiti, L. (2015) The African 'developmental state' is truly here with us – it takes the form of money-spinning Ethiopian Airlines. *Mail and Guardian Africa*, 26 August.

O'Connell, J.F. (2006) The changing dynamics of the Arab Gulf based airlines and an investigation into the strategies that are making Emirates into a global challenger. *World Review of Intermodal Transportation Research*, 1, 94–114.

O'Connell, J.F. (2011) The rise of the Arabian Gulf carriers: an insight into the business model of Emirates Airline. *Journal of Air Transport Management*, 17, 339–46.

Ozbeck, T. (2015) Turkish to expand African network. Accessed at: www.flightglobal.com/news/articles/turkish-to-expand-african-network-419334/.

Pirie, G. (2014) Geographies of air transport in Africa: aviation's 'last frontier', in A.R. Goetz and L. Budd (eds), *The Geographies of Air Transport*. Ashgate, Aldershot, pp. 247–266.

Smith, N. (2016) SAA emergency exits. *Financial Mail*, 4 February.

Surovitskikh, S. and Lubbe, B. (2008) Positioning of selected Middle Eastern airlines in the South African business and leisure travel environment. *Journal of Air Transport Management*, 14, 75–81.

Thome, W.H. (2012) Gulf carriers biggest threat to African aviation. Accessed at: www.eturbonews.com/27794/gulf-carriers-biggest-threat-african-aviation.

Williams, K. (1957) Commercial aviation in Arab states: the pattern of control. *Middle East Journal*, 11, 123–38.

6 The emergence of low-cost airlines in Africa

Charles E. Schlumberger and Rui Neiva

Introduction

Low-cost carriers (LCCs), epitomised by the likes of Southwest Airlines and Ryanair, have brought a revolution to the way people travel for business or pleasure, allowing large portions of the population to travel by air for the first time. In this century, the LCC market exploded, and there are now dozens of airlines, representing a significant share of available seat-kilometres offered. Initially bound to the air transport markets of developed countries, a significant push in LCC growth has resulted from the entrance of LCC in developing countries, particularly in Asia and in Latin America. Other regions, however, Sub-Saharan Africa and parts of the Middle East, have not witness the same growth in LCC availability.

Research has found that the entrance of LCCs has not only brought lower fares into the air transport market, but it has had a substantial contribution to a country's economy. Tourism, for example, has been a key beneficiary of the emergence of LCCs, as is the case of isolated island states or smaller cities. This would make the LCC business model especially valuable for developing countries.

In this chapter, we ask if the LCC model can also be successful in African countries with limited traffic. Additionally, we ask what conditions are needed in those countries to that model to be replicated. To answer these questions, the chapter explores the characteristics of the LCC model and highlights its impact on the aviation markets. Examples in Mexico and South Africa are also studied. Considering that model and the experiences of other countries, a series of pre-requisites for LCC development are identified. Air transport liberalisation is found to be a key for it to occur. Considering those pre-requisites, challenges and opportunities for LCC growth in the East African Community are discussed. A summary of issues concludes the chapter.

The low cost carrier business model

Although various definitions of LCCs exist, in essence LCCs are airlines that have achieved a cost advantage over full-service carriers, namely through operational changes. Oftentimes these definitions, however, stay silent on the matter of transferring these cost advantages to consumers in form of lower fares – sometimes referred as the "low-cost carrier" vs. "low-fare carrier" debate. This chapter will stay away from that debate, and a LCC will be defined as a carrier that translates those cost savings into lower, more affordable fares.

There are several key characteristics that can be found in most LCCs. These include:

- *À la carte, no frills, services:* LCCs offer a business model where the customer has the option to pay for the only the most basic service, i.e., a seat from A to B. Other services, like food and beverage, assigned seating, or baggage allowances, are regularly charged extra, the so-called "ancillary revenues".
- *Point-to-point routes:* LCCs generally operate with a point-to-point network rather than the traditional hub-and-spoke network, offering nonstop flights between city-pairs only. While still operating bases, which allow economies of scale, in contrast to traditional carriers, LCCs do not attempt to aggregate or 'bank' flights, nor do they offer connection opportunities for passengers. By doing this, they achieve higher level of use of facilities and employee services, thereby reducing costs.
- *Use of secondary airports:* LCCs in Europe and in the US have built up dense networks around secondary, rather than primary, airports, although this has changed somewhat as some of the bigger LCCs mature and look for more ways to expand. Secondary airports are more attractive as they offer lower charges, more slots, and less congestion. These characteristics help LCCs optimise their schedules and decrease turnaround time to maximise daily aircraft utilisation.
- *Fleet commonality:* LCCs typically use as little fleet types as possible, sometimes even one type, like Ryanair's exclusive use of the Boeing 737–800. This reduces the amount of ground support equipment, training, and spare parts inventories required. It also allows standardised handling and maintenance processes as well as flexible crew scheduling. Furthermore, bulk purchases increase the bargaining power of LCCs and thereby often result in considerable discounts from suppliers.
- *High-density one-class configuration:* LCCs traditionally operate with an all economy configuration with narrow seat pitches.
- *Low-cost distribution*: LCCs use direct distribution channels through their websites to reduce costs and avoid paying fees to intermediaries.

These principles are applied by each LCC differently, and the growth of many LCCs has translated in them adopting more hybrid models to capture other areas of the market with higher yields. Additionally, traditional carries have been adopting many of the LCCs principles and now offer "no-frills" fares in order to compete with them.

Impact of low cost carriers

It has been well documented in research that the development of air transport services can have a substantial impact on the aviation market and the overall economy (Button and Taylor, 2000; ICAO, 2003; ATAG, 2014; Button *et al.*, 2014). However, research on LCC entrance is also almost entirely focused on developed countries, particularly Europe and the US. This is mainly related to the more recent emergence of LCCs in emerging markets and the required data often not being available. A number of studies have, however, confirmed the positive impact of LCCs on air transport and the overall economy.

A heavily-cited work is the one by Bennet and Craun (1993), which studied the impact of the entry of Southwest Airlines on the market. The focus was on the LCC's impacts on three areas:

- The competitive effect in terms of passenger growth and fare reduction on a given route where Southwest had entered;
- The lowering of fares at surrounding airports through Southwest's entry;
- The impact Southwest has on the business models of new entries in other markets.

With a focus on California, the study presented evidence that Southwest's entry had a significant impact on all three aspects outlined above. On the Oakland-Burbank route, for example, where Southwest entered in 1990, prices dropped by 55 percent, and passenger traffic increased six-fold between its entrance and the third quarter of 1992. Since then, the impacts of a LCC entry into a market have been known as the "Southwest Effect". Similar effects were also seen in Europe (Alderighi *et al.*, 2012).

Those same effects have also been seen in developing countries, like Mexico and South Africa. In Mexico, since 2005 LCCs have provided a significant increase in domestic traffic, and in 2015 just two of them, Volaris and Interjet, carried more than 50 percent of the passengers (Statista, 2016). This market share was achieved by increasing traffic on existing routes, expansion of the domestic market, lower fares, and by attracting new flyers into the market. This allowed the LCCs to attract passengers from other modes of transportation, particularly long-distance buses.

In South Africa, LCC Kulula offered fares as low as ZAR800 (around US $80 in 2001) on the popular Johannesburg OR Tambo International Airport to Cape Town route, receiving 2000 bookings on its first day of operation (Townsend and Bick, 2011). The carrier is now South Africa's largest online retailer by annual sales value and carried almost 3 million passengers in 2015 (Comair Limited, 2016).

Another important effect of LCCs is their impact on tourism. The European Low Fare Airlines Association (ELFAA), a now-defunct trade association for the industry, grouped these benefits to tourism into three categories (ELFAA, 2004):

- Increase in tourist destinations due to usage of secondary airports;
- Less seasonality, with more even distribution of traffic throughout the year;
- Lower off-peak fares, enabling mid-week holiday travel.

The extension of the European Union liberalised market agreement to the new EU Member States, in Eastern Europe in particular, has resulted in a significant increase in LCC travel, with cities such as Krakow seeing a four-fold increase in foreign tourists in the 2003–2007 period (Dobruszkes, 2009).

In both Mexico and South Africa, tourism has also benefited from LCCs. For example, the Mexican LCC Volaris, for example, has expanded the offerings to Mexico's tourist destinations: in 2012, the Mexico City to Cancun route had a 39 percent growth. In South Africa, the entrance of the now-defunct LCC 1time on the Johannesburg-East London route increased traffic by 52 percent between 2004 and 2006. This played a major factor in revitalizing the city's tourism industry resulting in a 50 percent increase in holiday travel during that period (Schlumberger and Weisskopf, 2014). Morocco is another developing country that saw a boost in tourism from liberalisation in general, and LCCs especially. Since the country signed an Open Skies agreement with the EU, LCC growth between the two markets increased the number of Europeans visiting by almost double in five years (Dobruszkes and Mondou, 2013).

Several studies have also focused on other impacts of LCCs. Button and Vega (2008), for example, concluded that the reduced travel cost and increased accessibility that LCCs offers leads to a reduction of overall cost of international labour migration. Direct costs of transportation were only one of the components of those overall costs, as social costs resulting from the separation from their families were also part. These lower costs can even induce demand for migration that did not exist before. This is an observation that was also seen in the follow-up of the Eurozone debt crisis of the early 2010s, where LCCs were seen as enabling more intra-European migration, as they allow more frequent trips home for those migrants, thus reducing the cost of that migration.

The LCC model in developing countries

The success of LCCs in less developed markets needs certain market conditions to be in place. Economic growth, a sizeable middle class, and the liberalisation of aviation markets, are some of the needed conditions. In South Africa, domestic liberalisation was needed for LCCs to enter the market. The same has happened in Mexico, with the Aeromexico and Mexicana monopoly being broken and those companies privatised in the late 1980s (Schlumberger and Weisskopf, 2014).

Demand conditions

Demand is a crucial factor for any industry, but for LCCs even more. Without it, airlines would not be able to achieve the high levels of productivity necessary for their business model to work. While low fares might attract new passengers for air travel and shift existing customers to a given airline, underlying demand is driven primarily by two factors: the availability of disposable income to afford air travel, and conditions that encourage the use of air travel. LCCs are prone to attract a few particular markets, leisure and "visiting friends and relatives" trips (Mason, 2000).

Air transport liberalisation

Deregulated air transport markets, both domestic and international, are another essential condition for LCCs to thrive. Without it, Southwest, Ryanair, and others could not have had the success they have enjoyed. Especially in larger developing countries, the opening of domestic routes encourages the development of more efficient and affordable air services. Besides the case of Mexico and South Africa, Brazil offers another example in which deregulation of market entry and fares allowed LCCs such as Gol and Azul to enter the market (Evangelho *et al.*, 2005). In Southeast Asia, LCCs now represent more than 50 percent of seats available, and the number of airports served with commercial service grew by 15 percent from 1998 through 2013 (Bowen, Jr, 2016).

According to the World Trade Organization, intra-regional, short-to-medium-haul traffic, which is of importance for LCCs, is still very regulated in most developing countries (Schlumberger and Weisskopf, 2014). Liberalisation has mostly been the purview of individual countries or regional bodies, instead of global endeavours. The European Union, for example, achieved complete liberalisation between its member states in the late 1990s. In Asia, member countries of the Association of Southeast Asian Nations have also enacted, in 2016, an Open Skies agreement.

Air transport infrastructure

To optimise operations and minimise costs, LCCs tend to build their networks around airports with high capacity, low levels of congestion, and low airport charges. However, in developing countries, such necessary infrastructure, along with efficient management, might not be in place. The availability of air navigation services and safety and security facilities and equipment might also be problematic in many countries.

Airport charges, like landing and passenger fees, along with other taxation, can also be a major component in ticket prices. With less secondary airports available in developing countries, LCCs might be forced to operate from a country's primary airports. However, these major airports might not only have higher levels of congestion, but also often demand higher airport charges.

Airports in developing countries, and aviation in general, also prove to be an important source of foreign revenue for some governments, and are therefore seen as 'cash cows'. At smaller airports, the lack of landside infrastructure and limited opportunities for commercial revenue creates a larger dependency on air charges for airport funding. This can have a detrimental impact on ticket prices. Ground access to the airports is another issue, as many developing countries lack road conditions and public transportation.

Labour

Labour and fuel represent a major portion of an airline cost structure. Having qualified and affordable staff, along with a regulatory environment conducive for efficient labour utilisation, are crucial for airlines. Even in developed countries, lack of qualified personnel has become an issue, but it particularly affects Africa: the few qualified African persons are attracted by better wages in other regions.

Many airline employees require a high level of training, which is often not available or is very expensive. In some cases, unfavourable regulations and labour laws in developing countries further exacerbate this. Issues like restrictions to working hours, the mandatory use of overly expensive social security systems, high labour taxes, or very high minimum wages are often cited as problematic.

Safety and security

Safety and security are crucial for the airline industry. Besides the effect on the loss of life, air transport safety and security in a country also plays a critical role with regards to aircraft financing and insurance, with costs increasing when standards are inadequate. The aviation industry is now considered very safe in general, but some areas, notably in Africa and Asia, still have issues with safety. This is because of several reasons, including problems such as operational shortfalls, insufficient and defective equipment, inadequate maintenance of aircraft, and/or the lack of properly trained staff. These derive primarily from the lack of adequate infrastructure, insufficiently trained human resources, and poor oversight. Effective safety oversight is a must. It ensures that all the components of the aviation system, airlines, airports, and air navigation services comply with international safety standards.

Distribution channels

LCCs need to be able to sell their services effectively and inexpensively. For that, they have many times shunned the Global Distribution Systems that traditional carriers use, because of their high costs. But for that to happen, there must alternatives, with a knowledgeable population that can use the Internet and other channels to book directly with an airline. That might be problematic in developing countries with low Internet penetration and low use of technology in general.

Aircraft financing

The airline business is very capital intensive. To buy the fuel-efficient aircraft that LCCs prefer, solutions for aircraft finance are needed. (Although some LCCs have turned to buying older and less fuel efficient, but much cheaper aircraft. However, given the safety issues in Africa that route might be problematic.) Because commercial lenders might not be attracted to such markets, air carriers in developing countries have traditionally relied in export credit agencies, like the Export-Import Bank of the United States, to lower their financing costs.

In order to ameliorate the issue, the 2001 Cape Town Convention on International Interests in Mobile Equipment, and the accompanying Protocol to the Convention on International Interests in Mobile Equipment on Matters Specific to Aircraft Equipment, has acted on the issue. The convention, now ratified by 57 states, facilities the financing of aircraft by including among its provisions matters such as the right of a lender to deregister aircraft and procure its export upon default of a debtor or to take possession or control of aircraft (UNIDROIT, 2015).

Fuel

Fluctuations in the cost of fuel can determine if an airline is profitable or not. While the cost of fuel in general affects the airlines globally, local factors can have significant impacts on how much airlines pay for jet fuel. Levels of taxation, foreign exchange rates, and distribution infrastructure all affect the final price of fuel. Taxation is an issue in many developing countries. Under ICAO's policies on aviation fuel it should not be subjected to custom duties and excise taxes, many countries do not comply (ICAO, 2000). According to the International Air Transport Association (IATA), aviation fuel in Africa is about 21 percent more expensive than the global average, mainly because of government taxation not complying with ICAO principles (International Air Transport Association, 2013).

Governance

Good governance affects the general business environment in which any industry or service operates. Although several definitions exist, in this context good governance is the existence of an environment that does not stop or inhibit the growth of a business (UNESCAP, 2009). There are many instances where the inexistence of good governance has hindered the development of aviation markets. In African aviation, a good example of this was Virgin Nigeria. First established in 2004 as a partnership between Nigeria Airways and the Virgin Group, the experience would only last four years. The premature ending resulted from it being forced to change part of its operations in Lagos from its main terminal to a new remote terminal that was built at the airport, thus making connections between flights more difficult. Lack of transparency and good governance have been identified as crucial in this case (Thome, 2009).

The case of the East African Community

The East African Community (ECA) is a regional economic organisation formed between six East African countries: Rwanda, Uganda, Kenya, Tanzania, South Sudan, and Burundi. The region covers around 1.82 million square kilometres, and includes a population of 145.5 million. Its average GDP per capita was just over $1,000 (East African Community, 2016).

In its current iteration, the East African Community was formed in 2000 by Tanzania, Kenya and Uganda – it had existed before between 1967 and 1977. Rwanda and Burundi joined in 2007, while South Sudan joined in 2016. Initially just a customs union, the East African Community is developing a common market and aims to move to a common currency and, later, to a full political federation.

Air transportation is one of the areas of action of the East African Community, and it is the subject of Section 92 of the East African Community treaty. East African Community member countries are to "harmonize their policies on civil aviation to promote the development of safe, reliable, efficient, and economically viable civil aviation with a view to developing appropriate infrastructure, aeronautical skills and technology, as well as the role of aviation in support of other economic activities" (East African Community, 2007).

Demand

As in other developing nations, the air transport market in the East African Community is still very small. Most traffic is concentrated on the airports of Nairobi and Dar es Salaam. Mombasa and Entebbe are the other airports in the region with more than 1 million passengers per year (Table 6.1).

A few high frequency domestic routes represent a large share of overall traffic in the East African Community. They are primarily in Tanzania and Kenya, connecting their respective entry hubs in Dar es Salaam (DAR) and Nairobi (NBO) to its main economic and tourism centres. In Kenya, domestic direct traffic primarily links between Nairobi and Mombasa, Kenya's two largest cities and economic centres, with three airlines (including Kenya Airways' LCC subsidiary, Jambojet) offering services on the route with around 15 daily frequencies during summer 2016. High frequency domestic traffic also occurs between Dar es Salam (DAR) and Mwanza (MZW),

Table 6.1 Passengers by airport

IATA Code	*Airport*	*Passengers*
NBO	Jomo Kenyatta International Airport	6,271,922 (2012)[a]
DAR	Julius Nyerere International Airport	2,496,394 (2015)[b]
MBA	Moi International Airport	1,347,908 (2012)[a]
EBB	Entebbe International Airport	1,355,288 (2014)[c]
ZNZ	Zanzibar International Airport	878,789 (2015)[b]
JRO	Kilimanjaro International Airport	780,800 (2015)[b]
KGL	Kigali International Airport	580,505 (2015)[d]
MWZ	Mwanza Airport	444,215 (2015)[b]

a Airports Council International (2013).
b Tanxania Airports Authority (2016).
c Uganda Civil Aviation Authority (2015).
d Panapress (2016).

Kilimanjaro (JRO), and Zanzibar (ZNZ). This feeds tourism traffic from the country's capital airport to popular tourist destinations.

Air traffic, both domestic and within East African Community countries, is dominated by few carriers and competition is very limited. International intra-East African Community traffic is limited to a few key routes, primarily linking the East African Community's large and medium sized cities to the region's hub in Nairobi. In most markets a single carrier dominates routes.

Due to limited traffic in the region, most airlines use smaller turboprop, some regional jets, as well as a very limited number of narrow-body jets for few intra-regional routes. Although appropriate for these markets, these smaller aircraft offer higher costs per passenger that commonly used Airbus A320 and Boeing 737 narrow-body jets, creating additional challenges for these airlines.

New traffic for LCCs can come from a variety of factors, including economic growth, tourism, and migration or from modes of transport. East African Community countries have seen strong economic growth in the last decade, and pro-market market reforms eliminating restrictions on economic activity were introduced. However, income inequality and lack of disposable income are still serious issues. In a study about the region, the International Monetary Fund (IMF) has concluded that for it to achieve middle-income status, the region's real GDP per capita will have to grow at an average rate of 5.5 percent (two percentage points higher than between 2005–2010) until the end of the decade (McAuliffe *et al.*, 2012).

Tourism can offer another boost for traffic growth. East Africa has become more popular for international tourists, mostly from Europe and the US, who come to appreciate its national parks, mountain ranges, and scenic beaches. To facilitate this growth, the East African Community wants to introduce a common East African Community tourism visa and a common passport for East African Community member countries, but for now the visa is limited to Kenya, Rwanda, and Uganda (East African Community, undated).

In terms of ground transportation, road quality varies significantly in East African Community countries, but most roads connecting larger cities are believed to be in good condition (Ranganathan and Foster, 2011). There is also a well-connected intra-East African Community bus network, but air travel can compete significantly in terms of time, as bus travel between major cities in the East African Community can easily take eight to 15 hours (Schlumberger and Weisskopf, 2014).

Air transport liberalisation

The East African Community Treaty of 1999 provides a framework for cooperation on civil aviation. Its provisions on Article 92 include the harmonisation of civil aviation rules and regulation, merger of upper airspace air traffic management, and the liberalisation of passenger and cargo operation between the member states.

The East African Community has displayed great interest in and motivation toward liberalizing and developing air services within its territory. Being a relatively small regional compact, the East African Community relies mainly on mutual consent with respect to major decisions and programme implementation. Despite this, the latest news from the region on advancing air transport liberalisation came in 2013 (East African Community, 2013).

The existing bilateral regimes between East African Community states are nowhere near full liberalisation. For example, the air service agreements between Tanzania and other East African Community states (Table 6.2) show limits on frequencies and destinations.

Regarding internal liberalisation, several degrees exist, with Tanzania being the most advanced. Its internal market is fully liberalised, and competition from private operators exists, challenging the state-owned carrier Air Tanzania. In Kenya, the partial privatisation of Kenya Airways – the government is still the biggest shareholder, but 70 percent of the shares are owned by the private sector – and the appearance of the LCC Fly540 has also driven up internal competition. Across the region, internal liberalisation is seen as successful (Irandu, 2008).

Air transport infrastructure

Besides having airport infrastructure, there is a need for it to have sufficient quality and capacity, and to be affordable for the airlines. Most East African Community airfields are not suitable for commercial operations, so for now, they remain off-limits for LCC growth. Of the East African Community airports receiving commercial service, the majority have paved runways, taxiways, and aprons, but data on the quality of that ground infrastructure and on the landside infrastructure, like passenger terminals, is scarce. While runway capacity seems to be sufficient for foreseeable growth, the same cannot be said for passenger terminal capacity, which has already shown to be a constraint in some cases (Schlumberger and Weisskopf, 2014).

Table 6.2 Bilateral Air Services Agreements between Tanzania and East African Community countries

Country	*Frequency*	*Date of last review*	*Operating carriers*
Kenya	Unlimited frequencies on any point in Kenya to Zanzibar 42 on Nairobi – Kilimanjaro 42 on Nairobi – Dar es Salaam 14 on Kisumu-Mwanza 14 on Mombasa – Kilimanjaro Unlimited from any point in Tanzania to Mombasa 14 Nairobi – Mwanza 35 Zanzibar – Nairobi Any aircraft size	2011	Kenya Airways Air Kenya Express Five Forty Aviation Safari Link Precision Air
Uganda	As many as commercially viable Any aircraft size	2003	Air Uganda Precision Air
Burundi	Up to 14 per week No frequency and capacity restrictions on cargo	2009	Air Tanzania
Rwanda	Up to 14 per week Any aircraft size	2006	Rwandair
South Sudan	n/a	n/a	n/a

Source: Tanzania Civil Aviation Authority (2014).

While most airports in the region are government owned and operated, there are some examples of the use of public private partnerships becoming more common. Kilimanjaro Airport, for example, is operating under a concession arrangement with the Kilimanjaro Airport Development Company Ltd, a locally registered firm set up by the global airport operator Mott MacDonald (UK), Inter Consult of Tanzania, and the government of Tanzania.

Air navigation services infrastructure in the East African Community is still insufficient, like in the rest of the continent. This translates into the extensive use of flying under visual flight rules, where pilots rely on the "see and avoid" rule and are dependent on clear weather conditions that ensure visibility. Radar installations for surveillance and air traffic management are also rare due to the high equipment and maintenance costs. But, on this front, satellite-based navigation and surveillance offer interesting prospects, specially space-based satellite navigation that does not require ground infrastructure.

The Southern African Development Community (SADC) is expected to be the pioneer in the continent in using the technology starting in 2018 (Aireon, 2016). Tanzania, Rwanda, and Burundi already use SADC's very-small aperture terminal (VSAT) network for ground-to-ground communications, and it would be beneficial if they could join in in SADC's use of space-based satellite navigation. The use of this technology will allow these countries to manage traffic throughout the entirety of their territories, which they have not been able to do so before for lack of infrastructure. Based on the East African Community Treaty, the East African Community Secretariat has also been working towards a regional upper flight information region governing the upper airspace of all East African Community members, allowing for a more efficient and cost effective management of traffic.

Safety and security

Like the rest of Africa, the East African Community also suffers from a poor safety record. Causes of accidents include human error, aircraft overloading, unlicensed personnel operating aircraft, aircraft failure, and lack of navigational aids in mountainous areas. Although these causes are not only present in the developing world, the frequency of accidents in respect to traffic is very high and points towards an systemic deficiency in the air transport system (Schlumberger and Weisskopf, 2014).

According to the International Air Transport Association, the main influencing factors for accidents in Africa are related to the lack of effective regulatory oversight, the lack of data collection to perform Flight Data Analysis, and the lack of Safety Management Systems implementation. Poor regulatory oversight has been particularly critical with Africa performing significantly worse than other regions (Matschnigg, 2013).

The East African Community, with the help of US Department of Transportation's Safe Skies for Africa initiative has set up, in 2007, the Civil Aviation Safety and Security Oversight Agency (CASSOA). CASSOA is agency-mandated to help promote safety, ensure that the states meet the safety and security oversight obligation under the Chicago Convention, and create a forum for the states to coordinate their efforts related to the safety and security of civil aviation (East African Community CASSOA, undated).

Labour

Lack of qualified personnel is a major hurdle for the aviation sector in Africa. This include pilots and flight attendants, but extends also to maintenance engineers and technicians and regulatory staff. Kenya's flag carrier Kenya Airways, for example, is facing a shortage of experienced pilots, an issue exacerbated by the dozens of pilots the airline is losing to the Middle Eastern carriers (Eghwa, 2016). Officials in Tanzania and Rwanda have also identified issues with lack of qualified personnel to run their airlines and provide oversight (Schlumberger and Weisskopf, 2014).

There are a number of reasons for this. One is inadequate and underfunded training centres and civil aviation authorities. The other is poaching by overseas entities, for example, Middle Eastern carriers, that offer better pay and conditions to their employees. In the East African Community, regional training schools, such as the East African School of Aviation located in Kenya, and the East African Civil Aviation Academy at Soroti Airport in Uganda, have been able to promote some development of aviation professionals in the region, but due to lack of economies of scale, they have relatively high costs. There are several international initiatives that try to help developing countries in these issues, offering courses and seminars aimed at the development of human resources in the region. Examples include the Initiative on Human Resources Development by the African Civil Aviation Commission, the African Union's specialized agency for civil aviation matters, and ICAO's Next Generation of Aviation Professionals initiative (Schlumberger and Weisskopf, 2014).

Aircraft financing

Like it was mentioned before, aircraft financing is still a significant challenge in Africa, and the East African Community is no exception. However, most countries in the region have made progress towards the legal protection of borrowers and lenders. According to the World Bank, Rwanda and Kenya offer the best legal protections for borrowers and lenders. Burundi has the lowest score (South Sudan has not been classified) (World Bank, 2016a). Kenya, Tanzania, and Rwanda have ratified the Cape Town Convention, facilitating these countries' access to aircraft finance. Development institutions, such as the African Development Bank and the International Finance Corporation, as well as other private and public institutions, have also played a role in providing financing for airlines in the region.

Fuel costs and access

Access to competitively priced fuel is essential for an airline, much so for LCCs. In Africa, jet fuel prices have traditionally been higher than in other regions because as taxation is higher and there are not adequate transport and storage facilities. These factors lead to higher costs.

The East African Community is no exception. Government taxation and custom tariffs add to the cost of fuel. Still, East African Community countries have been complying with ICAO regulations, in that no excise or other taxes are applied to jet fuel, at least for international transport. Tanzania has abolished all excise duties for jet fuel. Some countries, such as Rwanda and Kenya, however, still apply value added tax and other taxes for domestic usage of jet fuel (Schlumberger and Weisskopf, 2014).

Another issue is the lack of adequate facilities at some airports, with many smaller airports not having any refuelling facilities. For example, in Tanzania, Iringa and Mbeya Airports have commercial service but no refuelling services. In Rwanda and Uganda, Entebbe and Kigali are the only airports with refuelling facilities (Schlumberger and Weisskopf, 2014).

Distribution

LCCs need a solid information and communication technology infrastructure and reliable and available payment methods to reach their customers. In Kenya, Internet use had by 2014 reached almost half of the population (according to the World Bank), the situation is quite different in the other East African Community countries, with only 1.4 and 4.9 per 100 people using it in Burundi and Tanzania, respectively (World Bank, 2016b). Poor infrastructure, costly services, lack of access to electricity, and low computer literacy are all factors limiting Internet access.

Mobile technology is promising in this regard. With more and more people connected via mobile devices, LCCs have a chance to use mobile technologies to reach their potential customers. Payments are also moving to the mobile world, and Africa has been the leader on those, particularly East African Community countries. Mobile payments allow users to make their transaction via their mobile without need for a bank account. Kenya's M-Pesa has been widely touted as the leader in these innovations, with the use of text messages to process transactions. The system is now available in 11 countries throughout Africa, Europe and Asia, and had more than 25 million customers in 2016 (Vodafone, 2016). Kenyan LCC Fly540 is just one of many companies that allows payments through M-Pesa (Mwangi, 2011).

Governance

Good governance is the essential component in any country for a competitive and transparent market. To assess how good governance is on the six East African Community countries, the World Bank's "Worldwide Governance Indicators" are used. Out of the six indicators in this index, five are particularly important in this context: political stability and absence of violence, government effectiveness, regulatory quality, rule of law, and control of corruption. (The one indicator left out was voice and accountability.) The dataset gives an estimate of the level of governance within a range of approximately −2.5 (weak) to 2.5 (strong) governance performance, with the latest data being for the year 2014.

In five of the six East African Community countries, the perceived level of governance is negative for most of the five indicators (Table 6.3) – the exception is Uganda, which gets a positive value for government effectiveness. Rwanda offers a different picture, as it only has a negative indicator: political stability. Political stability has been a known problem in many African countries, and the East African Community member states are no exception. The cases of violence in Kenya following the presidential election of late 2007 and the lack of political stability since South Sudan became independent in 2011 are just two, albeit extreme, examples of what political instability looks like.

Table 6.3 Good governance indicators

Country	Political stability	Government effectiveness	Regulatory quality	Rule of law	Control of corruption
Kenya	−1.27	−0.30	−0.34	−0.45	−0.94
Uganda	−0.93	0.18	−0.36	−0.39	−1.10
Tanzania	−0.54	−0.64	−0.34	−0.41	−0.80
Burundi	−0.89	−1.09	−0.77	−0.93	−1.19
Rwanda	−0.10	0.02	0.18	0.08	0.83
South Sudan	−2.54	−2.13	−1.63	−1.80	−1.61

(Columns are grouped under the header *Indicator*.)

Source: World Bank (2015).

Good governance and political stability are crucial for fostering the development of the aviation market, and providing conditions for the successful development of LCCs. Without them, it will be more difficult to achieve a striving market, and the East African Community countries still mostly lack on this front.

Concluding remarks

LCCs have proved to be a success in developed countries. They now represent a significant portion of traffic in markets like the US or Europe. But in less developed countries, the story is very different. While South Africa and Mexico can be considered successful in fostering LCC growth, many developing countries, including those in the East African Community, have lacked the key factors that allow LCCs to grow. These include liberalised markets, a strong middle class, and good governance.

LCCs are not the only way to achieve a bigger, more robust, aviation market in Africa. But these airlines have proved that they make markets grow at a pace that would be difficult to achieve without them. Thus, where LCCs can operate safely, efficiently, and cost-effectively, the economic benefits of air transportation can be achieved more rapidly.

References

Air Transport Action Group (2014) Aviation Benefits Beyond Borders. Accessed at: http://aviationbenefits.org/media/26786/ATAG__AviationBenefits2014_FULL_LowRes.pdf.

Aireon (2016) Aireon and ATNS Sign First Regional Commercialization Agreement for African Air Traffic Surveillance Data. Accessed at: http://aireon.com/2016/05/03/aireon-and-atns-sign-first-regional-commercialization-agreement-for-african-air-traffic-surveillance-data/.

Airports Council International (2013) Africa Airport Traffic 2012. Accessed at: www.aci-africa.aero/.

Alderighi, M., Cento, A., Nijkampd, P. and Rietveld, P. (2012) Competition in the European aviation market: the entry of low-cost airlines. *Journal of Transport Geography,* 24, 223–33.

Bennett, R. and Craun, J. (1993) The Airline Deregulation Evolution Continues: The Southwest Effect, U.S. Department of Transportation – Office of Aviation Analysis, Washington, DC.

Bowen Jr., J. T. (2016) "Now Everyone can fly"? Scheduled airline services to secondary cities in Southeast Asia. *Journal of Air Transport Management*, 53, 94–104

Button, K.J., Neiva, R. and Yuan, J. (2014) Economic development and the impact of the EU–US Transatlantic Open Skies Air Transport Agreement. *Applied Economics Letters*, 21, 767–70.

Button, K.J. and Taylor, S. (2000) International air transportation and economic development. *Journal of Air Transport Management*, 6, 209–22.

Button K.J. and Vega, H. (2008) The effects of air transportation on the movement of labour. *GeoJournal*, 71, 67–81.

Comair Limited (2016) 2015 Integrated Annual Report. Accessed at: www.comair.co.za/Media/Comair/files/2015/Annual-Report-2015.pdf.

Dobruszkes, F. (2009) New Europe, new low-cost air services. *Journal of Transport Geography*, 17, 423–32.

Dobruszkes, F. and Mondou V. (2013) Aviation liberalization as a means to promote international tourism: The EU-Morocco case. *Journal of Air Transport Management*, 29, 23–34.

East African Community (2007) About the Treaty. Accessed at: www.eac.int/treaty/.

East African Community (2013) Liberalization of Air Transport Market in East African Community on Course. Accessed at: www.eac.int/news/index.php?option=com_content&view=article&id=862:liberalization-of-air-transport-market-in-eac-on-course&catid=48:eac-latest&Itemid=69.

East African Community (2016) East Africa Community Facts and Figures Report. Accessed at: www.statistics.eac.int/index.php?option=com_docman&task=doc_download&gid=146&Itemid=153.

East African Community (undated) *East African Community: Visa.* Accessed at: www.visiteastafrica.org/visa-2/.

East African Community Civil Aviation Safety and Security Oversight Agency (undated) '*Mandate and Objectives*. Accessed at: www.cassoa.org/index.php?option=com_content&view=article&id=123&Itemid=92.

Eghwa, B. (2016) Kenya Airways Losing Pilots to Middle East, *Citizen Digital.* Accessed at: https://citizentv.co.ke/business/kenya-airways-losing-pilots-to-middle-east-135805/.

European Low Fare Airlines Association (2004) Benefits of LFAs. Accessed at: www.elfaa.com/documents/ELFAABenefitsofLFAs2004.pdf.

Evangelho, F., Huse, C. and Linhares, A. (2005) Market entry of a low-cost airline and impacts on the Brazilian business travellers. *Journal of Air Transport Management*, 11, 99–105.

International Air Transport Association (2013) Aviation: Strategic Driver of African Development. Accessed at: www.iata.org/pressroom/pr/Pages/2013-04-16-01.aspx

International Civil Aviation Organization (2000) *ICAO's Policies on Taxation in the Field of International Air Transport – Document 8632,* 3rd edn. International Civil Aviation Organization, Montreal.

International Civil Aviation Organization (2003) Economic Contribution of Civil Aviation – Ripples of Prosperity. Accessed at: www.icao.int/sustainability/Documents/EconContribution.pdf.

Irandu, E. M. (2008) The case of airline industry liberalization in East Africa. *Journal of the Transportation Research Forum*, 47, 73–88.

Mason, K. J. (2000) The propensity of business travellers to use low cost airlines. *Journal of Transport Geography*, 8, 107–119.

Matschnigg, G. (2013), *Safety: Focus on Africa*. International Air Transport Association. Accessed at: www.iata.org/pressroom/facts_figures/Documents/safety-gunther-agm2013.pdf.

McAuliffe, C., Saxena, S. and Yabara, M. (2012) The East African Community: Prospects for Sustained Growth, *IMF Working Paper*, International Monetary Fund, Washington, DC.

Mwangi, P. G. (2011) Fly540 Passengers to Pay for Tickets via M-PESA. Accessed at: www.thinkm-pesa.com/2011/07/fly540-passengers-to-pay-for-tickets.html.

Panapress (2016) Rwanda: Kigali International Airport Goes Digital to Improve Air Traffic Navigation. Accessed at: www.panapress.com/Rwanda—Kigali-international-Airport-goes-digital-to-improve-air-traffic-navigation—12–630465465–28-lang2-index.html.

Ranganathan, R. and Foster, V. (2011) *East Africa's Infrastructure: A Regional Perspective*. World Bank, Washington, DC.

Schlumberger, C. E. and Weisskopf, N. (2014) *Ready for Takeoff? The Potential for Low-Cost Carriers in Developing Countries*. World Bank, Washington, DC.

Statista (2016) Major airlines' domestic market share in Mexico in 2015. Accessed at: www.statista.com/statistics/572934/air-carrier-mexico-domestic-market-share/.

Tanzania Airports Authority (2016) Traffic Statistics. Accessed at: http://taa.go.tz/index.php/download/statisticts/16-traffic-statistics.

Tanzania Civil Aviation Authority (2014) The Status of Bilateral Air Services Agreements Concluded between the Government of the United Republic of Tanzania and the Government of other Countries as of 31 May 2014. Accessed at: www.tcaa.go.tz/files/Economic%20Regulation/Bilateral%20Air%20Services%20Agreements/BASA%20status%20by%2030%20June%202014.pdf.

Thome, W. H. (2009), 'Branson's Virgin Nigeria Nightmare', *eTN – Global Travel Industry News*. Accessed at: www.eturbonews.com/5010/branson-s-virgin-nigeria-nightmare.

Townsend, S. and Bick, G. (2011) Kulula.com: Now Anyone Can Fly in South Africa, *Emerald Emerging Markets Case Studies*. Accessed at: http://dx.doi.org/10.1108/20450621111126792.

Uganda Civil Aviation Authority (2015) Statistics. Accessed at: www.caa.co.ug/index.php?option=com_phocadownload&view=category&id=5%3AStatistics&Itemid=108.

UNIDROIT (2015) Protocol to the Convention on International Interests in Mobile Equipment on Matters Specific to Aircraft Equipment. Accessed at: www.unidroit.org/instruments/security-interests/aircraft-protocol.

United Nations Economic and Social Commission for Asia and the Pacific (UNESCAP) (2009) What is Good Governance? Accessed at: www.unescap.org/sites/default/files/good-governance.pdf.

Vodafone (2016) Vodafone M-Pesa Reaches 25 million Customers Milestone. Accessed at: www.vodafone.com/content/index/media/vodafone-group-releases/2016/mpesa-25million.html.

World Bank (2015) *Worldwide Governance Indicators*. Accessed at: http://info.worldbank.org/governance/wgi/index.aspx#home.

World Bank (2016a) Doing Business 2016 – Regional Profile 2016: East African Community (East Africa Community). Accessed at: http://documents.worldbank.org/curated/en/456461468186275656/pdf/103361-WP-PUBLIC-ADD-SERIES-DB2016-DB16-East-African-Community.pdf/.

World Bank (2016b) World Development Indicators. Accessed at: http://data.worldbank.org/data-catalog/world-development-indicators.

7 The evolution of African airline business models

Stephan Heinz and John F. O'Connell

Introduction

Africa covers more than 30 million square kilometres and is home to about a billion people. In terms of air transportation, the International Air Transport Association (2015) has forecast that seven of the ten fastest-growing passenger markets over the next 20 years will be Malawi, Rwanda, Sierra Leone, Central African Republic, Tanzania, Uganda, and Ethiopia. This study of airline business models indicates that Africa is set for strong expansion in air connectivity and that is expects passenger growth to average around 4.4 percent between now and 2034. By that time, the continent will have enlarged its intra-African and intercontinental passenger base to 294 million travellers in 20 years.

Euromonitor International (2014) reports that the sub-Saharan Africa's tourism industry is among the fastest-growing in the world. Between 1999 and 2013, international arrivals doubled to 36 million in 2013. Data extracted from MIDT reveals that around 90 million international passengers visited the continent in 2015, while over one-third of these passengers transited via a foreign hub to get to Africa. A mammoth 80 percent of this international traffic was carried on foreign carriers, while only 20 percent on African carriers, primarily with Air Algérie, Air Mauritius, Arik Air, EgyptAir, Ethiopian Airlines, Kenya Airways, Royal Air Maroc, Rwandair, South African Airlines, TAAG Angola and Tunis Air. Only 3 percent of global aircraft orders scheduled for the next 20 years are African bound, making it difficult to compete with established foreign carriers over the coming decades.

The operating environments in which airlines find themselves are far from homogeneous. The diversity of policies, geographies and economies across the world imply a need for a set of bespoke strategies that can be represented in broad templates or business models designed to respond to the challenges presented by specific operating environments. Simplifying and grouping airline strategies under common business model tags allows an examination of how these models evolve over time and change their key components. This chapter aims to assess the types of business models that exist in Africa, and specifically how they are evolving. Research by Heinz and O'Connell (2013) worked towards identifying a series of business models specific to Africa and delivered some conclusions on their relative business sustainability. Since then, a number of data points have been refreshed, allowing an analysis of how these business models have evolved over the past five years.

Although there is a considerable amount of literature on airline business models, and their evolution in changing global landscapes, there is a lack of research into the applicability of those models to the African environment. In the context of African aviation, chief bodies of research centre on the impact of liberalisation on the continent, not least of which was a comprehensive piece published for the International Air Transport Association (2014) on the economic benefits of implementing the Yamoussoukro Decision. The African Airlines Association (2015) states that there are about 660 regional and domestic city-pairs in Africa, however more than half are served by less than five flights per week hence potentially over 50 percent of the current city-pairs in Africa are underserved – clearly the restricted regulatory framework within Africa is constraining its development.

Much of the commentary on the impact of liberalisation, however, is limited in its reference to the evolution of airline strategies in response to these developments. Other salient research on African aviation has focussed on the challenges posed by the African operating environment, but no explicit link is made to any recommendation on suitable strategies for African airlines to overcome such challenges.

In a World Bank (2014) report entitled *Ready for Take-off*, the institution assesses opportunities for the low-cost carrier (LCC) business model to thrive in less-developed countries, including those in Africa and concluded that the prospect of profitable low cost carriers developing in the region is "questionable", identifying six key obstacles: limited existing air service network, high levels of economic inequality dampening demand, high infrastructure costs, limited human resources, high fuel costs, and restrictive air service agreements. In addition, poor safety, government interference, old aircraft, sparse demand over long sectors, low load factors, and currency valuations are all threats which need to be mitigated by African airlines if they are to remain economically sustainable, and they will shape any conclusions on sustainable business models on the continent.

A challenging operating environment

The challenges posed by the African operating environment are considerable and, although detailed discussion of them is beyond the scope of this chapter, it is important to take stock of them. Simply put, to remain as economically sustainable operating entities, airlines need to deliver sufficient returns to satisfy shareholders and re-invest in growth. In a notoriously challenging business, airlines the world over battle to deliver the types of margins that consistently deliver on this, and Africa is no exception. A look at how pressures in Africa impact both costs and revenues reveal the challenges that airlines need to overcome.

Revenue pressures

Yield and load factor

Although some routes in Africa show some of the strongest yields in the world (largely a function of government regulation and monopoly operators), load factors remain thin. One of the focal challenges which African airlines must overcome is sparse demand, specifically on intra-African routes. This is a direct result of high airfares on the continent and poor populations (Abrahams, 2002; Irandu, 2008; Chingosho, 2009; Ssamula, 2008, 2009; Schlumberger, 2010).

High air fares on the continent are a symptom of the general lack of competition from strong airlines on intra-African routes as well as the inequality of income across African populations. Air transport in Africa remains a luxury and generally air travellers still represent a very small, but lucrative, sector of top earners. Both the lack of available alternatives in terms of substitutes and the wealth of those travelling is reflected in the continent's lower-than-average price elasticity of demand. Figure 7.1 reflects some of the most recent research on air travel demand elasticities in Africa, presented by Chingosho (2009), and clearly illustrate Africa's position at the lower end for both business and leisure travellers, that is to say, demand for air travel in Africa is less sensitive to changes in price than in other regions. This picture is likely to have remained relatively unchanged since 2009, but it will evolve in the coming decades as Africa's middle class emerges.

Cost pressures

The cost pressures that African airlines face extend beyond the more generic ones found in aviation more generally.

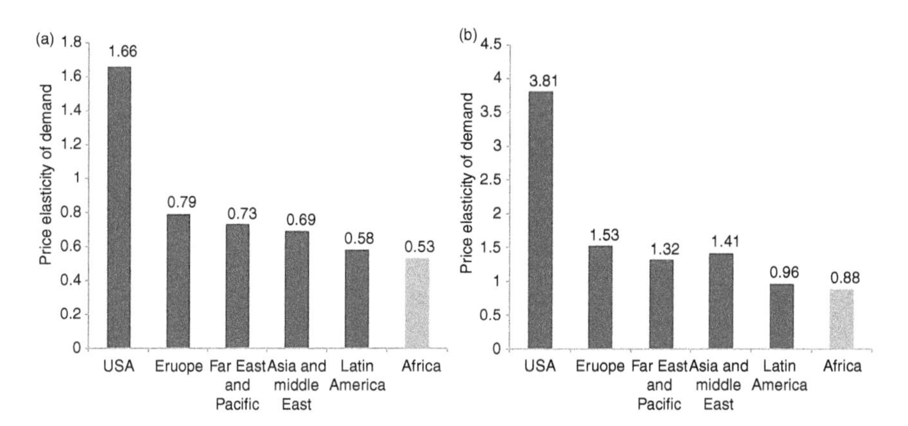

Figure 7.1 Price elasticity of demand for leisure travellers (left) and for business travellers (right).

Source: Chingosho (2009).

Airport and navigation charges

In most cases across Africa, service providers in this sector are typically government-owned monopolies. Despite poor service, this implies charges significantly higher than the world average. Overflying, navigation, landing, and parking charges are all higher in Africa than in the rest of the world. South Africa's airport operator Airports Company South Africa, for example, had announced in 2011 a significant tariff increase of 34.8 percent for passenger services, landing, and aircraft parking. Additional increases of 30.6 percent were applied in 2012; 5.5 percent in 2013; and 5.6 in 2014 (World Bank, 2014). According to the International Air Transport Association Airport and an ATC database the cost for landing and passenger charges for a 200-ton 777–200 aircraft in 2016 was $13,397 at Johannesburg, while in Addis Abba it was $12,837.

Fuel costs

With a quarter of countries on the continent land-locked, fuel needs to be transported over long distances, a problem exacerbated by poor infrastructure which increases transportation cost. Moreover, the small size of many of Africa's carriers means a distinct lack of bargaining power with large fuel companies. In addition, the small size of the aviation industry in Africa as a whole means that fuel companies have only a small market over which to spread their costs, resulting in higher costs per airline on the continent.

Distribution costs

The lack of technological development and Internet penetration throughout Africa means that most sales still occur through travel agents. *The Economist* (2013) reported that many Africans are purchasing items such as travel with their mobile devises through an e-commerce platform termed M-PESA. By 2013, it was used by over 17 million Kenyans, equivalent to more than two-thirds of the adult population. In fact, around 25 percent of the Kenya's Gross National Product flows through it. FastJet (2014) reported that 30 percent of its revenues were transacted through mobile money channels in 2014. There are currently 100 million Africans joining Facebook every month, with over 80 percent of these conducted by mobile interfaces.

Maintenance costs

Maintenance costs in Africa are significantly higher than in other parts of the world owing mainly to ageing fleets. Furthermore, the lack of credit worthiness of Africa's airlines means that often spare parts are paid for by cash.

Labour costs

Although, in general, salaries are lower in Africa than the world average, the low productivity means that often organisations are over-staffed.

Furthermore, the lack of a skilled workforce means that a significant amount of training is carried out per employee, which has obvious cost implications.

Insurance and ownership costs

Again, the relative small size of African airlines means that such airlines generally do not benefit from bulk purchase discounts. In addition, the continent is still perceived as "risky" in terms of investment, which implies that African airlines incur higher than average leasing, insurance, and financing costs. Restrictive government policies and lack of investor confidence in Africa also mean that raising equity finance from global markets is difficult, leaving airlines with shortages in liquidity and long-term capital. As a result, most African airlines are often financed by costly debt structures. Nevertheless, ratification of the Cape Town Treaty by numerous African states has gone some way to reducing the costs of such financing. This treaty serves to expand the sources and lower the costs of aircraft financing by establishing a central international registry for the creation and enforcement of interests in aircraft.

A classification of African airline business models

The research by Heinz and O'Connell in 2013 on developing a picture of sustainable business models for airlines in Africa was founded on a core piece involving classification of over 50 African airlines into a series of business models. Without any previous research in this area, the picture built up a static snapshot of these models at the time. This snapshot will be revisited before looking at what a refresh of the data taken over the subsequent four years shows regarding how these business models evolved.

The initial classification

In much existing airline literature, there is a general consensus that an airline's route network forms a fundamental component of its business model (Gillen, 2006; Mason and Morrison, 2008; among others). To this end, in building up a picture of the business models that exist in Africa, much emphasis was placed on metrics that summarise the sample airlines' route networks, most notably average stage length (weighted on seats flown per route) and connectivity (the average number of flights departing between one and three hours after each arriving flight at the airlines' hubs).

Connectivity is perhaps the most important core element that can distinguish between different airline business models because it implies a choice of network design that distinguishes hub-and-spoke (airline-supplied connectivity) from point-to-point (passenger-supplied) networks. Other variables included the Available Seat Kilometres (ASKs) as a measure of airline size and the Herfindahl-Hirschman Index (HHI), a measure of market concentration (where 100 percent is a perfect monopoly), to gain an understanding of a possible relationship between market structure and business models. Displaying these results on a platform with x-axis as seat stage length, y-axis as connectivity, and the point size as ASKs, builds a picture of common business models (Figure 7.2).

The graphical results were supported by the results of a hierarchical cluster analysis using the same metrics, largely delivering the same airline groupings. Ultimately, seven separate business model classifications were observed. These are detailed below.

Full-service network carriers (FSNC)

Referring to Figure 7.2, it is clear that a few very large carriers including South African Airways, Egyptair, Kenya Airways, Ethiopian Airlines, Royal Air Maroc, and Air Algérie dominate Africa. By virtue of their high connectivity values and slightly higher than average stage lengths, these carriers constitute Africa's FSNCs. They also have relatively high HHI values, often driven up by government-supported monopolies within domestic networks.

Established regional carriers (ERC)

These carriers include South African Express, Arik Air, Air Nigeria, Air Seychelles, Tunisair, and Afriqiyah. The services offered by regional carriers can be summarised in three forms: feeder services, own hub-and-spoke services, or point to point niche services. Overall, however, the regional carrier route networks are geographically confined. In this sense, South African Express and Air Nigeria are perhaps the two most obvious regional carriers. It is also evident that Africa consists of a number of carriers that may appear to be regional models but, as a result of a minimal long-haul service, cannot be accurately classified as regional carriers.

Long-haul niche carriers (LHNC)

These carriers rely heavily on long-haul point-to-point traffic from their home airports. Niche point-to-point demand from strong tourist, VFR (visiting friends and relatives) or business traffic is fundamental to these carriers' sustainability and is reflected in the generally low connectivity values. Air Mauritius is such a carrier focusing on serving the luxury tourism market as opposed to mass tourism – it strictly regulates its air transport services and in turn restricts air access to the Island (Seetarum, 2008). Over 60 percent of its fleet is composed of widebody aircraft and over 71 percent of its seat capacity was devoted to long-haul operations by the Summer of 2016, signalling its intent on capturing high-end tourists in mature markets such as Europe and in emerging markets such as China, where it serves four destinations. Its ambitions are evident as it has six A350s on order.

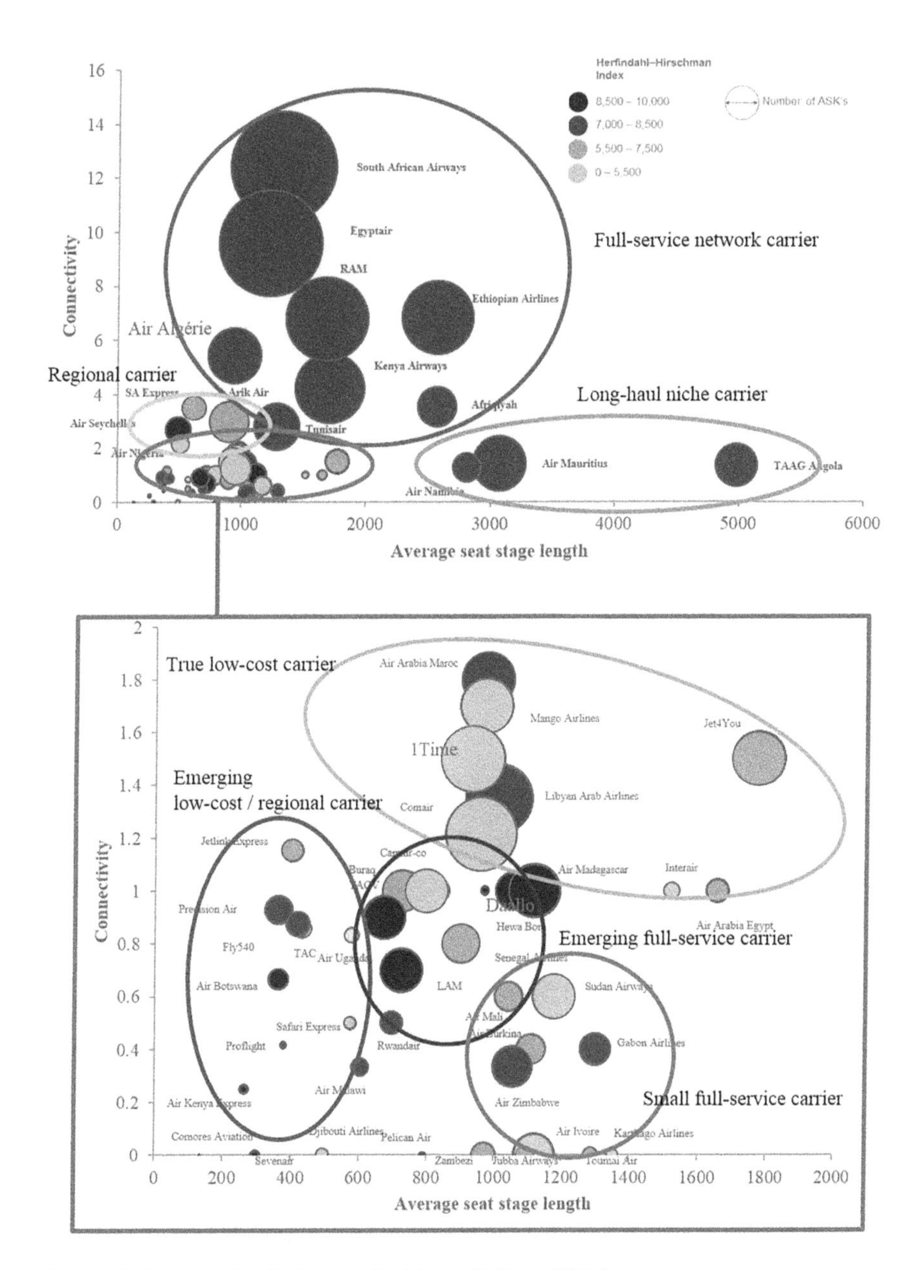

Figure 7.2 Geographical cluster of African Airlines (2011).
Source: Diio mi capacity data.

True low-cost carriers

Among the large group of smaller carriers with connectivity values below two, there is an obvious group including airlines such as Air Arabia Maroc, Mango Airlines, Comair (including low-cost carrier Kulula), 1Time (now ceased), FastJet and Libyan Arab Airlines. With the exception of the latter, these represent a selection of Africa's low-cost airlines. LCCs have been extremely slow at penetrating the African airline sector. There are currently only about 60 aircraft operated by African LCCs. About two-thirds of the continent's LCC aircraft operate in the domestic South African market, where they now account for about 50 percent of seat capacity.

The rest of Africa has experienced a wave of LCC start-ups over the last couple of years and by 2016 there were around ten African LCCs outside South Africa. But the new LCCs are all very small and still account for less than 3 percent of capacity in Africa's regional international market. With just five A319 aircraft, the FastJet pan-African LCC group has been expanding outside of its Tanzanian domiciled base as it has created FastJet subsidiaries in Zimbabwe, Zambia, and Kenya, with Fastjet Nigeria also in the pipeline for the future.

The rate of LCC expansion, though, is unlikely to gain mass momentum as liberalisation practices that would favour economic linkage are blanketed by protectionist policies favouring the incumbent national carrier. However, the research observed that these carriers reflect relatively low HHI values, consistent with the idea that true low-cost airlines in Africa can be found in regions with high demand and more competition, as opposed to less competitive, more sparse niche markets.

The emerging regional/low-cost carriers (ERLCC)

Among the smaller carriers in Africa, there appears to be a group with lower stage lengths and connectivity values of around one. In general, these are privatised airlines and this, combined with the overall short-stage lengths and small size, indicates that these carriers could be classified as privatised, emerging regional and low-cost carriers. The small size of these carriers means that, rather than being a by-product of high frequencies, the connectivity is created by clever scheduling, albeit resulting in only one connection on average. These airlines also have relatively high HHI values which, in some cases, may represent operations in monopolistic niche markets, in line with the regional carrier model. Although some carriers in this group, such as Fly540, may claim to be low-cost carriers, they are more representative of regional models or at least regional/low-cost hybrids.

Emerging full-service network carriers (EFSNC)

As with the emerging regional/low-cost carriers, the connectivity reflected among these carriers is likely to have been created through the set up of the timetable because the small size of these carriers means that, unlike the larger point-to-point carriers, connectivity as a by-product of size and frequency, is less likely. What is a salient characteristic of this model, however, is the longer-stage length which in some instances is reflective of a long-haul operation (Camair-co, LAM, Senegal Airlines). Essentially, the boundary between these carriers, and ERCs is somewhat blurred, and only maintained based on the contention that ERCs employ a geographically confined route network lacking any long-haul operations.

Small full-service carriers (SFSC)

A final business model consists of small, predominantly state-owned carriers with longer stage lengths but low connectivity, which could be representative of niche markets being targeted. This is contradicted, however, by relatively low HHI values with the exception of Air Zimbabwe and Gabon Airlines (now ceased), both of which operate a long-haul service. Despite an obviously larger size than the ERLCC (with average connectivity of around one), these carriers seem to lack any level of connectivity. This may be representative of fragmented and poorly planned schedules and route networks as well as small fleets, synonymous with weak state-owned African airlines. These airlines are likely to struggle with sparse demand on above average stage lengths, and seem to rely on point-to-point traffic despite operating in what appears to be more competitive markets.

Understanding the evolution of African airlines' business models

A simple analysis of the trends in seat capacity shares of the business models identified earlier, delivers a first view of how business models in Africa have developed over the past decade. Heinz and O'Connell (2013) used a similar view in 2011 as a basis for identifying sustainable business models for Africa. This was based on the assertion that the strong presence of a business model in the market, and, therefore, its associated inertia, contributes positively to its sustainability. The dominance of the full-service network carrier (FSNC) in Africa is clear and by virtue of these airlines' sizes, it is not surprising that this takes the highest share of seats on the continent. Between 2004 and 2011, the share of FSNC seats decreased as regional and low-cost carriers (LCC) gained ground as outlined in Figure 7.3. However, the marketplace landscape of FSNC enlarged from 2011 to 2015. This triggered by specific partnership strategies with smaller regional carriers.

There has been a growing collaboration between the two models in the form of joint ventures (e.g. code sharing, block space, etc.), cross border, and equity investments as witnessed by the partnerships between Ethiopian Airlines and Togo's Asky Airlines, for example, which gives the group access to almost 20 destinations in West Africa. Ethiopian also has a stake in Malawian, a smaller flag carrier with just six destinations, and is looking at several potential airline investments elsewhere in Africa.

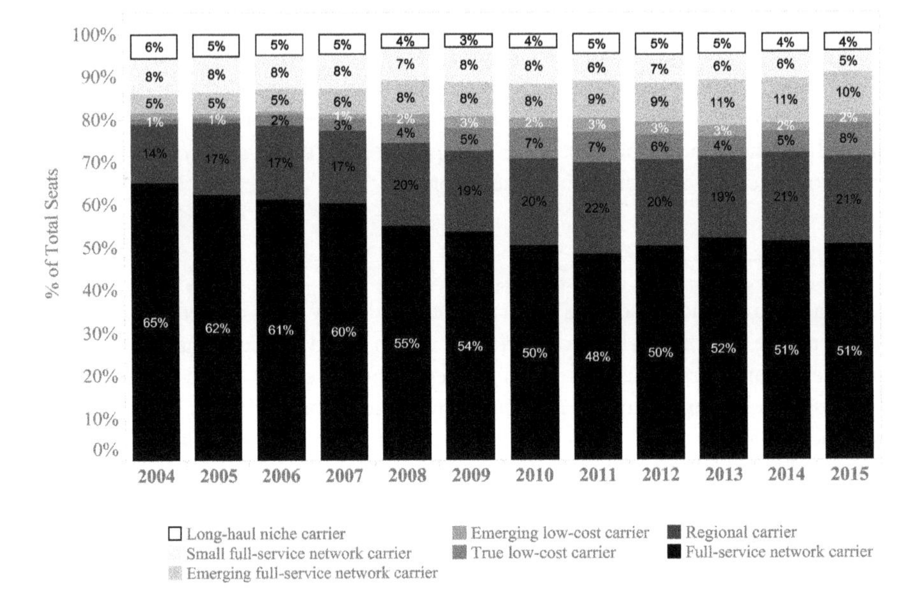

Figure 7.3 The evolution of African airline business models – a capacity perspective.
Source: Diio mi capacity data.

Meanwhile, Kenya Airways has partnered with Tanzania's Precision Air. These regional carriers were used as linchpins to redistribute traffic from the large network carriers and in turn feed traffic to the host's hub. These carefully planned networks with high hub-connectivity would overcome the challenges of serving long, thin routes profitably. Ethiopian Airlines has shown remarkable growth, with a compound annual growth rate (CAGR) between 2010 and 2015 of 16 percent. Kenya Airways showed the next strongest CAGR at 5 percent, followed by Royal Air Maroc at 4 percent.

The emerging full-service network carriers have also shown relatively strong growth over the past five years. In the Heinz and O'Connell classification in 2011, these carriers were identified as the "new wave" of FSNC's – although small, they were considered to have ambitious expansion plans based on building connectivity at their hubs and ultimately growing to offer a long-haul service (if not already available). The share growth of this model can be attributed to the successful launch of a new flag carrier, ECair of the Congo as well as growth by incumbents including Camair-Co, Rwandair, Air Ivoire and Air Seychelles.

Figure 7.3 illustrates that the true LCC share has stabilised since 2010, after showing strong growth from 2004. Much of this growth, however, was in localised markets such as South Africa, where the market dynamics are such that a European or North American-style LCC model is applicable.

With a stronger middle class than in other African countries and generally more wealth, the South African domestic market exhibits the type of traffic that drives LCC growth initially such as weekend, price-sensitive leisure traffic. Nevertheless, the market is highly competitive and in 2012 one of South Africa's (and Africa's) largest LCCs, 1Time, liquidated, citing tough operating conditions relating to high taxes and oil prices. 1Time's exit from the market drove down the true LCC share in 2012 and over the subsequent three years, only one other LCC emerged as a real player in the shape of FastJet, a British-based holding company for a group of African LCCs including Fly540 (which was acquired by the airline in 2013).

Githachuri (2013) found that around 38 percent of FastJet's passengers were first-time flyers, which indicates that the model is attracting passengers from other surface modes, particularly from buses. The authors view low-cost carriers as a future foundation for supporting the diversification of African air travel. Fastjet's growth has been notable, but it has been heavily restricted by glacial moving regulatory constraints that are suppressing its aspirations to emerge as a true pan-African LCC. However, financial problems are mounting as FastJet has amassed net losses of almost $100 from 2013 to 2015 due to liberalisation constraints, currency valuations, high operating expenses throughout every cost element at the carrier, a low pool of trained personnel and inadequate infrastructure. Meanwhile, Zimbabwe LCC based flyafrica with five B737–500 aircraft was grounded in late 2015 after just one year of operations highlighting the tough business and bureaucratic climate in the region.

Long-haul niche carriers, small full-service carriers, and emerging low-cost carriers all showed no growth or a decline in seat shares. Long-haul niche carriers (as indicated in their name) are limited in growth to core long-haul markets that serve a niche. These carriers typically offer point-to-point services catering to specific leisure or VFR traffic and thus their growth is tied to the performance of a relatively few number of markets. It is also very difficult for new carriers in this category to emerge, unless a specific, as yet unidentified niche market emerges. Both small full-service carriers and emerging low-cost carriers were identified as the business models with the smallest airlines and airlines offering little to no connectivity through a hub. Heinz and O'Connell (2013) cited this as a difficulty in Africa, given the sparse demand and low load factors. While emerging low-cost carriers may have a suitable value proposition with low enough fares to offset this, the same cannot be said for small full-service carriers, which are characterised usually by small state-owned carriers with few routes, low connectivity, and no significant value proposition. In both cases, however, growth has been difficult. In contrast, regional carriers – which build connectivity, either independently or with a larger partner (usually a FSNC) – have shown slight growth since 2012. These carriers may be as small as the emerging low-cost or small full-service carriers, but they place more focus on building connectivity and partnerships.

Considering that size and connectivity have been mentioned extensively in the discussion of these business models' evolution already, it may be significant to evaluate the evolution of these business models in terms of those metrics (essentially a moving view of the original model classification picture shown earlier in Figure 7.2).

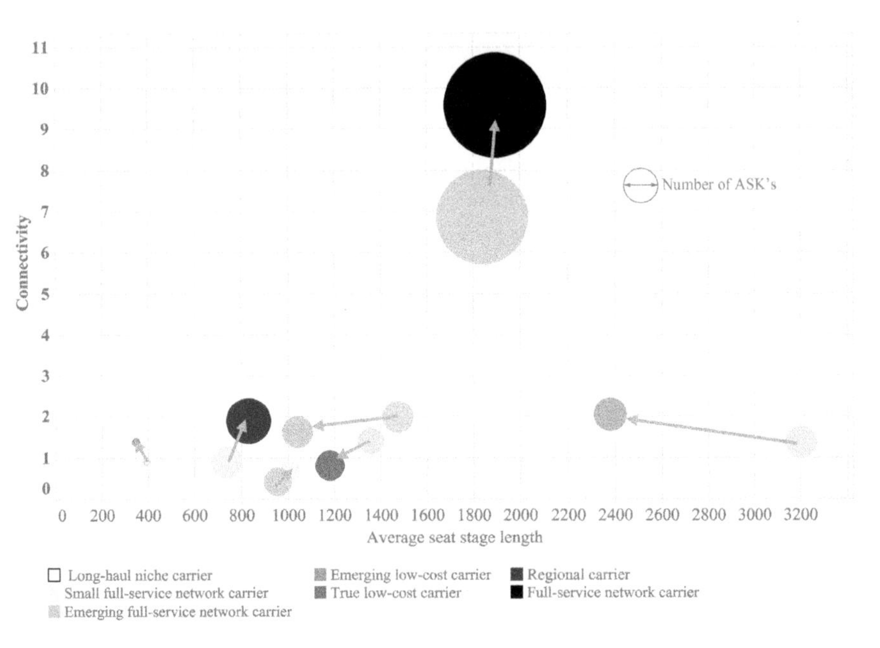

Figure 7.4 A network perspective of the evolution of African airline business models (2011–2015).

Source: Diio mi capacity data.

Figure 7.4 shows how African airline business models have evolved from 2011 to 2015. Each bubble represents the average of the airlines classified as that business model in 2011 and the arrow as indicative of the direction of movement to reach the average values observed in 2015. Heinz and O'Connell (2013) contested that connectivity was a fundamental component of successful business models in Africa. Developments among African airlines over the past four years appears to have echoed that contention, with five out of the seven observed model definitions all showing an improved connectivity value versus 2011. Africa's large full-service network carriers grew slightly in terms of ASKs produced but further increased their already-high connectivity value, consolidating further their strong hub positions.

Long-haul niche carriers appeared to have contracted their networks in addition to improving connectivity over the period. This could be indicative that they are focusing on more profitable regional routes, as well as improving hub bank structures such that regional flying can more easily feed historically challenging long-haul routes. Regional carriers also improved their connectivity and size, as well as slightly expanded their networks. Although small full-service carriers increased connectivity slightly, they also reduced in size and, overall, their connectivity values are still negligible. These carriers continue to show limited growth, together with emerging full-service network carriers and true low-cost carriers, which showed contracting networks and declining connectivity.

Of course, the dominance of the FSNC business model in Africa needs to be viewed in context with the regulatory environment in which FSNCs operates. This business model is dominated by large national flag carriers that have historically had their presence and growth in the market supported by government subsidies, even if that is no longer the case. For this reason, it is important to look more closely at the components of each business model and the extent to which they can be considered to contribute to its profitability.

Towards understanding what drives profitability among African airlines

Heinz and O'Connell (2013) selected a sample of around seven focus airlines to cover the major business models identified in the cluster analysis of Africa's airlines. The aim was to examine the components of those business models more closely and understand how they interplay to deliver profit and, therefore, sustainability. Given the general lack of data for African carriers, however, the sample included more full-service network carriers. These carriers publish annual reports consistently and therefore the data is abundant, introducing some inherent bias into the sample.

The following were key elements examined for each business model:

- Profitability
- Revenue performance
- Cost performance
- Connectivity
- Convenience (frequencies, punctuality, baggage service)
- Comfort (seats width and pitch)
- Fleet performance (utilisation, fleet commonality)
- Labour productivity.

The relevant benchmark items for each airline were calculated based on a "best in class" performance, whereby each airline was scored in relation to the best in class airline for that item. In line with the methodology proposed by Mason and Morrison (2008), two variations of calculation were employed, depending on whether or not the best in class for that item was the lowest or highest value. Once each benchmark item was calculated, the results were combined to compute the overall index, weighting each benchmark item to reflect the fact that some items in the index were more significant than others in their contribution. Consistent with the methodology, weights were based on a correlation of each benchmark item with profitability.

The final index score is then calculated by placing each airline in relation to the best performer in each benchmark area (profit, cost, labour, etc.).

Further, each index score is correlated with profitability, to gain an understanding of which areas of the business models of the airlines under analysis drive profitability. Carriers that perform best in these areas are considered to employ sustainable business models, given that continuity and economic sustainability are driven by profit and continuous returns. Index scores were also correlated with each other to gain an understanding of how they interrelate, highlighting a number of meaningful relationships. This process was completed for 2008, 2010, 2012, and 2015 data to gain additional data points and develop an understanding of how these business models have evolved over time.

A number of meaningful correlations were observed upon examining the evolution of key business model components and their link to airline profitability. Connectivity and fleet composition and utilisation showed the strongest impact on the airlines' profitability scores. Also notable was the correlation between the airlines' revenue and cost scores.

Revenue and cost leadership

Figure 7.5 shows that, among the performance of the seven African airlines chosen in the focused sample, revenue and cost leadership are mutually exclusive. In any one year, no carrier performs well in both indices, and usually a strong performance in one index is accompanied by a weak performance in another index. In some cases, this may be reflective of strong

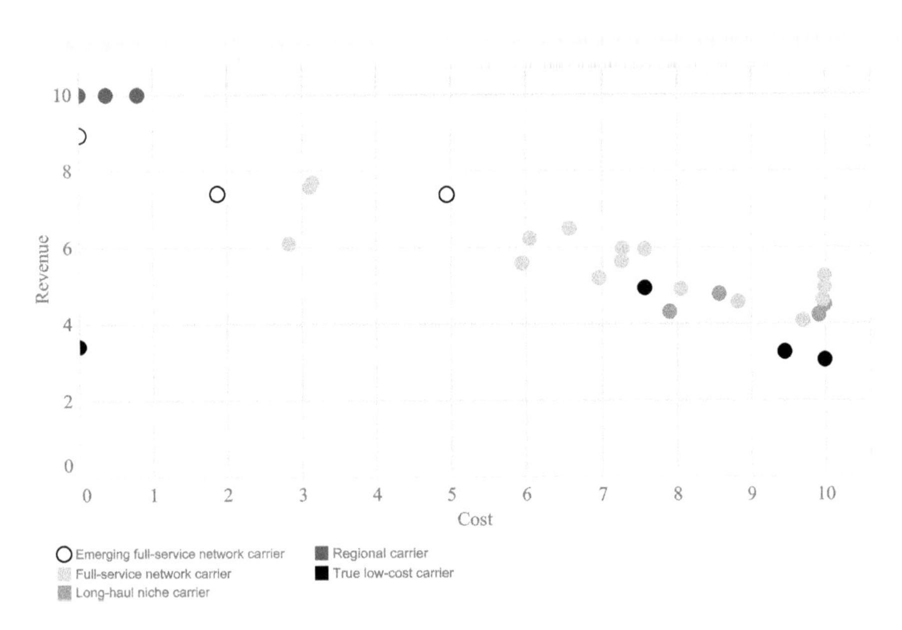

Figure 7.5 Relationship between revenue and costs.
Source: Airline annual reports.

intra-African yields resulting in a revenue focus, leaving cost performance somewhat neglected. In such cases, improving the cost position represents an opportunity to increase margins, but presents the risk of some yield erosion should such efficiencies lead to a real or perceived reduction in service.

Regional carriers show the worst cost performance but the strongest revenue performance, evidence of these carriers exploiting strong yields in highly regulated intra-regional markets. As expected, the true low-cost carriers show the best cost performance and lowest yield performance. The full-service network carriers are more evenly spread across the continuum but overall show slightly stronger cost than revenue performance. Combined with economies of scale, these carriers produce an overall higher ASK, meaning that their unit costs are driven down.

Connectivity and profitability

Generally, an increase in connectivity is accompanied by an increase in profitability. Taking into account metrics for each model for the years observed, this relationship becomes clear (Figure 7.6). It is more pronounced for the selected full-service network carriers in the sample, considering that these carriers are well positioned to profit from connectivity through their hubs. Further, if high connectivity of passengers through hubs is combined with convenience, then profit should be driven upwards yet further, which was supported by high and moderate convenience correlations (frequency of flights) with connectivity and profitability respectively.

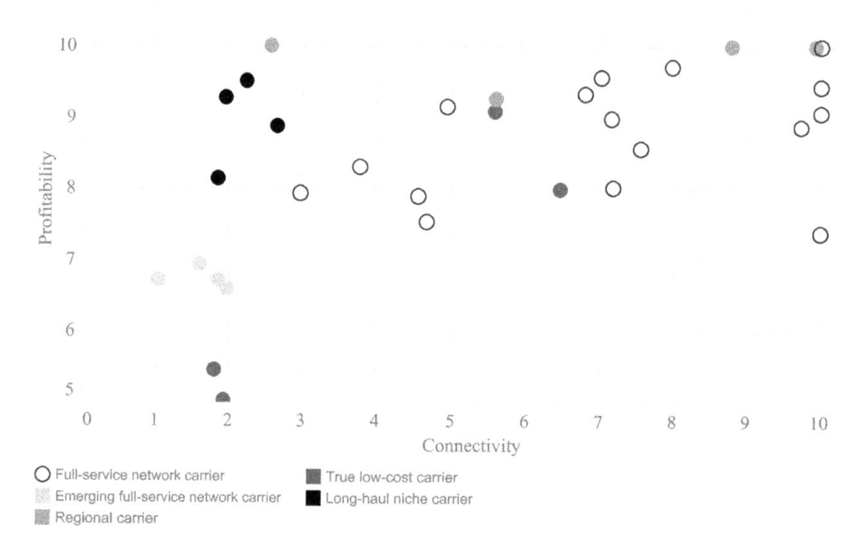

Figure 7.6 Relationship between connectivity and profitability.
Source: Airline annual reports.

Fleet composition and utilisation and profitability

The fleet score was derived as a function of utilisation and fleet composition (named "aircraft"). Airlines with high utilisation and high fleet commonality scored close to ten in the benchmark normalisation methodology. Fleet commonality shows a stronger correlation with profitability than utilisation, so this metric is weighted higher in the derivation of the overall fleet score. The correlation of this fleet score with profitability (Figure 7.7) reveals an inverse relationship. That is, over the observed years, airline business models performing strongly in the aircraft metric, and show a worse profitability score overall. This is driven, at least in part, by the LCCs (and particularly FastJet in recent years), which score very highly in fleet commonality but show weaker profitability.

The air transport markets in Africa mirror the diversity of its economies and it is this diversity that may go some way to explaining this relationship. The continent has an abundance of long, thin routes as well as a smaller number of shorter, high-demand routes. African airlines may struggle to serve these contrasting markets with a single aircraft type. This is evident in how some airlines structure their route networks, making use of fifth freedom rights and multiple stops to operate routes with sparse demand with single aircraft types.

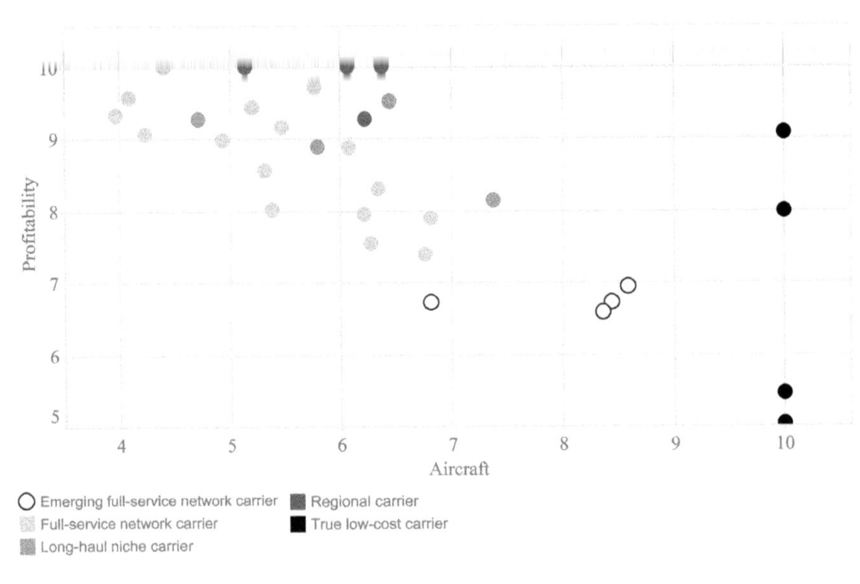

Figure 7.7 Relationship between fleet composition and utilisation (aircraft) with profitability.

Source: Airline annual reports.

Typically, this adds complexity to understanding segment profitability, and delivers a sub-optimal product for customers, with longer flight durations and sub-optimal timings. In contrast to the single-type fleets that serve the relatively homogeneous market dynamics in more developed regions like Europe and North America, there is an argument to be made that in an African context, mixed fleets could be one solution to more profitably serving a combination of local and regional niche markets and longer trunk routes. Full-service network carriers like Ethiopian Airlines, which has shown consistently strong profitability, operates 13 sub-types including both current and ordered aircraft types.

Evolution of business model components

In line with research conducted by Heinz and O'Connell (2013), the full-service network carriers in Africa perform best on those metrics that closely correlate with profitability. To examine this business model further, additional business model components were analysed with special attention given to pattern of changes since 2007. The level of detailed data available for full-service network carriers makes them suitable for this additional business model metric analysis.

Representing these metrics on a radargram gives an idea of the business model "footprint" of these carriers and comparing this footprint to 2007 gives an idea of how this model has evolved. Of course, in this case, the main full-service network carriers in Africa are considered and the footprint is an aggregation of their metrics. The carriers included are Ethiopian Airlines, Kenya Airways, South African Airways, and Egyptair, Africa's largest full-service network carriers. It should be noted, however, that the success of these carriers is mixed, and the aggregation should be considered with this in mind.

Figure 7.8 visualises how the business models of Africa's full-service network carriers have evolved since 2007. Most notable is the improvement in connectivity scores as these carriers further optimise their hubs and build connectivity. An improved cost position and a relatively consistent revenue position implies that these carriers are boosting margins by focusing on costs, relative to other business models in the sample. Although the connectivity metric increased, the convenience metric showed a strong decline in 2015 versus 2007. This metric is made up of the number of frequencies offered, baggage performance, and punctuality.

Overall, the carriers sampled show worsening punctuality and baggage performance, driving down this metric in 2015. Both Kenya Airways and Ethiopian Airlines have shown aggressive growth since 2007, which may have put strain on these carriers' operational infrastructure, in turn impacting their punctuality and baggage performance. The worsening labour score is a function largely of South African Airways that cut some capacity

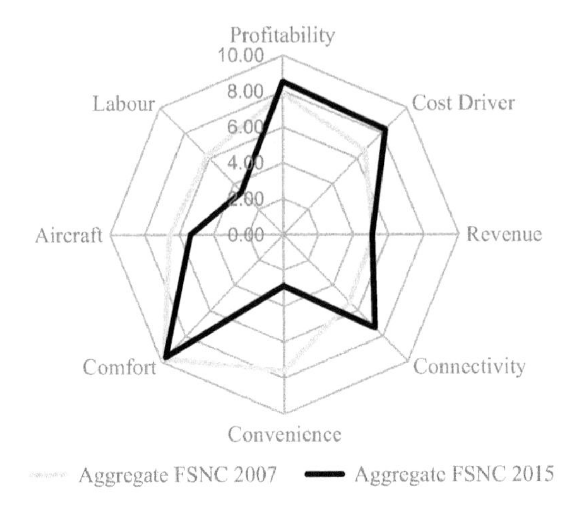

Figure 7.8 Evolution of the full-service network carrier model.
Source: Airline annual reports.

since 2007 but did not show the proportional reduction in workforce, echoing the airline's need to restructure again. In addition, carriers such as FastJet and South African Express showed strong labour scores in 2015, driving the relative performance of the full-service network carriers in this metric down.

Conclusions

Africa still only represents around three percent of global airline revenue passenger kilometres and the development of the industry on the continent is well behind that in more mature markets such as North America and Europe, although growth is strong. Market dynamics, influenced largely by regulation, mirror those of the pre-deregulation era in Europe and North America. This government protectionism and support for state-owned carriers has meant that historically the picture of business models on the continent was relatively homogenous, with the full-service network carriers dominating the landscape.

While this model's scale, inertia in the market, and support from government has supported, and continues to support, its dominance. Evidence suggests that its mechanics mean it will continue to remain relevant. Persistent strict regulation, high costs, and the nature of demand suggest that, for the moment, true low-cost carriers and other small carriers will find it difficult to gain a foothold in developing markets. The assessment presented above of how the seven African business model classifications evolved over the past five years is evidence of this.

Full-service carriers strengthened their positions and no real, viable low-cost carrier or other emerging model developed as a real alternative. In fact, in some sense it was observed that the other models have moved towards mirroring the key network characteristics of the full-service network model in Africa, including, most notably, improving connectivity. The evolution of business models in Africa is likely to continue as such and although in localised markets examples of low-cost carriers and regional carriers will continue to emerge, it will be decades before these models dominate the African landscape, as they do in other parts of the world.

References

Abrahams, T. (2002) Key Challenges facing air transport in Africa, to the 8th Aviation and Allied Business Leadership Conference, Johannesburg, South Africa.

African Airlines Association (2015) *Airline Business Outlook and Trends in Africa.* Accessed at www.afraa.org/index.php/media-center/sgs-speeches/sg-speeches-2015/584-airline-business-outlook-and-trends-in-africa-by-dr-elijah-chingosho-in-cairo-egypt-08th-dec-2015/file.

Chingosho, E. (2009) *African Airlines in the Era of Liberalisation,* 2nd ed. Nairobi.

Euromonitor International (2014) Sub-Saharan Africa How to Maximise Tourism Potential. Accessed at www.euromonitor.com/sub-saharan-africa-how-to-maximise-tourism-potential/report.

FastJet (2014) Annual Report and Financial Statements. Accessed at: www.fastjet.com/img/stand_alone_files/file/original/236678-fastjet-85.pdf.

Githachuri, E.N. (2013). Passenger Perceptions of Airlines in Africa, A case study of the East and West African traveller, MSc Thesis, Cranfield University.

Gillen, D. (2006) Airline business models and networks: Regulation, competition and evolution in aviation markets. *Review of Network Economics,* 5, 366–84.

Heinz, S. and O'Connell, J.F. (2013) Air transport in Africa: toward sustainable business for African airlines. *Journal of Transport Geography,* 31, 72–83.

International Air Transport Association (2014) *Transforming Intra-African Air Connectivity: The Economic Benefits of Implementing the Yamoussoukro Decision.* Accessed at: www.iata.org/whatwedo/Documents/economics/InterVISTAS_AfricaLiberalisation_FinalReport_July2014.pdf.

International Air Transport Association (2015) Air Passenger Forecast Shows Dip in Long-Term Demand. Accessed at www.iata.org/pressroom/pr/Pages/2015-11-26-01.aspx.

Irandu, E.M. (2008) Opening African skies: The case of airline industry liberalization in East Africa. *Journal of the Transportation Research Forum,* 47, 73–88.

Mason, K. and Morrison, W. (2008) Towards a means of consistently comparing airline business models with an application to the 'low cost' airline sector. *Research in Transportation Economics,* 24, 75–84.

Schlumberger, C. (2010) *Open Skies for Africa: Implementing the Yamoussoukro Decision.* World Bank, Washington, DC.

Seetarum, N. (2008) Mauritius, in aviation and tourism, in A. Graham, A. Papatheodorou, A. and P. Forsyth (eds.) *Aviation and Tourism: Implications for Leisure Travel.* Ashgate, Aldershot.

Ssamula, B. (2008) Strategies to Design a Cost-Effective Hub Network for Sparse Air Travel Demand in Africa, PhD Thesis, University of Pretoria.
Ssamula, B. (2009) Sustainable Business Models for the State-Owned African Airlines. *Sustainable Transport*, 28th Annual Southern African Transport Conference. Pretoria.
The Economist (2013) Why does Kenya lead the world in mobile money? Accessed at www.economist.com/blogs/economist-explains/2013/05/economist-explains-18.
World Bank (2014) The Potential for Low-cost Carriers in Developing Countries. Accessed at: https://openknowledge.worldbank.org/bitstream/handle/10986/20191/905860PUB0Box3014648028290Sep102014.pdf?sequence=1.

8 Pan-African strategic alliance, global competition

A case study of air Afrique

Joseph Amankwah-Amoah

Introduction

Over the past 50 years or so, scholars of economics and political economy have become increasingly interested in the role of air transport in facilitating economic development (Belobaba *et al.*, 2009; Pirie, 2014; Button *et al.*, 2015). At the same time, governments have also experimented with forming and developing state-owned enterprises with mixed outcomes (Goldstein, 2001; Doganis, 2006). Indeed, the desire for faster economic development has historically provided the impetus for governments in newly established and newly independent states to inject their scarce resources to sustain state-owned airlines and their operations (Heymann, 1962; Doganis, 2006).

One growing branch of research has examined this role of the nation states as champions of economic development through new firms' formation (Doganis, 2006). For decades, many enterprises have flourished in the developing world, whilst others have failed to meet governments' expectations and subsequently collapsed. Despite the impressive and surging stream of scholarly works on state-owned enterprises (Bruton *et al.*, 2015), our understanding of why and how such firms fail remains limited. Such analysis has the potential to enrich not only strategy research, but also debate in the economics and political economy areas about the role of state-owned enterprises in the 21st century.

The main purpose of this chapter is to examine why some state-owned enterprises fail despite having government backing. The chapter focuses on the case of Air Afrique, which was a "multi-national airline" in the civil aviation sector, jointly owned and operated by multiple nations (Barrett, 1969). The case is particularly important because the airline was among the very few in this group of firms that "outlived" its rivals with similar ownership structures across the globe (Fadugba, 1985; Yacouba, 2002; Amankwah-Amoah *et al.*, 2016). This chapter holds that Air Afrique was one of the first quintessential international businesses in post-colonial sub-Saharan Africa. This chapter is concerned with the ways in which a firm supported by multiple states can become so mismanaged and eventually cease operations. It draws heavily on Amankwah-Amoah and Debrah's (2014) paper on the airline and adds new perspective, extensions and insights, which extend our understanding of the causes of business failure. This research on business failure has largely focused on multi-national or small businesses with little emphasis on multiple state-owned enterprises.

The rest of the chapter is organised along the following lines. In the next section, a review of the literature on bankruptcy is presented. This is followed by an examination of the historical backdrop to the Air Afrique story, 1961–2002. An examination of factors that contributed to its demise is then presented. The final section discusses the theoretical and policy implications.

Theoretical underpinnings: business closure research

For decades, scholars have grappled with the question of what constitutes a business failure and have employed terms such as demise, closure, and exit to refer to failure (see Mellahi and Wilkinson, 2004). In the context, business failure is taken to mean a situation where the firm ceases operations, loses its legitimacy, and closes its doors (Hager *et al.*, 2004). The theoretical understanding of the causes of business failure is reflected in three schools of thought on the subject (Table 8.1). Each of these schools of thought presents a competing explanation for business failure. The first schools of thought exemplified by Delacroix and Carroll (1983) and Carroll and Huo (1986) argue that business failure is an outcome of free market competition which forces less adaptive firms to exit the market. Political interference and market competition have been identified as contributory factors in the demise of firms (Amankwah-Amoah and Debrah, 2010).

The second line of research exemplified by Nutt (1999) and D'Aveni (1990) contends that business failure is attributed to management and decision-related variables, which ultimately create conditions for business failure to occur. In other words, business closure stems from actions and inactions of managers, strategy, and implementation of the strategy (Amankwah-Amoah

Table 8.1 Theoretical underpinnings

Theoretical perspectives	*Explanations*
The voluntaristic perspective subsumes theories such as the resource-based perspective	Business closure is caused by managerial or decision-specific factors
The deterministic perspective	Business closure is caused by market forces such as competition and deregulation
The integrated perspective	Business failure stems from interactions of firm-specific and environmental factors

Sources: Synthesised from Mellahi and Wilkinson (2004); Amankwah-Amoah (2014a,b, 2015c); Amankwah-Amoah and Debrah (2010, 2014), and Amankwah-Amoah and Zhang (2015).

and Zhang, 2015). Studies have suggested that business failure stems from factors such as human capital decay (failure to update employees' knowledge), poor decision-making, managerial inexperience, and incompetence (Amankwah-Amoah, 2015c). This is in line with the resource-based view of business failure (Thornhill and Amit, 2003), which focuses on the resources and capabilities of the focal firm as a possible explanation for poor business performance and business failure. According to research anchored in this perspective, one prerequisite for business failure to occur revolves around inefficient and ineffective deployment of organisational resources and capabilities of the focal firm (D'Aveni, 1990; Thornhill and Amit, 2003).

Since the 1990s, the second view has gained prominence and many scholars have sought to identify firm-level factors that create conditions for business failure to occur (Amankwah-Amoah, 2015b). In recent years, the accumulating research on business closure has brought to the fore the pivotal role played by superior human capital (i.e. knowledge, skills, and abilities) in firms' ability to mitigate decline, failure, or generate a turnaround (Headd, 2003). Studies have shown that it is the misallocation of resources that then triggers the process of decline which over time brings about business collapse (Ranger-Moore, 1997).

Both lines of research have been explored for decades but recent lines of research, however, indicate that the integrated approach offers a more complete understanding of the causes of business failure (Mellahi and Wilkinson, 2004). To put it differently, failure can be better explained by looking at internal and external factors of the firm. Firms that fail to identify and respond quickly to customers, suppliers, and partners' concerns are often selected out by the force of market competition (see also Freeman, 1984).

There are two views on the relationship between firm size (internal factor) and business failure advanced by Ranger-Moore (1997). The first view argues that as firms grow, they accumulate experiences, and acquire and develop resources which equip them for future challenges and therefore render them more able to weather environmental upheavals (Baum, 1996; Ranger-Moore, 1997). Cumulatively, this helps them to improve their survival chances. The second perspective contends that as firms age, they "plant the seeds of their own destruction" by creating and developing complex and ineffective processes and bureaucracy (Ranger-Moore, 1997, p. 903). These may also impede their ability to learn. In other words, business failure for older firms stems from events and processes that occur later in the life of the organisation (Baum, 1996). In the case of state-owned enterprises, failure may stem from the actions and inactions of employees, governments, and policy makers (Doganis, 2006).

Air Afrique: the making of a pan-African airline

In this section, a brief profile of the airline will be provided. Across the continents many countries gained independence in the 1950s and 1960s, and they immediately embarked on a journey of economic and political development. Africa's transition from colonial rule to post-colonial environment was clouded by the various countries adopting several different political systems. These ranged from socialism to democracy and then to totalitarianism (Jackson, 2004).

The range of governments was also reflected in how national resources were marshalled towards economic development and growth strategies. Although the path to democracy differed for countries such as Ghana and Nigeria, their paths were propelled and shaped by their colonial experience with British rule and, as such, the nature of the policies adopted bears that imprint (Amankwah-Amoah and Debrah, 2014). These included reliance on a central system and use of chiefs. Around the same time, several francophone countries also gained independence from France and set out to pursue a policy of development also shaped by their past experiences. For these countries, their policies emphasised unity and collaboration by combining their limited resources.

One of the unique features of this policy was the case of Air Afrique, an airline established to advance the pan-African dream of unity and collaboration. From an aviation standpoint, whilst many former Anglophone nations took steps to dismantle multi-nation airlines such as West African Airways Corporation (including Nigeria, Ghana, Gambia, and Sierra Leone) and East African Airways (1946–1977) (including Tanzania, Kenya, and Uganda), the former French colonies in Africa largely opted to combine their resources towards the formation of Air Afrique (Amankwah-Amoah and Debrah, 2011a).

Buoyed by the spirit of independence and the opportunity to chart their own course and shape their futures, the newly independent former French colonies decided that an effective means of projecting their image as well as advancing the new-found spirit of collaboration was to establish a pan-African airline – Air Afrique. After achieving political autonomy, the 11 former French colonies in West and Central Africa met at the 1961 Heads of State Summit in Yaounde and decided to marshal their resources towards the establishment of a multi-national airline capable of competing and projecting its image not only in Africa, but also across the world (Kromah, 2008). The airline was born in 1961 and was heralded by each of the contracting states as the "new beginning" for Africa – a symbol of post-colonial collaboration and unity. Over time, it came to exemplify multi-national unity.

Table 8.2 provides details of the contracting states. In the post-colonial era of the early 1960s, many countries sought means to concurrently project their newly found independence whilst concurrently exploring means to pool their resources with similar nations to achieve economies of scale. To appear local as a "national airline", each of the contracting states had an office and ground handling with the staff composition within each state attempting to reflect each country's contribution to the airline (Kromah, 2008). Although there was demand for domestic air travel within each of the contracting states, this was not enough to sustain a viable air service.

Table 8.2 Contracting nations of Air Afrique from 1961–2002

Founding members	*Period*
Dahomey (contemporary Benin); Upper Volta (contemporary Burkina Faso); Central African Republic; Chad; Congo-Brazzaville; Ivory Coast; Mauritania; Niger; Senegal	1961–2002
Mali	1992–2002
Togo (expressed interest in 1964 to become a member)	1968–2002
Cameroon (formed autonomous carrier, Cameroon Airlines in 1971)	1961–1971
Gabon (Formed Compagnie Nationale Air Gabon in 1977)	1961–1977

Source: Amankwah-Amoah and Debrah (2014, p. 521).

One of the notable exceptions was the case of Cameroon, which had to two major cities – Yaounde and Douala, with demand for Air Afrique to offer services (Kromah, 2008). One of the key selling points of the airline was the direct services it offered on the Dakar–New York route. Its prices were relatively low compared to Western carriers, which helped it grow passenger numbers from 300,587 in 1966 to around 757,000 by 1985 (Kromah, 2008). In the earlier years, the airline was an outstanding example of the benefits of African unity and strategic collaboration between nations.

From 1980 to 1989, the policy of "Africanisation" was pursued geared towards replacing the predominantly French nationals in the top management team of the airline (Farah, 2001; Amankwah-Amoah and Debrah, 2014). The main thrust of the "policy of Africanisation" was the replacement of French nationals with locals who were politically well connected, thereby diminishing the human capital (i.e. expertise and individually held knowledge of the workers) and social capital (i.e. relationships with customers, clients, suppliers, and foreign governments) base of the firm putting it on a permanent path to decline and demise (Amankwah-Amoah and Debrah, 2014). In the following sections, other factors that contributed to the closure of the business are examined.

Liberalisation, market forces and the Yamoussoukro Decision

Although there was a growing awareness among policy makers and governments across the continent that liberalisation would be beneficial during 1970s, it was not until the 1980s that countries began to offer a concrete commitment towards a common aviation market (Amankwah-Amoah *et al.*, 2007; Abate, 2016). In 1988, the Yamoussoukro Declaration (YD) was adopted at the Yamoussoukro Convention on Market Access for Air Transport in Africa in 1988 as a blueprint for liberalising civil aviation. This ushered in a new environment towards market competition (Amankwah-Amoah and Debrah, 2011b; Abate, 2016). One of the driving forces behind the YD was the creation of conditions for ingenious new entrants as well as the expansion of existing airlines in the intra-African market (Clark et al., 2015). Another main driver was the potentials inherent in harnessing economic growth and development by creating conditions for African airlines to expand into intra-African routes to help link people and markets (Belobaba *et al.*, 2009; Njoya, 2015).

In the mid-1980s, the airline accredited its declining revenues and increasing costs to high fuel bills and unrestrained growth of rival airlines on its key Abidjan and Dakar routes (Amankwah-Amoah and Debrah, 2014). As a comprehensive strategic response, the airline sought to reduce debts of more than $250 million by seeking agreements to reduce competition with rival airlines such as UTA (Yacouba, 2002; Amankwah-Amoah and Debrah, 2014). This came in the wake of the adoption of the YD. One of the many barriers to growth in the late 1980s and 1990s was the failure to fully implement the Yamoussoukro Decision which hampered intra-African connectivity, thereby forcing many African airlines to focus on and exploit opportunities on inter-African routes, especially Europe and North America. Given the competition on the inter-African routes, diversification of Air Afrique's activities on intra-African routes was warranted to broaden its risk portfolio and improve its long-term survival, but this failed to materialise. After the adoption of the YD, it was expected that major carriers such as Air Afrique and Nigeria Airways would capitalise on the opening of the regional markets to expand across the globe. For Air Afrique, this largely failed to materialise.

Throughout its decades of operation, the Yaounde agreement helped to stifled competition and constrained the entry of new airlines (Yacouba, 2002; Kromah, 2008). This lack of competitive pressure, in tandem with the safety net offered by the states through subsidies and financial assistance, meant that its survival depended more on obtaining the support of the contracting states rather than delivery of quality, affordable, and reliable services as a means of attracting and retaining customers. The protection and support to a large extent "disguised the cumulative problems" of Air Afrique for decades (Kromah, 2008). The airline utilised the institutional supports and government subsidies to deter competition and carve out a large portion of the African aviation market. The start of the liberalisation process through the YD started to change all of this by creating conditions for many new airlines to emerge on Air Afrique's key routes. With increasing regional and global competition, the continued reliance on government protection and subsidies as a source of competitive advantage was no longer sustainable.

Liability of ageing, decision process, and resource misallocation

Less obvious, but an equally important factor in the firms' demise, was "liability of ageing" (see also Ruef, 2002, for discussions on the effects of ageing). Liability of ageing provides a route through which inertia and bureaucratic structures can become a constraining force to growth and development leading to decline and exit. By structural attributes, we are referring to the formalised routines, processes, decision structure, and systems through which the airline was administered (Nightingale and Toulouse, 1977). Although the age and decades of experience of Air Afrique bestowed legitimacy on its operations and enabled it to gain travellers' patronage, by the late 1990s and early 2000s, the age and complex structure had become a liability in its ability to respond to environmental jolt. The liability of ageing unfolded over time as complacency stemming from decades of experience meant that customers were often taken for granted as quality of services declined further, overbooking became common and flight cancellations at short notice came to characterise its operations (Amankwah-Amoah, 2015a). One feature was that it increased prices with limited implication on passenger numbers. However, as more competitors emerged, the strategy of increasing prices to respond to rising costs and fuel prices became increasingly unstainable (Kromah, 2008). The sources of competitive advantage of the business were rooted in protection and government support were also weakened (Kromah, 2008).

In addition, the airline was accountable to and served the interests of multiple governments, which created a structure reflecting the interests of the state rather level of expertise available. Accordingly, responding to changes in the business conditions required the consultation of top executives as well as ministers from the contracting states. This slowed down the airline's ability to respond and compete in a timely manner. Because the airline became complex and bureaucratic in tandem with conflicting interests of multiple states, its decision-making process was coloured with political interference as each government fought its own corner.

The complex decision-making structure also meant that the firm was slow to change, slow to make decisions and slow to implement decisions, which enhanced its vulnerability to adverse change in the business environment such as high oil prices, currency fluctuations, and political inability of one of the member states (Amankwah-Amoah and Debrah, 2014). The main rationale behind the member's decision to opt for such a decision-making structure was that such an approach would allow consensus to emerge and minimise and reduce ill-conceived ideas from being implemented – which could lead to misallocation of the states' resources and devaluing of their assets.

Perhaps the most striking factor in the demise of the firm is the inherent over-staffing that characterised its operations for most of its lifespan. The political structure of the business created conditions which made it difficult to reduce staff numbers. The firm also faced resistance form unions and managers who enjoyed considerable benefits and travel concessions to maintain the status quo. For most airlines, route networks are determined by the number of their customers and profitability. However, largely due to the structure of the airline representing multiple states, its route network was largely designed to service the national capitals of the contracting states (Amankwah-Amoah and Debrah, 2014). Consequently, routes were maintained even in the face of continued loss-making operations. In addition to this, cancellation of routes to any of the national capitals became a political rather than economic issue that required consultation of national ministers. The power structure and decision-making processes favoured maintaining the status quo to the detriment of the airline's longevity.

Over time, such old firms "become less efficient and effective, and thus less competitive" and ultimately "lose their ability to respond quickly or appropriately to changing environments" (Ranger-Moore, 1997). At the same time, the emergence of new airlines and expansion of Air France meant that they exploited the market opportunities to expand, thereby equipping themselves to be able to outwit and out-compete Air Afrique in many of its key routes connecting Africa to the west. Although the system of bilateral arrangement to an extent benefited Air Afrique because the contracting states designated it as their national airline, in the long term it created conditions for complacency and inefficiency given the limited competition on the key routes.

Conclusions

This chapter has presented an analysis of the demise of a pan-African airline, Air Afrique. Drawing on the literature on business failures, a narrative was developed to account for some of the precipitating factors in the airline's demise. Based on this analysis, at least two conclusions can be drawn. First, the collapse highlights and provides support for the contention that external factors can act as a constraining force on the firm's ability to respond to market conditions. Through the actions of the contracting states, the airline's ability to cancel routes and reduce staff levels was curtailed by the actions of the states. This set of findings suggests the ability to ease external political constraints on state-owned firms can empower managers and decision-makers of state-owned enterprises to pursue a long-term objective of profitability.

A second conclusion concerns the effects of firm-specific factors in precipitating the closure. The inability to curtail the external forces can be traced to a lack of highly skilled individuals after the introduction of the Africanisation concept. The depleting of scarce human capital from the organisation created conditions for "mediocre", but politically well-connected, individuals to emerge to manage the operations as well as perpetuate the status quo against a backdrop of a changing business environment.

From a policy maker's perspective, the findings suggest that a more suitable strategy for dealing with such constraints may be the establishment of an independent organisation to manage such airlines with multiple state owners and multiple parties with conflicting and competing interests. In addition, it is suggested here that public ownership necessitates the development of an autonomous management structure capable of withstanding political interference (Doganis, 2006). Overall, these findings suggest that the ability to navigate and charter a path towards achieving the common good would have helped to improve the survival chances of the firm.

From a theoretical standpoint, scholars in the last three decades have reiterated at length the causes of business closure, yet relatively few studies have offered little insight geared towards a better understanding of the processes and systematic steps inherent in business closure. This oversight has allowed misunderstanding to occur. In this direction, the case of Air Afrique offered a promising setting to illuminate our understanding of this complex issue. This chapter adds to the growing voice that the study of state-owned firms and their failure can help inform governments' policies aimed at reducing waste and improving efficiency (Millward, 2005; Doganis, 2006). In recent years, some governments are still reluctant to ensure full implementation of the Yamoussoukro Decision (Abate, 2016). Indeed, the limited intra-African flight connectivity has stifled the economic development of the region (Clark *et al.*, 2015).

References

Abate, M. (2016) Economic effects of air transport market liberalization in Africa. *Transportation Research Part A*, 92, 326–37.

Amankwah-Amoah, J. (2014a) A unified framework of explanations for strategic persistence in the wake of others' failures. *Journal of Strategy and Management*, 7, 422–44.

Amankwah-Amoah, J. (2014b) Old habits die hard: a tale of two failed companies and an unwanted inheritance. *Journal of Business Research*, 67, 1894–903.

Amankwah-Amoah, J. (2015a) Against all odds! A strategic analysis of the failures of three state-owned firms, in P. Konara, Y.J. Ha, Y. Wei and F. McDonald (eds) *Achieving a New Balance? The Rise of Multinationals from Emerging Economies and the Prospects for Established Multinationals*. Palgrave, Basingstoke.

Amankwah-Amoah, J. (2015b) An integrative review of the antecedents and consequences of lateral hiring. *Journal of Management Development*, 34, 754–72.

Amankwah-Amoah, J. (2015c) A unified framework for incorporating decision-making into explanations of business failure. *Industrial Management and Data System*, 115, 1341–57.

Amankwah-Amoah, J. and Debrah, Y.A. (2010) The protracted collapse of Ghana Airways: lessons in organizational failure. *Group and Organization Management*, 35, 636–65.

Amankwah-Amoah, J. and Debrah, Y.A. (2011a) The evolution of alliances in the global airline industry: a review of the Africa experience. *Thunderbird International Business Review*, 53, 37–50.

Amankwah-Amoah, J. and Debrah, Y.A. (2011b) Competing for scarce talent in a liberalized environment: evidence from the aviation industry in Africa. *International Journal of Human Resource Management*, 22, 3565–81.

Amankwah-Amoah, J. and Debrah, Y.A. (2014) Air Afrique: the demise of a continental icon. *Business History*, 56, 517–46.

Amankwah-Amoah, J., Debrah, Y. A., Mmieh, F. and Ituma, A. (2007) Globalization, liberalization and air transport in Africa: constraints and challenges. Presented at the 8th IAABD Conference, London.

Amankwah-Amoah, J., Ottosson, J. and Sjögren, H. (2016) United we stand, divided we fall: historical trajectory of strategic renewal activities at Scandinavian Airlines System, 1946–2012. *Business History*, 59, 1–23.

Amankwah-Amoah, J. and Zhang, H. (2015) "Tales from the grave": what can we learn from failed international companies? *Foresight*, 17, 528–541.

Barrett, D. M. (1969) Multi-flag airlines: a new breed in world business. *Columbia Journal of World Business*, 4, 7–14.

Baum, J.A.C. (1996) Organizational ecology, in S.R. Clegg, C. Hardy, and W. Nord (eds.) *Handbook of Organization Studies*. Sage, London, pp. 77–114.

Belobaba, P., Odoni, A. and Barnhart, C. (eds.) (2009) *The Global Airline Industry*. Wiley, Chichester.

Bruton, G. D., Peng, M. W., Ahlstrom, D., Stan, C. and Xu, K. (2015) State-owned enterprises around the world as hybrid organizations. *Academy of Management Perspectives*, 29, 92–114.

Button, K.J., Martini, G. and Scotti, D. (2015) African decolonisation and air transportation. *Journal of Transport Economics and Policy*, 49, 626–39.

Carroll, G.R. and Huo, Y.P. (1986) Organizational task and institutional environments in ecological perspective: Findings from the local newspaper industry. *American Journal of Sociology*, 9, 838–73.

Clark, O., Dunn, G. and KIngsley-Jones, M. (2015) Africa still to flower. *Airline Business*, 31, 46–7.

D'Aveni, R. A. (1990). Top managerial prestige and organizational bankruptcy. *Organization Science*, 1, 121–42.

Delacroix, J. and Carroll, G.R. (1983) Organizational foundings: an ecological study of the newspaper industries of Argentina and Ireland. *Administrative Science Quarterly*, 28, 274–91.

Doganis, R. (2006) *The Airline Business*, 2nd ed. Routledge, London.

Hadugha, N. (1985) United we fall, divided we fall. *Flight International*, 3976, 38–40.

Farah, D. (2001) Air Afrique's fall to Earth: politics has bankrupted the soaring dream of 11 African Nations. *Washington Post*, July 31: E01.

Freeman, R.E. (1984) *Strategic Management: A Stakeholder Approach*. Pitman, Boston.

Goldstein, A. (2001), Infrastructure development and regulatory reform in sub-Saharan Africa: the case of air transport. *World Economy*, 24, 221–48.

Hager, M. A., Galaskiewicz, J. and Larson, J. A. (2004) Structural embeddedness and the liability of newness among non-profit organizations. *Public Management Review*, 6, 159–88.

Headd, B. (2003) Redefining business success: distinguishing between closure and failure. *Small Business Economics*, 21, 51–61.

Heymann, H. (1962) Air transport and economic development: some comments on foreign aid programs. *American Economic Review*, 52, 386–95.

Jackson, T. (2004). *Management Change in Africa: A Cross Cultural Perspective*. Routledge, London.

Kromah, A. (2008) Aviation and Regional Cooperation in Africa. Accessed at: www.alhajikromahpage.org/alhajiairafrique.htm.

Mellahi, K. and Wilkinson, A. (2004) Organizational failure: a critique of recent research and a proposed integrative framework. *International Journal of Management Reviews*, 5, 21–41.

Millward, R. (2005) *Private and Public Enterprise in Europe: Energy, Telecommunications and Transport, 1830–1990.* Cambridge University Press, Cambridge.

Nightingale, D.V. and Toulouse, J. (1977) Toward a multilevel congruence theory of organization. *Administrative Science Quarterly*, 22, 264–80.

Njoya, E. T. (2015) Africa's single aviation market: the progress so far. *Journal of Transport Geography*, 4–11, 50.

Nutt, P. C. (1999) Surprising but true: half the decisions in organizations fail. *Academy of Management Executive*, 13, 75–90.

Pirie, G. (2014) Geographies of air transport in Africa: aviation's 'last frontier', in A.R. Goetz and L. Budd (eds.), *The Geographies of Air Transport.* Ashgate, Aldershot, pp. 247–66.

Ranger-Moore, J. (1997) Bigger may be better, but is older wiser? Organizational age and size in the New York life insurance industry. *American Sociological Review*, 62, 903–20.

Ruef, M. (2002) Unpacking the liability of aging: toward a socially-embedded account of organizational disbanding, in M. Lounsbury and M.J. Ventresca (eds.) *Social Structure and Organizations Revisited.* Emerald, Bingley, pp. 195–228.

Thornhill, S. and Amit, R. (2003) Learning about failure: Bankruptcy, firm age, and the resource-based view. *Organization Science*, 14, 497–509.

Yacouba, N. (2002) My era Africa. Accessed at: www.airafrique.eu/mon-ere-afrique-2/.

Index

For Product Safety Concerns and Information please contact our EU representative GPSR@taylorandfrancis.com
Taylor & Francis Verlag GmbH, Kaufingerstraße 24, 80331 München, Germany

www.ingramcontent.com/pod-product-compliance
Ingram Content Group UK Ltd.
Pitfield, Milton Keynes, MK11 3LW, UK
UKHW020948180425
457613UK00019B/583